Make Better Landings

.Alan Bramson, FRAeS

Chairman of the Panel of Examiners
Liveryman of the Guild of Air Pilots and Air Navigators

Illustrations and photographs by the author

VNR VAN NOSTRAND REINHOLD COMPANY
NEW YORK CINCINNATI TORONTO LONDON MELBOURNE

For Miriam

Copyright © 1982 by Alan Bramson

Library of Congress Catalog Card Number 82–2754

ISBN 0–442–21308–5

Printed in Belgium

Published in the United States in 1982
by Van Nostrand Reinhold Company Inc.
135 West 50th Street
New York, NY 10020, U.S.A.

First published in the United Kingdom in 1982
by Martin Dunitz Ltd, London

16 15 14 13 12 11 10 9 8 7 6 5 4 3 2 1

Library of Congress Cataloging in Publication Data
Bramson, Alan Ellesmere.
  Make better landings.

  Includes index.
  1. Airplanes–Landing. I. Title.
TL711.L3B75   629.132'5213   82–2754
ISBN 0–442–21308–5   AACR2

Contents

Acknowledgements

My thanks to the Aviation Safety Bureau, Transport Canada, the South African Department of Transport, the Director of Aviation Safety at the US Federal Aviation Administration, The Air Safety Investigation Department of Australia and the UK Civil Aviation Authority for providing details of accidents during the approach and landing phase for inclusion in the appendix to this book.

I am grateful to Captain P. Dallosso and Training First Officer T. Carver for their valued advice on landing swept wing jets.

For expert advice on the specialist activity of ski flying I have been fortunate in obtaining the valued help of Giles Kershaw, a young airline pilot who since 1974 has spent most winters flying a Twin Otter in support of the British Antarctic and Transglobe Expeditions.

And finally I am happy to acknowledge that the idea of a book devoted to the various problems of landing was that of Martin Dunitz who kindly invited me to write *Make Better Landings*. My thanks to him and his splendid team.

Abbreviations

agl	above ground level
ASI	Airspeed Indicator
ATC	Air Traffic Control
CAA	Civil Aviation Authority
CAS	Calibrated Airspeed (American term. *See* RAS)
C of G	Centre of Gravity
DG	Directional Gyro (American term)
DI	Directional Indicator (British term)
ESHP	Equivalent Shaft Horsepower (relating to turboprops)
FRAeS	Fellow of the Royal Aeronautical Society
ft	feet
HF	High Frequency
IAS	Indicated Airspeed
ICAO	International Civil Aviation Organization
IFR	Instrument Flight Rules
ILS	Instrument Landing System
ISA	International Standard Atmosphere
ITT	Interstage Turbine Temperature
kg	kilogramme
km	kilometre
kt	knot
lb	pound
L/D ratio	Lift/Drag ratio
m	mile
M_{ne}	Never Exceed Mach Number
mph	miles per hour
N_1	Relates to gas generator turbine on a turboprop or the fan turbine on a fan jet
N_2	Relates to the propeller driving turbine on a turboprop or the gas generator turbine on a fanjet
OAT	Outside Air Temperature
PAPI	Precision Approach Slope Indicator
PPL	Private Pilot's Licence
psi	pounds per square inch
QDM	Magnetic bearing to a station or destination
RAS	Rectified Airspeed (British term. *See* CAS)
RCAF	Royal Canadian Airforce
RPM	Revolutions per Minute
SHP	Shaft Horsepower
STOL	Short Take-Off and Landing (relating to an aircraft class)
TAS	True Airspeed
VASI	Visual Approach Slope Indicator
VFR	Visual Flight Rules
VOR	VHF Omnidirectional Range
VSI	Vertical Speed Indicator
WED	Water Equivalent Depth (a reading related to contaminated runways)

V-code related to landing

V_{at}	Target Threshold Speed (approach speed over the threshold. British term. *See* V_{ref})
V_{mcl}	Minimum Control Speed, Landing
V_{ref}	Reference Speed (approach speed over the threshold. American term. *See* V_{at})
V_s	Stalling Speed

Preface

Most people imagine the Wright brothers to have been small-town cycle repairers who, by diligence and sound workmanship, managed to build the first heavier-than-air machine capable of taking off under its own power. Popular belief is often spiced with a sneaking satisfaction that these splendid, simple, country folk were able to solve a problem that had defied all men through the ages, one that had driven some of the finest scientific talent of the day to build complex 'aircraft' which ended in failure. Some of these failures were spectacular, while others might have been capable of flight had the 'operator' (the word 'pilot' was then not in use) known how to fly.

There are several reasons why Wilbur and Orville Wright became the first men to fly under power and control. First, and contrary to popular belief, their mathematics and physics were good, while the conduct of their experiments was to the highest scientific standards; they took nothing for granted. Second, they were fortunate in being possessed of great practical engineering skills, which enabled them quickly to translate their ideas into hardware. But third, and most important, from the start of their experiments at the turn of the century the Wright brothers recognized one vital fact that had escaped the great majority of aviation pioneers – having designed and built a flying machine, the inventor must then learn how to control it. So while others were making flimsy wings and jumping off balloons or mountains (often breaking their necks in the process), the brothers from Dayton, Ohio, went about their task cautiously, step by step. Then they lay in their frail, wire-braced creations, restraining ropes pulled taut in the steady winds of Kitty Hawk, while experience was gained with their unique method of control. Next came free gliding, short hops at first followed by longer ones, so that when the time came to fit an engine of their own design and manufacture, the Wrights were probably the most experienced glider pilots of the time.

On studying the various Wright letters and diagrams, one finds no particular reference to the problem of landing; in fact, such mundane exercises as entry to a turn and the subsequent return to level flight were, during their early powered flying days, regarded by them as hurdles of a magnitude to equal the sound barrier of half a century later. Of course, the aircraft of the day, often with wing loadings of less than ½ lb per sq ft (2.44 kg per sq m), had a touchdown speed of 20 knots, or considerably less when a wind was blowing, and such breakages that occurred were usually of a minor nature, which could be repaired on the spot.

It was a long time before dual controls and formalized instruction became available, and the student pilot of dim and distant 1910 could only learn by example. The French had a manually tilted simulator that vaguely resembled an Antoinette, and, if nothing else, it enabled the student to learn the effects of controls, at the same time giving an impression of what attitude to adopt during climbs, descents and turns.

You may ask: what has all this to do with landing? The point is that in those far-off days, when flying machines alighted at a fast walking pace, it was considered quite normal to let a student attempt his first landing on his own. Indeed, the aircraft of the period offered no alternative. But it is interesting to contemplate whether even the Wright brothers would have been able to teach themselves how to land if, instead of 20 knots or less, their 'flyer' had, of necessity, to touch down at two, three or more times that speed. The modern two-seat trainer lands at more than double the maximum speed of those early 'flying machines', and contemporary passenger jets must approach to land faster than the cruising speed of 1930 vintage airliners. Personally, I doubt if the early pioneers would have been able to land a modern aircraft without previous experience or tuition – certainly not one of the few tailwheel designs that remain in present-day production.

This brings me to the purpose of my book, which is devoted to the problem of landing. Few flying instructors would disagree that the most difficult exercise a student pilot has to learn is landing. True, one occasionally meets the trainee pilot who sails through this part of the flying course without trouble; it comes as easily to the fortunate few as, for example, climbing, descending or medium-level turns. But the great majority who have gained a pilot's licence, myself included, did not take readily to judging the approach, checking the descent and holding off, all of these functions demanding a good eye and above average co-ordination.

My early training with the RAF was on Tiger Moths in the days before electric intercom. We had Gosport tubes (a form of Victorian in-house telephone), which allowed us to hear one word in ten. I had a bad habit of undershooting, which must have tried the patience of my instructor. If he had known then what many of us in flying training understand now, my problem would have been recognized, corrected and cured. As it was, my instructor adopted drama as a means of making his point. During one approach I was alarmed to see him undo his harness and stand up in the front cockpit. 'What are you doing, sir?' I enquired somewhat anxiously through the speaking tube. 'I am going to open the bloody gate to let you in,' he replied. I never undershot an approach again.

This book is intended to advise the pilot under training on aspects of landing, to assist the instructor with a student who seems unable to learn how to cope with the problem, to offer a few hints to qualified pilots who are going through a bad patch with their landings (most of us do at one time or another), and to explain how to handle those difficult landing conditions.

Some readers may be surprised at the absence of a section dealing with instrument approaches but this book is confined to the landing process and, autoland excepted, all instrument approaches must terminate in a visual touchdown as described in Chapter 2. Likewise, very little is said about night landings because, other than the interpretation of angle of approach indicators, the final act of touchdown in the dark is, with minor modifications, very similar to daytime landing. Yet again I have said very little about asymmetric landings because most of the special techniques involved when an engine quits are related to shutdown, make-safe and clean-up procedures which often occur many miles from the point of landing. Where I have departed from the confines of the landing process is in the chapters on turboprops, jets and skiplanes because these types of aircraft will very likely be a closed book to most readers.

My book sets out to be all things to all men, a dangerous aim for any writer, but, judging by the number of accidents that continue to occur throughout the world (sometimes at the hands of experienced pilots), there is a need for a work of this kind, one devoted entirely to the problems of landing. I therefore hope that *Make Better Landings* will encourage the student who is having trouble with this phase of flight, offer advice to the inexperienced on how to tidy up their arrivals and (dare I suggest it?) offer the older hands a few techniques aimed at improving their already high standards of landing.

A. E. B., January 1982

1. The problem that provoked this book

On the face of it, one could be forgiven for questioning whether there is a need for a work devoted entirely to the approach and landing or even if there is enough information on the subject to fill a book of this size. After all, various flying training manuals deal with the subject, and since the earliest days of formalized pilot training the student has been shown how to land and how to cope with various situations demanding special techniques (crosswind and short landing being two examples that spring to mind). Unfortunately, all is not well on the landing front, and a few moments' study of the approach and landing accident statistics shown in the appendix will explain more eloquently than my most persuasive prose why it was thought necessary to publish this book. Opinion is one thing: fact is another. And the facts of the matter are that over a five-year period 38.56 per cent of all notifiable accidents in Canada occurred during the approach and landing phase, while the corresponding figure in the United States was an even higher 46.16 per cent. Within the ten-year period 1970 to 1979 almost 40 per cent of all South African accidents took place during the approach and landing, while over the same period in Britain half of all accidents have, more or less as a matter of tradition, been enacted in that brief interlude between turning on to finals and bringing the machinery to a dignified halt at the end of the arrival. In Australia, over the years spanning 1975–9, a staggering 74.26 per cent of all accidents happened during the approach and landing.

While, in the main, accident statistics are prepared in accordance with ICAO recommendations, the various states have their own ways of presenting the information. In compiling the simplified charts shown in the appendix, I have tried to list the numbers vertically according to accident type (e.g., hard landing, ground-loop, undershoot, etc.). In the United States, where more flying activity takes place than in the rest of the world combined, sheer numbers make it possible to break down the statistics in great detail and to cross-reference them against phase of flight (e.g., round-out/touchdown, landing roll, VFR final approach, etc.). The Canadian authorities provide similar information.

These statistics are worthy of study because although the problem varies from one country to the next, a degree of uniformity may be detected here and there. For example, in all cases hard (heavy) landings are a major cause of accidents, as the following extract shows:

Country	Percentage all accidents
Canada	5.40
United States	7.14
South Africa	8.20
Australia	13.00
Britain	14.38

This seems to indicate that in Australia and Britain pilots are not averse to dropping their aircraft on to the runway. However, when we consider ground-loops/water-loops and loss of control on the ground the league table takes on a different look:

Country	Percentage all accidents
Britain	5.90
South Africa	7.57
Canada	8.72
Australia	10.12
United States	10.60

Then there are the various odd national pastimes, such as the British passion for collapsed landing gears (7.98 per cent), the plethora of overshoot/overrun accidents in the United States (5.47 per cent) and the remarkable number of accidents in Australia caused by flying into objects on the approach, which, at 17.98 per cent of all notifiable accidents, is the biggest single approach and landing problem 'down under'.

In an effort to confine these statistics to pilot-induced accident, I have removed those attributable to such mechanical problems as engine or airframe failure. By the same token, I have included the gear-retracted accident because, as is the case with its near relation, the wheels-up accident, in most cases the pilot might have avoided the problem. On the other hand, burst tyres are usually (but not always) beyond the control of the pilot, and the few landing accidents that are known to have resulted from that cause are not included in the figures.

A breakdown of approach/landing accidents according to phase of flight, reveals that in the United States there were 3,264 accidents during the round-out and touchdown over the period 1975–9 (an average of 653 such accidents a year). So during those brief seconds at the end of what are usually uneventful flights, almost 19 per cent of all American flying accidents occur. Once the pilot has flown the approach without hitting anything, completed the round-out and made the touchdown with the aircraft intact and his reputation untarnished, it would be nice to say 'end of story', but not a bit of it. In the United States there were 2,735 landing-roll accidents during the five-year period under review – almost 16 per cent of all flying accidents.

An interesting feature of both the American and the Canadian statistics is the very small number of accidents that occur during an IFR approach.

	IFR initial approach	**IFR final approach**
	(*percentage all accidents*)	(*percentage all accidents*)
United States	0.20	0.99
Canada	0.06	0.49

In fact, over a five-year period there were only 17 IFR approach accidents in Canada and 206 in the United States, which, having regard to the amount of flying that takes place in these countries, is not very many.

This brings me back to my question: why a book devoted to landing? If any justification is needed for writing a book, none is more pertinent than need. And the need for (to use the legal phrase) 'further and better particulars' on the subject of landing must surely be underlined by the statistics shown in the appendix, some of them highlighted above. No doubt a statistician would read all manner of trends and root causes into these figures, but the fact that relatively few accidents occur during an IFR approach – considerably fewer than during a VFR approach – is revealing. Because an IFR approach presupposes that the pilot making it holds an instrument rating. And an instrument rating is a demanding qualification to acquire, one that entails professional attitudes even when the holder is an amateur pilot. Could it be that the pilots involved in the much greater number of VFR approach accidents are not instrument-rated and their attitudes rather less than professional?

This is the point where I depart from cold fact supported by statistical evidence and indulge myself in opinion, although the views I am about to express are, I believe, shared by many experts engaged in flying training. In my view, although instructional methods have improved over the years, we are all guilty of being a little complacent about the approach and landing – as the accident statistics would appear to confirm. Particularly since the advent of simple-to-land nosewheel aircraft, this critical phase of flight has been treated as just another exercise, like climbing, descending or medium-level turns. If you think about it, the act of flying down the approach, fighting off the weather and arriving over the runway at the right place, at the right speed and at the correct height are in themselves no push-over. And the complex juggling feat of transfer from air to ground we casually refer to as 'landing'.

Now, landing is a manoeuvre demanding great skill and judgement on the part of the pilot. Yet, in the main, the teaching of this complex exercise and the approach that precedes it is accorded no more emphasis or priority than how to set up the VOR. You think I exaggerate? Then look again at the statistics, and ask yourself how much better we would all be if the 7990 approach and landing accidents that occurred in the United States between 1975 and 1979 could have been reduced to, say, 1,000 or an average of 200 a year. Impossible, you may say, but study the Australian figures, which are broken down into type of flying operation, and note that very few approach and landing accidents occurred among commuter or business operators.

And the worst offenders are not students, under training and never far from the beady eye of their chief flying instructor. Trouble starts when these students gain a licence, buy their own plane and fly without guidance or supervision, something they are entitled to do as private owners. Over a five-year period this category of Australian pilot suffered 441 approach and landing accidents (an average of 88 a year) representing a massive 38.48 per cent of all flying accidents. My understanding is that a similar private-owner problem exists in most countries because, for reasons best known to themselves, many such people regard it as beneath their dignity to submit themselves for continuation training or even a periodic check-ride. Their attitude seems to be: 'I've got a PPL. I am capable enough in my own profession or business to have the means of buying my own plane, and flying instruction is for student pilots anyway!' The fact that professionals, civil and military, spend much of their time being checked out, refreshed, criticized (a *nasty* word nowadays) is lost on the 'know-it-all' private-owner breed I have in mind.

I am sure that some readers will consider these remarks to be unduly harsh. They might even accuse me of expecting professional standards from amateur pilots whose ambitions in aviation are limited to the pleasure of admiring the scenery from above on a nice sunny day. I would be the first to champion their right to that little pleasure, provided it is not at the expense of others with more serious aims in aviation. Because be in no doubt: these landing accidents, however trivial, affect us all. They send up the cost of aviation insurance, and they provide newspapers with material for the kind of sensational reporting that gains more readers for them and encourages the anti-flying lobby.

The pattern is surely familiar. Joe Bloggs makes a mess of the approach, swings off the runway and hits a fence. The wheels disappear from under him, and he finishes the landing several feet lower than when he started. Next day the local newspaper carries a banner headline: PILOT CRASH-LANDS AT LOCAL AIRPORT. It may have happened in Timbuktu, yet the national newspapers of the world will most likely carry a brief report. And when such accidents occur in the so-called 'developed' countries (I regret to admit, Britain in particular) pompous little men on the local council start jumping up and down demanding an end to 'this dangerous activity called private flying'. It is not unknown for the ill-informed rantings of such people, aimed at vote-catching from among the anti-aviation pressure groups, to influence the aviation authorities in directions that do not further the cause. Flying accidents, even amateur ones, are the business of everyone involved in aviation because they affect us all. Reduce the accident rate and down will go the cost of insurance.

There may even be a gradual process of public enlightenment towards light and general aviation. None of us should be under any illusion that private flyers are popular among their fellow citizens. Of course, the more intelligent man in the street is perhaps moderately aware that all pilots are not irresponsible playboys (or -girls) with too much money and the time to spend it. But to a lot of folk the private flyer (and they are all private flyers if they pilot anything smaller than a 707) evokes envy. To them there is nothing wrong in Mr X falling off a mountain and coming to a full stop 3,000 ft lower down, of Mr Y going out in a small boat when the sea is rough and having to be rescued at great cost as a result. But if Joe Bloggs leaves his wonderplane in a heap at the local airfield (at no cost to anyone but himself), cries of anguish go up:

'All pilots are layabouts,' and 'Houses should be built on the airport.'

Over a period of almost forty years I have flown with many pilots in the course of testing them for instructor ratings, multi-engine ratings and various other qualifications. Often the more advanced exercises have been expertly flown, but I never cease to be astonished by the lack of consistency displayed during the approach and landing. Even some of the professionals (admittedly, of relatively limited experience) seem unable to carry out two approaches in the same way, on the same glidepath and at the same speed. Too often the plane is flying them, not (as it should be) the other way round.

If you are an airline pilot flying large jets into all but the longest runways, each arrival is a 'performance' landing – something akin to the kind of short-field landing which forms part of the training syllabus for a PPL. And just as a light plane flying into a private strip must be accurately positioned on the approach so that the threshold is reached at the correct height and speed, so the pilot of a passenger jet must keep within the height/airspeed slot. To the light-plane pilot performance landings are usually rare incidents; to the airline captain they are everyday events. The fact that it is almost unknown these days for an approach and landing accident to involve a passenger aircraft may partly be explained by the fact that such operations are flown by highly experienced professionals, but that is not to say that amateurs or the relatively low-hour professionals are to be excused if they land too far down the runway and finish the trip going by road: consistency is attainable by *all* with the will to subject themselves to a little self-discipline.

When I learned to fly, the landing was taught by a process of example and practice; the instructor 'pattered' a landing, and there followed repeated so-called lessons, when I flew circuit after circuit with very little improvement in the accuracy of my approach or the tidiness of my arrival. Other than a pained 'You're too high again' or 'We are supposed to be landing on this airfield, not the next', there was little attempt at analysing the approach, explaining how to correct departures from it or where to look during the landing. I know my experiences were typical, and while it could be claimed that the 'example and practice' method taught a lot of wartime pilots how to land (and has produced many more pilots since), there were landing accidents aplenty after we gained our wings because few of us were equipped to achieve *consistency*.

When it became known that I was writing this book, I had a letter from Macarthur Job, editor of *Aircraft* magazine in Australia. Mac used to run the government-produced *Aviation Safety Digest,* and he has considerable experience on a wide variety of aircraft. He had this to say about the act of landing:

> I have felt for many years that no adequate training is given on the technique of actually setting an aeroplane down on the ground – as distinct from such considerations as circuit planning, correct angle of approach, under or overshooting, etc. Most low-time pilots seem content to come over the fence, haul back on the pole, shut their eyes (metaphorically speaking) and wait for the crunch! I think I was a bit like this myself once, but when I began my first flying job (flying a medical-service Dragon in the outback) my chief pilot, an old hand who had learned to fly in the early 1930s, took me in hand and taught me where and how to look when rounding-out for a landing. The result was a transformation in my ability to land. Even today, when I do little flying, I can still pull off a greaser virtually every time – not because I am a hot pilot but because I have been adequately taught!

. Like Mac, I do not fly as much as I would like these days but in the course of writing aircraft-evaluation articles for a number of magazines throughout the world, a great variety of flying hardware comes my way. One day I might flight-test a new light trainer or a pressurized twin. Next week there could be a turboprop or a business jet – they arrive in all shapes and sizes. But I am just as fussy about flying an accurate approach in a Cessna 152 as I would be in a Falcon 10 or a BAe 125.

According to the statistics sent to me by the aviation authorities of Canada, South Africa, Australia, Britain and the United States, over a five-year period there were 10,952 approach and landing accidents in those countries alone, and no doubt France, Germany and other countries could swell that number. So the answer to the first question at the beginning of this chapter is that since the approach and landing phase produces about half of all notifiable accidents, a book devoted to the subject is long overdue. As to the second question, whether or not the subject warrants a book of this size, I am happy to let readers form their own judgement.

The rewards of getting it right during an approach and landing are fewer accidents, leading to lower insurance rates and greater public acceptance of light and general aviation. Then there are the more immediate advantages – like avoiding damage to your beautiful aircraft and not becoming the captain of a wheelchair.

2. The engine-assisted approach and landing

Even the most ardent supporters of aviation can hardly claim that the air is man's natural environment, although a few pilots manage to convey the impression that they are more at home flying around a loop than catching the early-morning train. Most of us find it difficult to do more than one thing at a time, even when the functions are of a simple nature, requiring no special judgement. With practice, people of quite average ability learn to steer along the road with one hand while the other changes gear in co-ordination with the clutch, which must be operated by one foot, the other being committed to the accelerator (although always ready for a quick shift to the brake pedal).

If you think about it, these are quite complex functions, the more so because, while following the routine of changing gear according to engine and road speed, there are highways to follow, traffic lights to obey and other vehicles to avoid. Of course, all of this is happening in familiar surroundings, and subconsciously there is always the reassuring feeling that you are firmly (and relatively safely) on the ground.

Translate what has just been described into manoeuvres in a light aircraft approaching to land, and imagine the variables involved:

1. There is no road. It is replaced by an imaginary glidepath.

2. There is no reassuring feeling of being firmly on the ground.

3. Conditions at the time may be totally dissimilar to those prevailing when last you landed. Then there was a 20-knot wind. Today it is dead calm, and the runway threshold seems to be coming closer at a much faster rate.

4. There are no houses, trees or other nearby objects, so that until the aircraft has descended to near the landing area it is impossible to assess speed, and one must constantly refer to the airspeed indicator.

5. On a hot day turbulence will rock the aircraft, so while trying to fly down the imaginary glidepath at an accurate speed, it becomes necessary to level the wings and to steer back towards the runway extended centreline.

6. At a busy airfield, particularly one where flying training is in progress, it is vital to guard against the unexpected appearance of other aircraft which threaten to cut in on your approach.

7. There will probably be constant chat on the radio. If you are learning, this will make it difficult for you to concentrate on the job in hand and may swamp what your instructor is trying to tell you.

8. As a newcomer to aviation, not yet the proud owner of a pilot's licence, odds are that every bump, however gentle, feels as though the magic of flight is about to cease, leaving you and your favourite plane to drop like a stone.

9. On top of all this – the need to steer down a two-dimensional road while avoiding others, fighting the bumps and taking in only that part of the constant radio traffic that concerns you – there are vital actions to complete and recheck.

It is often said that a good landing must be preceded by a good approach, and while this is perfectly true, our tantalizingly elusive, smooth and well-placed arrival – surely one of flying's most prized achievements – is dependent upon foundations that go deeper than that part of the act where you point your wonderplane in the general direction of the runway. Because you are unlikely to enjoy a good, crisis-free approach if the base leg is wrong. And the base leg will be misplaced, or perhaps too short, if the downwind leg is incorrect. If you are practising circuits or joining one from outside, there is a right and a wrong way of positioning the aircraft.

Revision

Before considering the all-important approach, here is a little advice on the various stages leading to it. These comments are directed at rusty pilots as well as those under training.

Around the circuit

When you are fortunate enough to do your pilot training at a relatively peaceful airfield, it is not uncommon to have the circuit to yourself. But there are many airfields throughout the world where several schools have the same runways (at Biggin Hill, the famous Battle of Britain airfield near London, there are no fewer than twelve schools of various sizes). When the winds are light, the circuit can just about cope with the usual stream of traffic, but come 'circuit-and-bump' time, when 20 knots or more blow down the runway, all manner of problems can arise because, for reasons I have never been able to understand, instructors insist on adopting the usual 'light-wind' circuit, which entails a climbing turn when 500 ft has been attained after take-off.

In a strong wind 500 ft may be reached by the time you have crossed the airfield boundary, and unless corrections are made during the next stage, the aircraft will drift during the climbing turn and crosswind leg. These stages will be followed by a downwind leg flown at a groundspeed that rivals that of a passenger jet. First, this aircraft must of necessity adopt a longer-than-usual approach; then, one by one, others, who through lack of foresight find themselves crowding the man in front, have to edge further downwind until some are faced with motoring down an approach long enough for a Jumbo Jet. One school with a reputation for this technique was the Norfolk and Essex Flying Club, so-called because its circuits took in most of the county of Norfolk and all of Essex.

Fig. 1 shows the kind of situation I have described, but the remedy would be simple if only the schools could get together with their local airfield control and agree that in winds of 15 or 20 knots and above there will be no climbing turn at 500 ft. Instead all aircraft flying circuits should climb straight ahead to the height prescribed for that airfield, level out, settle into straight and level flight and only then turn crosswind.

Having adopted this procedure – which, by pushing the circuit upwind, ensures that a normal approach will follow instead of a mini cross-country – the advantage must be consolidated by tracking into wind and so preventing the aircraft from drifting in a way that will shorten the downwind leg (Fig. 2).

Positioning the downwind leg

Whatever the wind conditions, it is important not to crowd the downwind leg by flying along the airfield boundary, because such a practice will store up evil for the next stage.

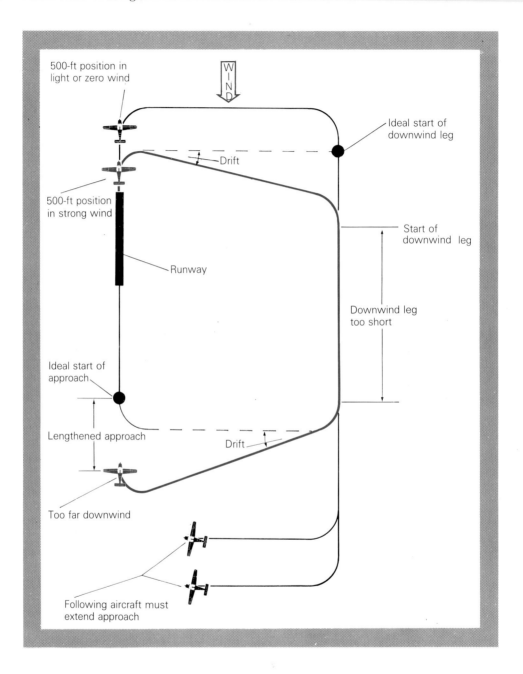

Fig. 1: Planning the circuit according to wind conditions.

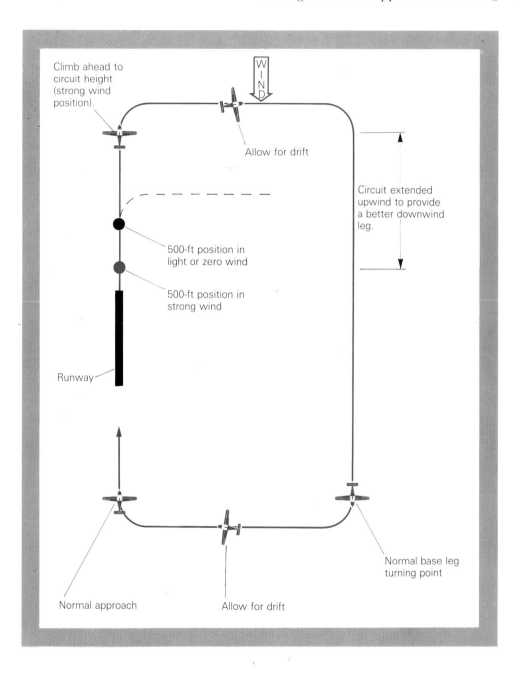

Climb ahead to circuit height (strong wind position).

WIND

Allow for drift

Circuit extended upwind to provide a better downwind leg.

500-ft position in light or zero wind

500-ft position in strong wind

Runway

Normal approach

Allow for drift

Normal base leg turning point

Fig. 2: Ideal circuit in conditions of strong wind.

Along with a tendency to converge with the runway while flying downwind (a common fault, by no means confined to those under training), the practice of hugging the airfield is bound to shorten the base leg and lead to cumulative faults, which combine on the approach and lead to one of 'those landings'.

We are back to the imaginary road problem again – the fact that there are no white lines and kerbs to guide the pilot. Nevertheless, there are other external and internal cues at your disposal:

1. You can determine distance from the airfield by making sure that the wingtip is tracking down the runway. This is illustrated in Fig. 3. Situation A, while incorrect, is acceptable, provided you are unlikely to turn into other traffic at the end of the downwind leg. It may even enhance separation from slower aircraft flying closer to the airfield – but keep them in view at all times. Situation B is ideal, but C cannot be tolerated and you must correct it *immediately*. By running the wingtip down the runway, as shown in B, there is no danger of converging with the extended centreline and so reducing the length of the base leg.

2. The direction indicator (directional gyro in the U.S.) should be checked at intervals to ensure that the reciprocal runway heading is being flown. This will help you to avoid the problem illustrated in Fig. 4.

A major difficulty that has to be faced by most student pilots is that although the early basic exercises are tranquil, perhaps almost leisurely experiences, all this changes when circuits and landings become the order of the day. At times the aircraft can seem so far ahead of the student that there is little hope of catching up. Certainly, there is a lot to occupy the mind – circuit shape to monitor in relation to the runway, height and speed to adjust, other traffic to watch and, of course, the aircraft to control. While all this is in progress, the radio will be competing with the instructor.

One way to reduce the workload is to learn thoroughly the vital actions so that they may be completed speedily while flying downwind. However, although there is the obvious advantage of being able to concentrate on the circuit pattern and on other traffic when the pre-landing checks have been completed, speed of execution must not be at the expense of safety, so a word of warning here. While running through the vital actions, first

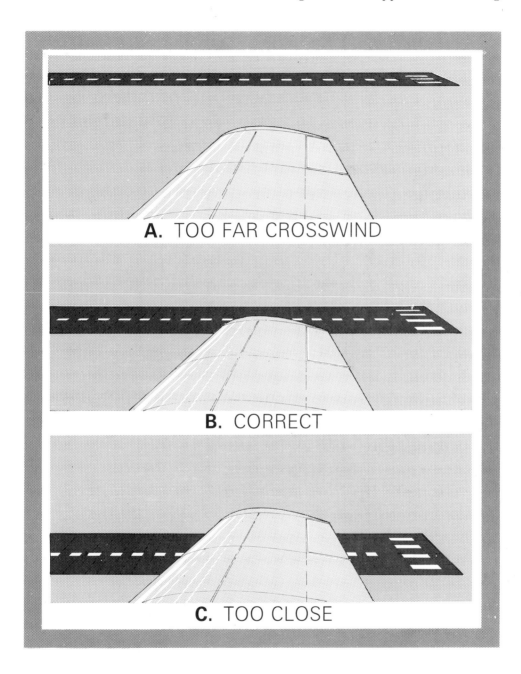

Fig. 3: Positioning the downwind leg.

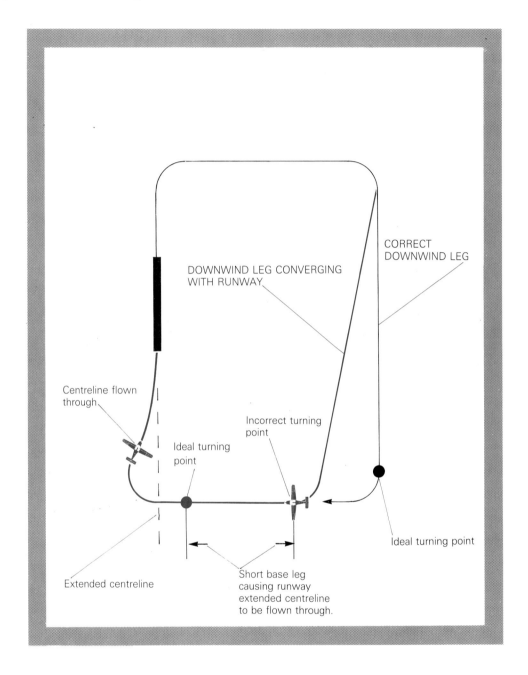

Fig. 4: The effects of a badly flown downwind leg.

have a good look outside the aircraft, then run through the checks deliberately. There is little point, for example, in reciting 'Fuel pump on,' only to leave it off. And when checking 'brakes off,' try them. If the pedals go down to the floor, you have lost the anchors, and it will be necessary to make for a big runway capable of handling your brakeless bird.

Avoid keeping your eyes inside the cabin while completing the vital actions. From time to time, have a look outside for other traffic. And, throughout the circuit, check your height. If you are too low or too high, you must make appropriate corrections.

Clearly, your workload on the circuit will be reduced if the vital actions are thoroughly learned and executed in a slick, competent manner. Another important and often underestimated pilot's friend is accurate trim. At enormous expense, the manufacturers have provided elevator trim, sometimes backed up with rudder, and even aileron trim. Make full use of these essential controls.

Turning on to base leg

Provided the downwind leg has run parallel with the runway and is located at the correct distance from it (using the technique illustrated in Fig. 3), the problem shown in Fig. 4 should not arise, because a base leg of comfortable length is assured. It now only remains to establish the base leg in the correct position relative to the runway threshold and so ensure a proper approach that is neither too short nor too long.

What is a proper approach length? Well, that depends on the type of landing. Broadly speaking, these fall into three categories:

1. Engine-assisted.   2. Glide.   3. Short-field.

Short-field landings are described in Chapter 5, while the glide approach and landing will be explained in Chapter 3. The engine-assisted approach and landing, however, is regarded as the standard method of arrival; others are variants of the basic technique. The following text relates to the standard engine-assisted approach and landing.

Time to turn on to the base leg may be determined when the runway threshold lies somewhere between the wingtip and the tail surfaces. More precisely, start the turn when an imaginary line between the front seats and the runway threshold is at 45° to the lateral axis of the aircraft (see Fig. 5).

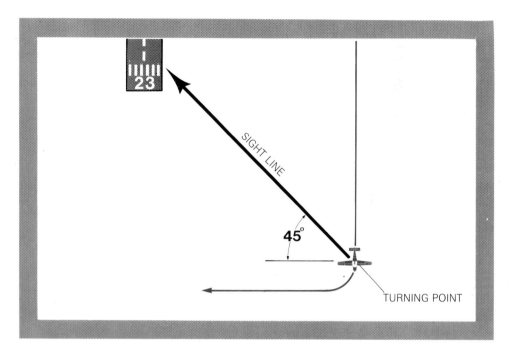

Fig. 5: Determining the turn on to base leg.

While you are flying downwind, most airfields require a radio call, although there are exceptions, and since local training regulations may vary slightly, I will confine myself to recommending you to use the radio according to local requirements.

Before turning on to the base leg, ensure that it is safe to do so and that you will not be heading into another aircraft on long finals. Remember, bigger aircraft make bigger circuits and longer approaches. So WATCH OUT – TAKE NOTE and avoid crowding yourself with other traffic.

A word about crowding. If you are driving in a stream of traffic, and the vehicle in front starts getting closer, he is probably moving more slowly than you. Instinctively, I hope, you will let up on the accelerator and prepare to cover the brakes. The odd thing is that when even experienced drivers learn to fly, they will sit back and watch the plane in front draw closer until its wings fill the windscreen. Then the realization that aircraft, like vehicles on the road, do not all move at the same speed usually prompts ineffective action, which eventually sends the ace at the back of the queue on another fly around the airfield.

When you are catching up with another plane ahead, there is a natural

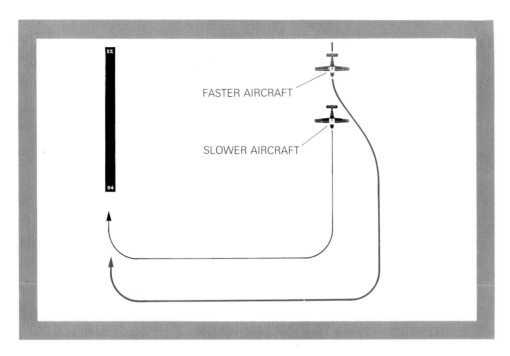

FASTER AIRCRAFT

SLOWER AIRCRAFT

Fig. 6: Dealing with a slower aircraft ahead while flying in the circuit.

temptation to fly a '360', but unless you are requested to orbit by the tower, never do that – it brings on the pains in those following, who will be apprehensive of your next move.

When you are obviously closing with an aircraft ahead, reduce power, slow down a little and, if more separation is required, edge away from the runway while flying downwind, thus extending your forthcoming base leg and allowing the aircraft in front more time to land and clear the runway (Fig. 6). Correct spacing while flying in a busy circuit is an art that can only be learned by experience. Obviously, the problem is aggravated when circuit traffic contains a mix of fast and slow aircraft. These days, when any licensed pilot with the means to pay can get his hands on 160-knot singles or 220-knot twins, there is a tendency for the relatively inexperienced to enter the circuit like a tornado, the pilot frantically trying to complete his checks while training aircraft flash backwards at an alarming rate.

At busy airfields handling mixed traffic the message is clear. Slow aircraft should consider the problems of their faster brothers and must not crawl around the circuit or carry out long, straight approaches at a speed of 5 knots above the stall (unless as a training exercise previously agreed with ATC). And fast aircraft will help everyone, themselves included, if they slow down to a gallop while in the circuit. It is good practice when flying more rapid hardware to lower, say, 15° of flap while on the downwind leg. There are these advantages:

1. Stalling speed is lowered slightly, thus providing a bigger safety margin while flying at reduced speed.

2. At any particular IAS, nose attitude is lower with flap, thus improving the view ahead.

3. Since lowering even 15–20° of flap increases drag, power will have to be added, and the additional slipstream that follows from opening the tap finds its way over the tail surfaces and ensures positive pitch and yaw control at a time when the airspeed is low. Without additional slipstream, some aircraft exhibit reduced elevator and rudder response at low airspeeds.

Having reached the 45° position illustrated in Fig. 5 and checked for other traffic, the turn on to base leg may now commence.

Flying the base leg

At this stage of the circuit, the pilot must concern himself with the following factors, each of them important:

1. Base leg must track at 90° to the runway extended centreline; consequently, in conditions of strong wind it will be necessary to head in towards the threshold so countering the drift that would otherwise distort the approach.

2. Speed must be reduced, half-flap applied (or as recommended for the aircraft type), and the aircraft should then be retrimmed. Ideally, speed should be similar to that for the initial approach, although at busy airfields the tower may ask pilots of slower aircraft to maintain 'X knots'. (Think of all those faster aircraft falling out of the sky like confetti as they struggle to stay behind your 70-knot tin parachute!)

3. Power must be adjusted to set up a rate of descent that will allow you to start the final turn at about 600 ft. In most aircraft it will be necessary to readjust the trim after power has been reduced.

The final turn

Prior to turning finals, it is essential to check that some eight-engined monster is not roaring in on a long approach to the runway. Remember, big aircraft mean big circuits, etc. Assuming that it is clear to turn – and that means looking to see if the approach is clear between you and the runway – time will have arrived to point the aircraft in the general direction of the airfield. Here are some of the considerations:

1. Since you are (or should be) flying at a low airspeed, and since stalling speed increases with angle of bank, limit the final turn to no more than 30° of roll.

2. Plan the turn so that you are lined up with the runway, wings level, at a height of 400 ft above ground level (agl) and *no lower*.

3. Plan a *gradual* turn towards the runway. Avoid the common error of flying until the extended centreline is on the nose before heading inbound for the landing. That way you are certain to fly through the extended centreline, and while a modest infringement may be corrected by making a *gentle* 'S' turn (see Fig. 7), a badly misplaced final turn will demand missed-approach action (see page 64).

Throughout the foregoing paragraphs no mention has been made of crosswind conditions, because that subject will be dealt with in chapter 4. No doubt some readers will by now feel that the subject is complex enough without introducing yet another factor to worry about. I quite agree. It has always been my belief that even the most complex of subjects can be explained clearly, provided step-by-step simplicity is maintained.

Teach the straightforward first – leave the fancy work until after the basics have been mastered. To those who, even at this stage of the book, feel that being a pilot is akin to being one of those performers who juggle eggs with one hand while playing the trumpet with the other I say, you are right – it is. But practice and experience rapidly turn all the individual actions, checks and corrections so far described into instinctive reactions and control inputs, just like typing a letter, or changing gear while the world threatens to collide with you and spread your pride and joy in small pieces across the highway.

Having arrived in line with the runway at approximately 400 ft, half-flap applied and aircraft trimmed so that the airspeed is correct, we

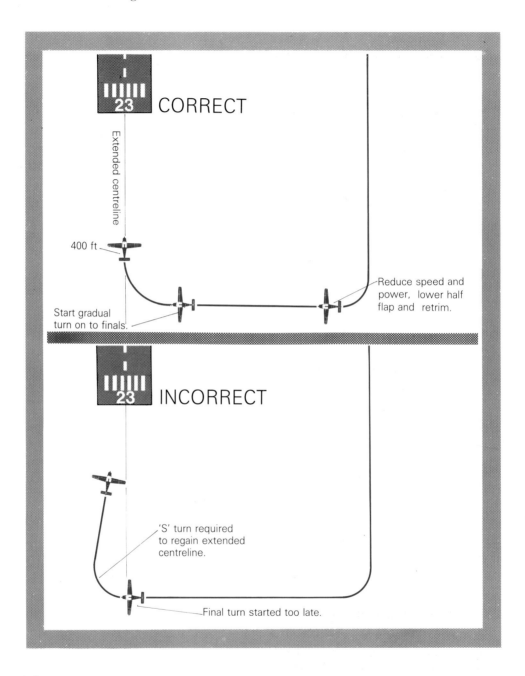

Fig. 7: Planning the final turn on to the approach. Top illustration shows the correct method; bottom picture indicates the effects of flying through the extended centreline.

are really at the start of *Make Better Landings*, all previous text being revision and an amplification of why a good landing demands a good approach, demands a good base and downwind leg, etc.

Flying the approach

There was a time when we could all go to sleep at night secure in the knowledge that on the approach a pilot controlled airspeed with the elevators, while adjusting the glidepath on the throttle. Why not, indeed? One basic law of aerodynamics stated that for a given weight every airspeed is related to a particular angle of attack, while another taught us that rate of climb was determined by the amount of surplus power available over and above that required for level flight at best climbing speed (usually attained when the wing is at its optimum lift/drag ratio angle of attack). Indeed, countless thousands of US military pilots, RCAF and RAF pilots were trained that way during World War II, and so were those of most other countries.

Along came jets and highly sophisticated autopilots that were pro-grammed to think rather differently; among the breed of pilots brought up in these high-powered surroundings many proclaimed that 'power controls speed and elevators control height.' In a jet there is a case for thinking in such terms, because when you operate the power lever, thrust is adjusted direct, whereas the throttle on a piston engine alters power, thrust being affected indirectly. Also on an ILS approach it is convenient to maintain the glidepath by moderate tweaking of the elevators, up or down as the case may be. Of course, in cases of persistent overshooting or undershooting, use of the elevators alone will not suffice; power must be adjusted too. This brings me to the point where I must concede that in practice, adjustments of power and elevator should be co-ordinated on the approach in order to conform with the ideal glidepath. Indeed, the RAF has been looking at a well-reasoned paper entitled *The Total Energy Concept*, which goes into the process of power/elevator control during various phases of flight in a way that must delight those seeking to turn what is a practical skill into an academic study. I do not belittle such papers – far from it. I just consider that they should be confined to the fountainheads of flying training for discussion at learned level, per-haps as a vehicle for debate. This book comes down heavily in favour of controlling speed on the approach with elevator and rate of descent with the throttle(s). There are three reasons why: the method works; it conforms with principles of flight; most flying training authorities known to me agree with it.

To be pedantic about it, the approach should be regarded in two parts:

1. The initial approach.

2. The final approach.

Initially, the pilot's task is to get himself lined up with the runway and on the glidepath (most landings these days have nothing to do with the glide!). Much confusion has arisen in recent years over the use of flap, and a separate section is therefore devoted to the subject.

Use of flap on the approach

Although flap characteristics differ as widely as airfoils themselves, in the main they share the same habits, which are these: The first 15° to 25° of depression confer a lift increase (and, in consequence, a decrease in stalling speed) allied to a modest addition in drag. Further depression brings with it a smaller lift increase (and therefore a further but only modest decrease in stalling speed), but drag builds up markedly with some designs of flap, rather less so with others. A typical example is illustrated in Fig. 8.

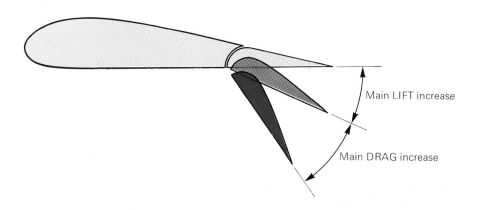

Main LIFT increase

Main DRAG increase

Fig. 8: Main lift increase with most flaps comes during the first 15 to 25° of depression. Further flap application causes a modest lift increase and a significant build-up in drag.

Earlier models of one trainer in widespread use had flaps like barn doors, which made one feel that the bird had flown through a haystack when they were dumped to the full extent. Unfortunately, they brought with their undoubted advantages trim changes that demanded the grip of an all-in wrestler when power was added for an overshoot, so it became common practice among instructors to limit flap in these aircraft to around 25°. There was a case to be made for the technique with this particular aircraft during training. However, the practice spread, and in more recent times a breed of pilot has emerged that is reluctant to use full flap for any landing in any conditions.

Strong crosswinds apart, you will rarely see a professionally flown transport aircraft land without full flap, and there are several reasons for this. First, you have more control over the approach angle when additional power must be used to combat the drag of full flap. Power can be used to adjust from the flattest 'power-on' to the steepest 'power-off' descent path but *only when full flap is applied*. Second, stalling speed is at its lowest. Finally, with full flap you get the best transition from air to ground, followed by good deceleration after landing.

So, assuming that there is no crosswind and that a gale is not blowing down the runway, during normal conditions select full flap when established on the approach, and concentrate on maintaining a steady airspeed and a good glidepath.

Flying down the glidepath

The two factors affecting the approach at this stage are: (1) visibility/cloud base and (2) wind strength.

Factor 1 really belongs to a book on instrument flying, and it is not the purpose of this work to do more than mention that a low sun can be a nuisance when it glares at you from the other end of the runway. There is no simple answer to the problem, particularly when the sun blots out the runway, but judicious use of sun visors/glasses can help, and you should avoid looking directly into the sun. Plant the vision to one side, and remember that during the landing itself the eyes will be deflected towards the ground and away from the sun.

Factor 2 will naturally affect your groundspeed and therefore the steepness of the glidepath for any particular power setting. This is shown in Fig. 9, and, basic as it may seem, I mention it here only to explain why on some days you need more power on the approach than on others. In a strong wind, power must be added unless you wish to visit a local

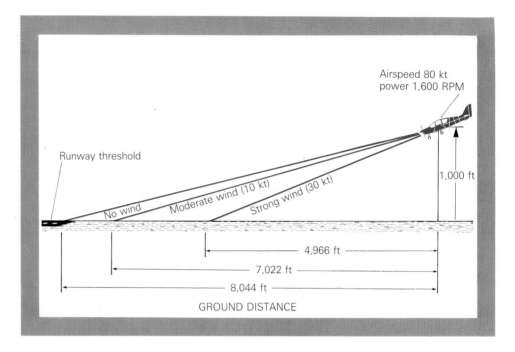

Fig. 9: The effects of wind on the glidepath.

farmer on the way in.

At this stage a landing area should be chosen. Many pilots, often because they cannot bring themselves to apply full flap, touch down between one-third and half of the way along the runway. This is bad enough at any airfield; at a small one you could land up off the end of the runway, through the fence and across the road with a ticket for dangerous driving.

The touchdown zone should be just past the runway numbers. To achieve it, the round-out will have to be made as the threshold slips underneath the aircraft. Clearly, if you are to position the hardware with such precision (and there is no reason why not), the approach will have to be flown with great accuracy. It is all done by relating the situation to a picture framed by the windscreen. Study Fig. 10a, and note the position of the runway threshold relative to the top of the glareshield.

Your aim should be to maintain both threshold relative to the windscreen and the aspect of the runway (neither long, standing up or short and flat) all the way down the glidepath. Of course, the runway will become bigger and must eventually fill the vision as you fly nearer to the airfield, but nothing else should change.

Take a look at Fig. 10b. The threshold has drifted up the windscreen and runway aspect has flattened, giving a clear indication that the aircraft is undershooting.

Remedy: Add power; maintain the airspeed with elevator; and if necessary, retrim.

When the original picture has been restored, it will be necessary to reduce power slightly, otherwise the situation depicted in Fig. 10c will develop. Here the threshold has moved down the windscreen, and the runway is beginning to stand on end, warning the pilot that he is overshooting.

Remedy: Reduce power; maintain airspeed with elevator; and if necessary retrim.

As the correct picture emerges (Fig. 10a), be prepared to add a little power, and avoid sinking into the situation shown in Fig. 10b.

Note that I have said 'If necessary, retrim', because with many aircraft power adjustments bring with them appropriate nose-up/nose-down tendencies that automatically maintain a steady airspeed. Usually only minor elevator and trim adjustments are required.

The importance of close glidepath control cannot be overemphasized, and if the picture changes, never wait for a crisis to develop – get after it and restore runway threshold and runway aspect through the proper use of the controls at your disposal. More bad landings are born at this stage of the ritual than at any other.

Maintaining a steady airspeed

Another major factor contributing to bad landings is common among even quite experienced pilots – erratic airspeed. Recommended approach speed will be found in the aircraft manual. In the case of simple types (e.g., trainers, low-powered tourers), one speed is usually recommended for the initial approach with, in some cases, a lower one for finals. In this class of aircraft, landing weight cannot vary very much, but when one becomes involved with turboprops, big jets and, in particular, large passenger aircraft, the flight manual must provide a range of approach speeds to cater for different weights. This is hardly surprising when one considers that at the end of a 4,000 nm journey, a DC10 will most likely be 65 tons (66,000 kg) lighter than when it took off; fuel in these aircraft represents a major proportion of their total weight. All this is by the way

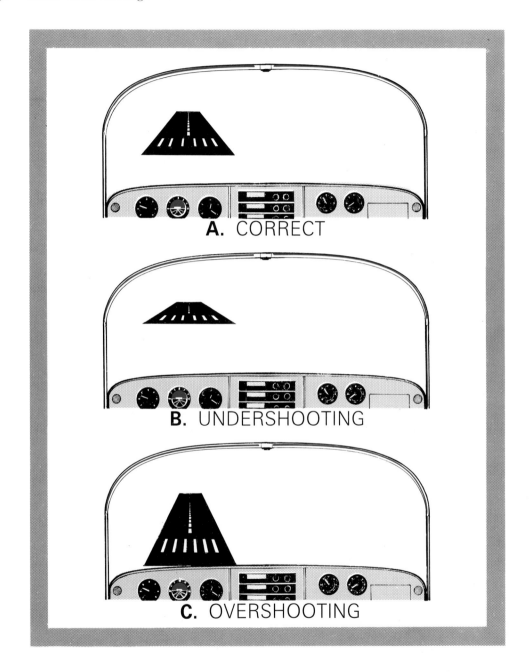

Fig. 10: Judging the approach according to visual cues provided by runway aspect and the position of its threshold relative to the windscreen.

and dealt with in Chapters 7 and 8, so let us return to our light planes and their single recommended approach speed.

There is, of course, no reason why the initial approach should not be flown at a higher speed, provided flap limit is not exceeded. This will be shown as a white arc on the airspeed indicator. Indeed, at a busy airfield there may be a need to maintain a higher speed during the initial approach so that other, faster aircraft in the circuit are not baulked. But for the purpose of this explanation, let us assume that we have a nice, clear day, 10 knots blowing down the runway and only a little circuit traffic. You have selected full flap and positioned the aircraft so that the windscreen presents a picture similar to that shown in Fig. 10a.

Airspeed too high

The aircraft manual recommends 70 knots for the initial approach, but a quick glance at the ASI reveals 80 knots. If you hold up the nose and leave the power where it is, the situation pictured in Fig. 10c will rapidly develop, so what is the correct action to take?

Remedy: Reduce power slightly; hold up the nose and regain 70 knots; retrim; and check threshold position and runway aspect (see Fig. 10a).

Airspeed too low

You look at the ASI, expecting to see 70 knots on the clock, and find yourself 10 knots too slow. To gain speed the nose must be lowered, but this action taken in isolation will provide the undershoot situation illustrated in Fig. 10b.

Remedy: Increase power slightly; lower the nose and regain 70 knots; retrim; and check threshold position and runway aspect (see Fig. 10a).

By now it will be clear that glidepath and airspeed corrections are closely interrelated, since one can affect the other and co-ordinated power–attitude–trim adjustments are required. Since the initial approach must place the aircraft in an ideal position for the final approach and landing, it is important in its own right, and if much of what has been said in the previous few pages would appear to state the obvious, I am afraid there will be no apologies from the holder of this pen. Too often I fly with 1,000-hour-plus pilots who make a mess of the approach (and, as a result, arrive rather than land) because they have never been entirely clear about which does what, how the situation should appear through the windscreen or what they should do about it when the picture changes. Here are a few do's and don'ts for relaxed pilots on the approach:

Do

1. Use the flaps. They are part of the kit, requested by the designer for very good reasons.

2. Line up with the runway centreline. To one side is not good enough, because you need runway left and right of the aircraft during touchdown, so that if a tyre bursts (or a swing develops), there is somewhere to go without ploughing the field.

3. Trim the aircraft accurately, particularly after changes in power or attitude. The trimmer is almost as good as an autopilot when used correctly.

4. Keep the wings level, otherwise you will depart from the runway-extended centreline.

Don't

1. Indulge in large power–attitude variations. All alterations should be small. Avoid going from crisis to crisis – it is quite unnecessary.

2. Allow a bad situation to develop. If the runway threshold moves up or down the windscreen, action is called for. As soon as the picture changes take *immediate* but *moderate* steps to prevent over- or undershooting.

3. Chase the airspeed. Remember that your wonderplane, like any other vehicle, suffers from inertia, and a few seconds will be required for airspeed changes. So fly attitudes, retrim after any changes and give the bird time to settle at the new airspeed.

4. Emulate a low-level attack on the airfield, where, possibly due to strong winds and insufficient power for the prevailing conditions, the aircraft is low down, nose up and a long way from the runway threshold. By then a lot of power will be needed to make the airfield, but, more important, visibility ahead will be seriously degraded, with the attendant risk of hitting something on the way in. Creepers are for creeps. And creeps do not make good pilots.

Having positioned the aircraft at the correct speed, on the extended centreline and on the glidepath, it remains only to carry on the good work until, at about ½ mile (800 m) from the runway, the final approach can begin.

The final approach

During training most instructors give their students one approach speed, and this is used from start of approach to over the threshold. However, it is usual practice, certainly with aircraft of higher performance, to quote a lower speed at which to arrive just before commencing the landing. In the United States they call it reference speed (V_{ref}) but many other countries, Britain included, use the term target threshold speed (V_{at}). It is good training practice to teach today what might be needed tomorrow, when the student may find himself flying a King Air or a BAe 125 or even a Jumbo Jet. An example of this is the manual for the Piper Tomahawk, which prescribes an initial approach speed of 70 knots, followed by a final approach at 62 knots. Of course, it would not be the end of the world if you held 70 knots all the way to the airfield. The worst that could happen is that there would be an additional 8 knots to lose during the landing process.

For the purpose of this chapter, let us imagine that, having made the initial approach at 70 knots, the manual recommends 65 knots for finals (a more sensible figure than 62 knots, which is not easy to read on most instruments). Even the simple act of ridding yourself of 5 knots can displace the aircraft from the glidepath, so here is the procedure that should be adopted while setting up the final approach:

1. Assuming there is little turbulence (dealt with later) check that you are lined up with the runway and that its aspect looks good (see Fig. 10a).

2. Reduce power slightly; raise the nose a little; allow the airspeed to settle at 65 knots; and retrim.

3. Adjust the power to maintain a correct glidepath, with the runway threshold fixed in relation to the windscreen, and hold a steady 65 knots with the elevators.

Many pilots have a habit of entering short finals, leaving on half-flap and holding up the nose to reduce speed, a sequence of actions that can only place you above the glidepath (Fig. 11).

When for any reason, full flap is not being used, it is particularly important that power must first be reduced slightly before holding up the nose to reduce speed for the final approach.

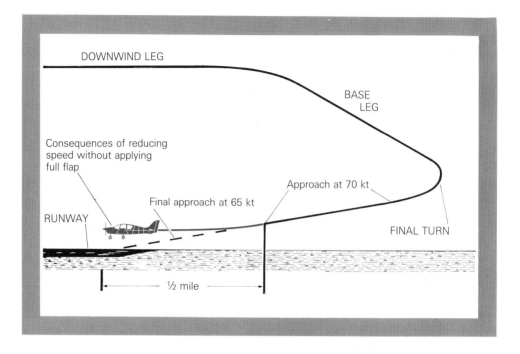

Fig. 11: Problems that follow an incorrect speed reduction on final approach.

Factors affecting the approach and landing

Here are some of the variables that can affect the aircraft in this phase of flight. Some apply to the approach, or at least the latter part of it, while others have a direct bearing on runway-length requirements.

Density altitude

Unlike the take-off, during which engine power has a profound influence on the distance required to clear that ever-present, invisible hurdle of aviation, the '50-ft screen', airfield elevation and ambient temperature assume less importance while landing. In the case of most light aircraft a temperature rise of 10° C adds only 20–30 ft to the landing distance.

In so far as airfield elevation is concerned, a light two-seat trainer tends to add 20–25 ft to its landing distance per 1,000-ft increase in airfield elevation, while the Piper Turbo Seminole, a light twin of respectable touring performance, is affected even less. So we are talking in penny numbers, and while all the figures for landing distance are in the performance section of the aircraft's manual, if you allow 2.5 per cent per 1,000 ft and 2.5 per cent per 10° C (rise in temperature above ISA), you will not be far out.

Aircraft weight

In a two-seat trainer, weight cannot vary to a great extent, but as the aircraft becomes larger and more advanced (turboprop or jet), landing weight assumes greater importance. It works this way: Greater weight = higher stalling speed = faster approach; faster approach = higher touchdown speed = more energy to stop = longer landing roll.

To put some numbers on it, a Piper Turbo Seminole, at 2,500 lb (1,135 kg) weight, should approach at 61 knots, whereas at 3,500 lb (1,590 kg) speed must be increased to 72 knots. Assuming a sea-level runway and a standard temperature, the nil-wind landing distance at the lower speed is 1,210 ft and at 72 knots 1,360 ft, a 150-ft difference. In the case of a long-distance passenger jet, which, as we have noted, could be 65 tons (66,000 kg) lighter than its departure weight at the end of a journey, landing distances can vary by as much as 1,100 ft, according to its weight at time of landing.

Landing distances at various weights are shown in the aircraft manual.

Wind strength during the approach

For any particular power setting, the stronger the wind, the steeper the approach. Obviously, the wind component will affect groundspeed during the approach, but it is not always realized that rate of descent is not affected by a constant wind. Fig. 12 compares the descent path of an aircraft approaching at 65 knots in conditions of no wind, 10 knots, 20 knots and 30 knots. In each case the same power has been set (i.e., to produce a descent rate of 400 ft/min), and the diagram shows the effect of wind on the distance covered while descending from 400 ft to ground level, together with the glidepath angle that will result.

In essence, Fig. 12 shows that to achieve a satisfactory glidepath, power must be added according to the windspeed during the approach.

Wind strength during the landing

This topic will receive more detailed analysis later in the chapter. At this stage, the pilot should have in mind that when there is no wind, he will probably float for some distance before touching down at a relatively high groundspeed, but that wind has the effect of shortening the float period and reducing the landing roll. If it is necessary to land with a

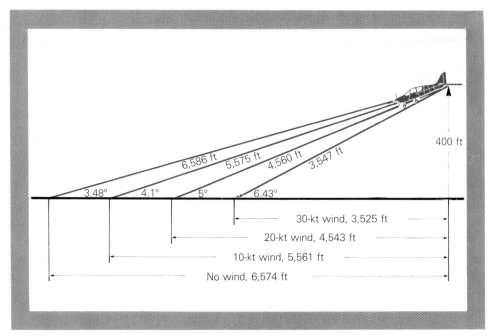

Fig. 12: The effects of a 10-, 20- or 30-knot wind on the final approach at 65 knots.

tailwind (a situation to avoid if at all possible), the landing roll will increase, figures often quoted being a 20 per cent increase in landing run for a 10 per cent increase in groundspeed, but much depends on type of aircraft, braking efficiency and – that ever-important link in the chain – the skill of the pilot.

Wind gusts and turbulence

Although a steady wind is of some benefit during landing (because it obligingly reduces touchdown speed and the length of the landing roll), wind delivered in gusts can be unpleasant and, to inexperienced pilots, a distraction that could, in really bad conditions, present a hazard.

Turbulence is the result of thermal currents (uneven heating of the surface on a sunny day) and eddies caused by trees, uneven ground or buildings near the approach. The most violent gusts are associated with thunderstorms and line squalls, but pilots of little experience, certainly those under training, should not be flying under these conditions. Apart from causing the usual wing rocking and lurching about, gusts (which may reach the aircraft from a direction other than that of the general flow of wind during the approach) have these effects:

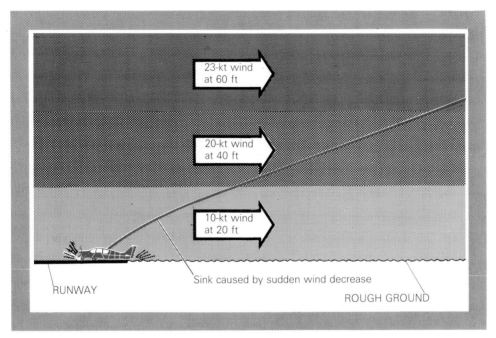

Fig. 13: The hazards of wind gradient.

1. A sudden increase in airspeed.

2. A sudden decrease in airspeed.

3. A sudden change in angle of attack.

   While the first will cause an equally sudden increase in lift and will therefore decrease the rate of descent (or even cause a small gain in height), an abrupt decrease in airspeed, followed by a decisive sink while near the ground, could be dangerous. So when gusty conditions are encountered, it is good practice to add, say, 10 per cent to your approach speed and, in very bad cases, to use only half-flap.

Wind gradient

This factor is subtly different from gust effect, in so far as it is not a product of eddies. Wind gradient (alternatively known as wind shear) is caused by the retarding effect of rough ground on the lower layers of moving air (wind). To some degree, wind gradient is always present (other than in dead calm), but under certain conditions it can be very pronounced during the final stages of the approach, as the ground is neared. Fig. 13 shows that on entering the lower (and slower) levels of air, a sudden decrease in wind speed will bring with it the risk of a rapid sink.

When the runway being approached is known to exhibit wind-gradient behaviour, be prepared, particularly when the wind is strong. Use an approach speed 10 per cent higher than usual, and at the first suggestion of an increase in descent rate, add power to check the trend. In the words of the famous advertisement: 'It prevents that sinking feeling.'

By now, and as a result of good management, the aircraft is aligned with the runway centre; it has no drift; the wings are level; and you have arrived over the runway threshold at the correct speed (in this case, 65 knots). The next stage is about to begin.

The round-out

The one phase that can cause the majority of student pilots to question why they took up flying (and make their instructors wish they had stuck to golf) is the transition from approaching down the gentle glidepath to that brief flit over the runway, wheels just above the ground, power off and airspeed decreasing. Much has been said and written about when the round-out should take place and, more out of interest than in support, I quote a few examples here, together with my comments. Although I may appear rather less than enthusiastic about some of the advice that is to follow, it may help readers who are experiencing difficulty with their landings. As a personal opinion, I have long felt that we do not teach landing in the most effective way – but more about that later. Here are the more common hints offered in the various established textbooks, some of them old, some new.

At a reasonable height, move the stick gently back and make the aircraft fly just above the ground. While I would not fall out with that, one man's 'reasonable' is another man's 'outrageous'. Also, what might be 'reasonable' for one aircraft may well have the legs off another.

When the ground is coming up rapidly and you must do something about it. . . . Nothing like a little drama to make the point, but there is some value in this one, because as you near the correct round-out height, proximity with the ground does increase the sensation of speed. A variation on this one is: *When the ground seems to open up and come towards you. . . .* or *When you suddenly become conscious of movement of the ground. . . .*

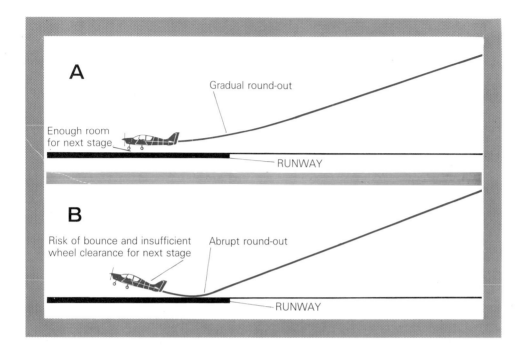

Fig. 14: Dealing with the round-out, (A) painlessly or (B) with certain risks.

Many instructors like to say 'Round-out at the height of a double-decker' (which is all very well if you have ever been on the top deck of a London bus – not everyone has) or 'Ease back on the elevators at 20 ft above the ground', whereas experiments seem to indicate that experienced pilots begin the transition from approach to hold-off rather higher than that.

In truth, there is little point in quoting a height above the ground, because 20 ft up if you are standing on a tall ladder seems different from 20 ft up when you are seated in an aircraft flying at 60–120 knots, according to type. The correct position above the ground for starting the round-out can only be learned, in my opinion, by visual experience, demonstrated by the flying instructor. Here are some of the more common pitfalls I have encountered while training pilots:

1. **Bouncing**. This is usually the result of aiming for perfection at too early a stage. Better by far to start the transition a little sooner and make a gradual round-out (Fig. 14a) than continue the final approach to within a few feet of the ground before easing back on the stick/ wheel. That way (Fig. 14b) you risk flying into the ground. Also, if

the wheels are very near the ground after rounding-out, you will probably touch down prematurely at too high a speed, a problem that will be discussed shortly.

2. **Ballooning**. This problem is often the result of adopting the technique shown in Fig. 14b. In an effort to avoid flying into the ground, inexperienced pilots are sometimes inclined to over-rotate the aircraft during the round-out, when the situation depicted in Fig. 15 will develop. The risk at this stage is that the airspeed will rapidly decrease, and unless steps are taken to add power immediately and go round again, the aircraft will sink heavily on to the ground. Given enough height following the 'balloon', this will cause expensive airframe damage. Faced with such a situation, an experienced pilot would most likely add a little power and gently ease back on to the runway. But whatever your experience, when dealing with the abnormality shown in Fig. 15, *never* be tempted to move the stick/wheel forward without adding power. Remember your position – nose high, speed low and a lot of air between you and the runway. Unless there is ample room ahead for you to ease down with skilful use of power, open the throttle fully and go round again. (These remarks apply equally to correcting a bounce.)

The correct sequence of events at the end of the final approach is:

1. At the appropriate height above the runway, ease back on the elevators and gradually change from a descending glidepath to one parallel with the ground.

2. Close the throttle.

Note that power is left on until the aircraft is near the ground. A common fault among inexperienced pilots is their passion for turning an engine-assisted approach into a glide during the final stages, while at a considerable height above the ground. They may get away with such abysmal technique in a two-seat trainer. But in faster, more powerful aircraft, operating at near-maximum weight (and even in high-performance singles), sudden removal of power while at low speed will provoke a rapid sink, which could have expensive consequences when the runway comes up to meet the wheels.

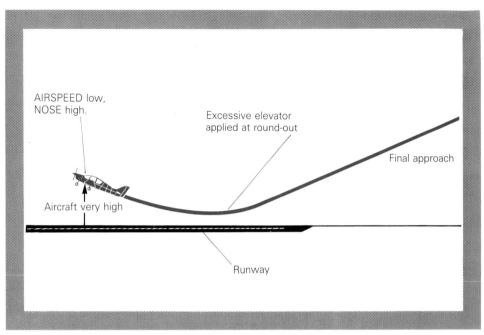

AIRSPEED low,
NOSE high.

Excessive elevator
applied at round-out

Final approach

Aircraft very high

Runway

Fig. 15: Ballooning caused by excessive use of elevator at the round-out.

The hold-off

At this stage of the landing, the aircraft is several feet above the runway, with power off, and gliding more or less parallel with the ground. Having arrested the descent by rounding-out, the airspeed will now begin to decrease. Unless steps are taken to compensate for the decrease in lift by increasing the angle of attack, the aircraft will sink and will make fairly decisive contact with the runway, probably on all three wheels simultaneously but possibly nosewheel first – and herein lies the danger.

In the days when all aircraft were 'tail-draggers', the landing demanded greater skill than that required for a modern nosewheel design. Reasons for this are explained in Chapter 6, 'Tailwheel Techniques', but the relative simplicity of handling that we all now enjoy, thanks to the nosewheel landing gear, has been the signal for some pilots to give up trying. Any busy training airfield will bear witness to the fact that many pilots, some of them instructors, are content to arrive rather than land. They motor in, make a gesture of rounding-out and then fly on to the ground, all wheels making contact with the runway at the same time.

Here are the risks and disadvantages of such slovenly flying:

1. Because the aircraft 'arrives' in the level attitude, touchdown speed is needlessly high, causing unnecessary tyre, wheel-bearing and brake wear.

2. There is every possibility that you will arrive nosewheel first. The nosewheel and its strut are not designed for that purpose. Their prime functions are to safeguard the propeller and to provide a means of manoeuvring the hardware while it is on the ground. You may land nosewheel first without invoking anything more undignified than a bounce. In fact, you may get away with landing that way on a number of occasions, but sooner or later metal fatigue will have its say, and the time will come when someone (perhaps an innocent, well-trained pilot) will make a perfectly good landing only to have the nosestrut collapse during the ground roll. The damage that follows can be quite considerable – bent propeller blades, shock-loaded engine, bent firewall, damaged cowlings – all for want of correct pilot technique.

3. The habit of landing nosewheel first brings with it another risk, one that can cause even more damage than that just described. 'Wheelbarrowing' (as it is called) has afflicted all types of aircraft, large and small, but those with stabilators (all-flying tailplanes) are perhaps more prone to such an encounter than those with fixed tailplanes and separate elevators.
    Imagine the aircraft has touched down nosewheel first, mainwheels off the ground. It only requires a crosswind to pivot the airframe around its one and only contact with the runway for the situation to get well and truly out of hand (Fig. 16). With most of the keel area behind the nosewheel, an unstable weathercock action will develop, which, if not arrested by moving back the stick/wheel and planting the main landing gear firmly on to the runway, will very likely wreck the aircraft. This is because as the swing develops there is a natural tendency for the centre of gravity to come up from behind the nosewheel and take charge of the situation (Fig. 17).

The aim must be to touch down mainwheels first, nosewheel clear of the ground, because only then will a good landing be assured. Such a landing has these advantages:

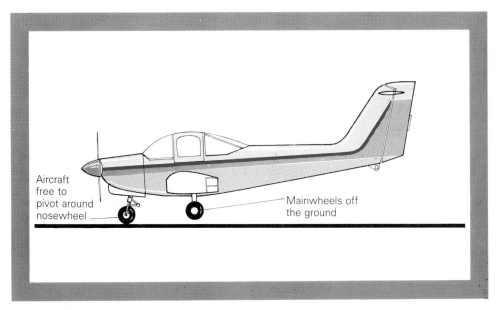

Fig. 16: Wheelbarrowing, first stage.

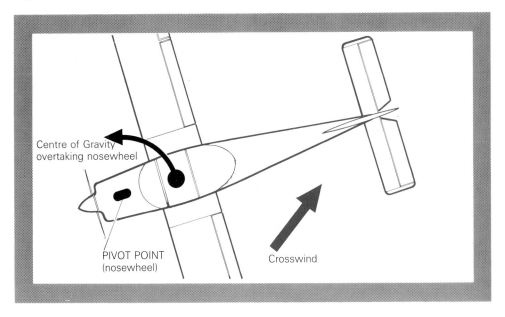

Fig. 17: Wheelbarrowing, second stage.

1. The risk of wheelbarrowing is removed because point of contact (mainwheel) is behind the centre of gravity.

2. A slightly or moderately heavy arrival is unlikely to cause much of a bounce because there is a natural tendency for the aircraft to pitch forward, reduce its angle of attack and therefore to decrease the amount of lift being generated at the time.

3. Because the aircraft is in a slightly nose-up attitude, the large angle of attack ensures a relatively low touchdown speed.

The technique to be adopted following the round-out entails holding-off, a lost art among many modern pilots. During this procedure, the aircraft is kept in the air by progressively easing back on the elevator control, increasing the angle of attack step by step with the decrease in airspeed. Furthermore, the process must be enacted so that when the correct attitude is achieved, the mainwheels are allowed to make gentle contact with the ground. Nice work if you can get it. But you *can* get it if you try (Gershwin could have written his famous song with pilots in mind). There are, however, a couple of problems:

1. **What is the correct attitude?** I would rather not talk in terms of X number of degrees, because the only way you can measure that angle is to look at your artificial horizon (or attitude director, if it is a high-class plane). But think in terms of the lift-off attitude and you will not be far out.

2. **How do we know when the wheels are near the ground?** This is the kind of question that often provokes a long silence, but since we have now reached the moment of truth (the ingredient that is most difficult to teach, hardest to learn and most elusive to explain) I shall do my best to provide a lucid answer.

Assessing the proximity of the ground

Some student pilots experience little difficulty in recognizing when the wheels are close enough to the runway for a greaser of a landing. They are fortunate. In my own case, I found the going hard, and even after my first 1,500 hours I could, on occasion, make an untidy job of the landing. True, most of the aircraft that came my way, even the larger ones, were of the period – tail-draggers, which demand more skill to land than nosewheel aircraft. Strange thing is, on looking back over the years I have no recollection of any instructor actually teaching me how to land in a detailed, analytical manner, either in England (where I started learning with the RAF) or in Texas, USA (the scene of my military training). I was given several demonstrations of how it was done and then told to have a go myself. Occasionally, there were pungent comments, like 'You're too bloody high!' or, in Texas, 'Yo'all tryin' to kill me, lootenant?' But there was no real attempt to explain *why* I was too high or, more important, how I was supposed to know.

Judging wheel height above the ground is hard for the student to learn and difficult for the instructor to teach, so here are a few thoughts on the subject.

The round-out has already been explained (page 44), but, you may recall, my advice was that the descent should be checked so that there was a reasonable distance between the wheels and the ground. Note that I am avoiding the trap of saying 'Complete the round-out with the main gear 3–4 ft above the runway' because (a) you cannot see the wheels, and (b) there are no means of taking such measurements from the pilot's seat.

The hard answer is that you must learn that bit from experience – there is no other way. But what follows can be explained in more tangible terms. There will be a few seconds while the aircraft becomes aware of the fact that it is no longer coasting downhill, then its momentum (mass × velocity) will begin to be overcome by drag, and the hardware will commence to slow down; there will be a reduction in lift, and the aircraft will *sink*. Here is your signal for action. By completing the round-out a little higher (but not a lot higher) than some instructors like to teach, you get two bites at the cherry; that additional air between you and the ground permits the aircraft to sink a little and to give you warning that time has come to start the hold-off (Fig. 18).

The fact that there has been a sink not only signals that deceleration has started; it also places the wheels nearer the runway, and your task is to prevent them from touching until a tail-down attitude has been attained.

Use of elevator while holding-off

If the elevators are moved back too far while the aircraft retains near-

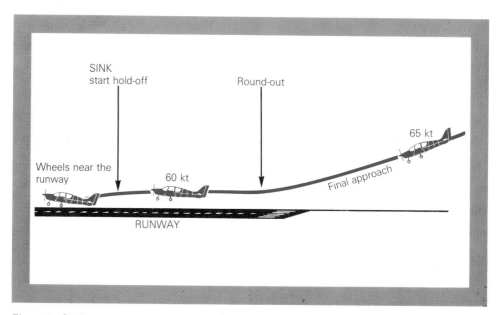

Fig. 18: Sink, a warning to start the hold-off.

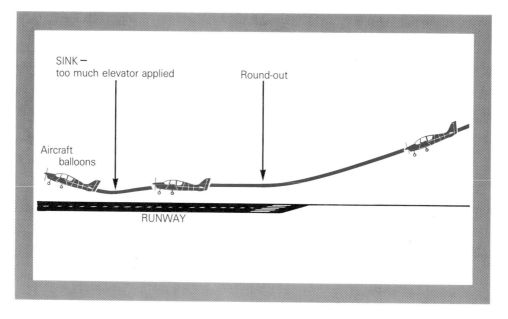

Fig. 19: Excessive use of elevator during the hold-off. Because of the low speed involved this is more dangerous than the situation illustrated in Fig. 15.

approach speed, excess energy will cause it to balloon (Fig. 19). Conversely, insufficient back pressure on the stick/wheel will allow premature touchdown at an unnecessarily high speed, with the attendant risk of nosewheel strain or even wheelbarrowing already mentioned on page 48.

In the early stages of training, students must learn from experience how much up-elevator pressure is required. Indeed, accident statistics indicate that many qualified pilots experience difficulty with this part of the landing, because they are unable to react correctly to visual cues being presented at a time when speed is decreasing and angle of attack should therefore be increased. From the moment one receives the hold-off signal, progressive back pressure on the control stick/wheel is required.

Where to look?

This important question is seldom answered during training. At this stage the pilot is interested in two things: landing attitude and height above the runway. Landing attitude is best determined by looking well ahead towards the end of the runway, but this in itself is not enough. Height above the surface is more easily recognized by looking just ahead of the aircraft, but not so close that the ground is a blur due to forward speed. As the airspeed decreases, so the closest point of distinct vision will come back towards the aircraft, but the eyes should be kept moving back and forth between the far end of the runway (aircraft-attitude cues) and the nearest point where movement can be recognized without features becoming blurred (height appreciation). Above all, avoid staring at one fixed distance. Look too close, and you may let a wing go down or you may balloon through lack of a horizon. Concentrate the gaze to the far end of the airfield, and you will have little appreciation of where the ground is in relation to the wheels.

An alternative method favoured by some is to fix the eyes on a point, sometimes described as 'the length of two cricket pitches away', from which the eyes are moved back and forth to achieve the same appreciation of aircraft attitude, direction (relative to the runway) and height. Well, the Americans and many other nationalities do not play cricket, so I am forced to put a number on the distance – 130 ft or 40 m. And the best way to recognize that is to pace it out, assuming you know how many paces to take for that distance, place an object on the ground then take a good look for future reference.

It goes without saying that whichever method is used, you will have to look along the left of the nose (unless you are landing from the right-hand seat). I only mention the obvious because it is not unknown for pilots to try their luck looking over the nose, a sure way to lose sight of the ground as the correct landing attitude is attained.

Exercises for improving ground-proximity appreciation

Simplistic as it may sound, great benefit may be derived from sitting in the aircraft with the nosewheel standing on a small beer crate to simulate the landing attitude as it will be seen on touchdown. Spend time adjusting the gaze back and forth along the left of the nose – 30 minutes or more is not too long. This method has the double charm of being effective and remarkably cheap!

The second exercise, one that I have found to be very successful over a period of many years, is illustrated in Fig. 20. It requires the pilot under training (licensed or otherwise) to sit, lightly holding the controls, while the instructor, by prior arrangement with ATC, flies low and slow down the runway at hold-off height. As he deliberately undulates the aircraft above the runway, the student must look along the left of the nose in the manner already described and repeat 'Rising', 'Sinking', etc., throughout these slightly eccentric feats of aerial navigation. It may be undignified, but it works like a charm, and after a few such demonstrations those experiencing trouble with their landings will have learned:

1. How and where to look along the left of the nose.

2. How to recognize aircraft height above the ground while holding-off.

Fig. 20: Ground proximity training exercise.

3. How little control movement is required to achieve the correct atti-
tude/height prior to touchdown.

Final correction

Assuming the round-out was handled correctly and the hold-off was a
continuous process that allowed the aircraft to adopt a tail-down (i.e.,
initial lift-off) attitude, the mainwheels should make gentle contact with
the runway. What if the hold-off was a little high? All is not lost. As the
aircraft drops, simply reduce the rate of sink by further back pressure on
the elevator control; the landing that follows should not disgrace anyone.

Factors affecting the hold-off

Several years ago I became involved at the tail-end of a long, drawn-out
club discussion which, I was told later, had been going on for months by
word of mouth and through the club's excellent monthly news magazine.
Why was it, some club members had questioned, that on a windless day
the aircraft floated for what seemed to be an age before sitting down on
the runway, while in a moderate to strong wind a landing occurred
almost immediately after the round-out? After all, they reasoned, the
same approach speed is used on each occasion, so why the difference?

The point is this. While the airspeed may well be the same in both
cases, the aircraft does not take account of that during the hold-off.
Remember, the power is off, and the hardware is no longer coasting
downhill. So what makes it continue to fly parallel to the runway? The
answer is – momentum. Imagine that there is no wind and that you are
flying an aircraft weighing 3,000 lb (1,361 kg). Speed after round-out is
70 knots, and on a speed × weight basis, you and your wonderplane are
possessed of a lot of energy in that instant of time. According to a
gentleman named Newton, your plane is intent on continuing forever at
70 knots, and so it would in outer space; but, fortunately for the aviating
public, we are surrounded by air. And the same air that generously gives
us lift also provides drag.

Assuming your touchdown speed is 50 knots, drag has to remove 20
knots before you can land, and that might take, say, five seconds. Some
days later you are landing with a 15-knot wind blowing down the runway,
so although the ASI indicates 70 knots, immediately after round-out
groundspeed is only 55 knots. And by the time your touchdown IAS of 50
knots has arrived, groundspeed will be 35 knots. While that leaves drag
with the same task as before – to get to grips with the airframe and slow

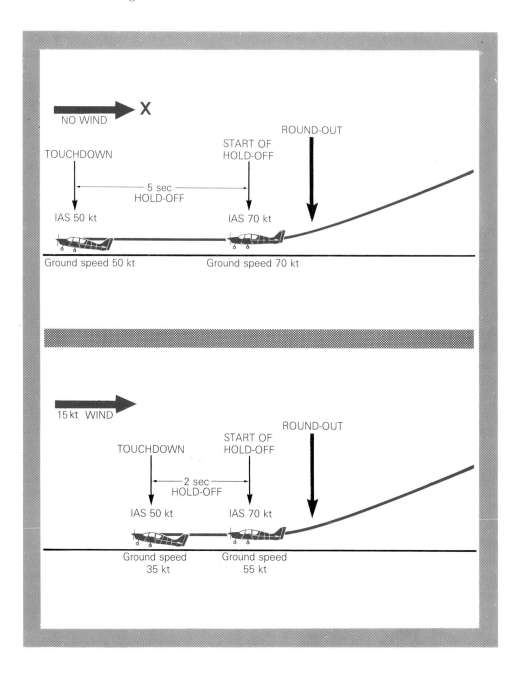

Fig. 21: Wind effect on the hold-off.

it down by 20 knots – on this occasion there is less momentum. You will recall that in still air there was the product of 3,000 lb × 50 knots to retard, but now a 15-knot wind has reduced the task to 3,000 lb × 35 knots, which is 30 per cent less of a battle for drag to fight. Fig. 21 illustrates the hold-off under conditions of nil wind and 15 knots, but pilots should always remember the following:

1. Touchdown at the correct attitude (i.e., mainwheels first) is related to airspeed.

2. Length of hold-off (i.e., float) is proportional to aircraft landing weight × groundspeed at the end of the round-out.

3. Pilots should therefore be prepared for a relatively long float in conditions of nil wind and a progressively shorter hold-off period as the wind becomes stronger.

4. In any wind conditions, the float period may be increased by adopting a higher approach speed and reduced by adopting a lower one.

5. Since aerodynamic drag provides the retarding force during deceleration, it follows that amount of flap will affect the hold-off period, which will be at its longest (other things being equal) in the flaps-up configuration.

The landing roll

Because the point of touchdown (mainwheels) is behind the centre of gravity, there is a natural tendency for nosewheel aircraft to pitch nose-down following a landing. While this is beneficial in so far as angle of attack is reduced and the corresponding decrease in lift ensures that the aircraft will stay on the ground, the nosewheel must be kept off the surface at this stage. This applies to light singles and twins, but not all aircraft, because techniques are rather different with larger types. But the advantages of safeguarding the nosewheel by keeping it off the runway until the nose lowers of its own accord during deceleration are the obvious ones of less wear and tear, lower demands on the brakes (because of the retarding effect of drag with even a slightly nose-up attitude) and the avoidance of wheelbarrowing.

Even after the nosewheel is on the runway, the stick/wheel must be held back to relieve the strut/wheel assembly of unnecessary load. This is particularly important when landing on grass airfields or on any surface where rough patches may be encountered.

Braking

In the days when aircraft were fitted with cable-operated drum brakes, they could be relied upon to fade at the very moment when most needed. Then along came disc brakes, which greatly reduced fading by exposing the braking area to cooling air.

Disc brakes may be a great improvement on the old drum units, but that is not a licence to abuse them. It should be remembered that when you hammer the brakes, tyre wear increases too, so here are a few hints on avoiding unnecessary wear and obtaining the best results from your brakes.

Surface

Best braking will occur on a hard, dry surface free of grease or other contamination. It therefore follows that caution should be exercised when braking on a wet runway, since there is a risk of aquaplaning (a wedge of water can build up between tyre and runway surface, turning your favourite plane into a water skier). Likewise, the brakes must be used with caution when ice is present. Snow, on the other hand, can have a retarding effect unless it has become compacted, when it should be treated as ice. (This is all explained in Chapter 9.)

It is often not realized that wet grass can act like ice, particularly if harsh braking is applied immediately after touchdown.

From the foregoing it will be obvious that pilots who find it impossible to land before a third or more of the runway is behind them are in trouble when the surface is likely to offer poor braking effect. The moral is clear:

1. Land near the threshold.

2. Exercise careful speed control.

3. Touch down on the mainwheels only, and hold off the nosewheel after landing. That way you will keep the main landing gear firmly planted on the ground and enjoy the assistance of aerodynamic braking.

4. Delay applying the brakes until the aircraft is rolling at a low speed, and use them very sparingly.

Use of brakes

1. Never apply the brakes until the nosewheel has lowered to the runway unless you want to see the nosestrut make a sudden, spectacular appearance through the top of the nose.

2. Apply the brakes in short bursts, using more prolonged applications as the speed reduces. Never allow a wheel to lock on a slippery surface.

Raising the flaps

Some manufacturers advise raising the flaps during the landing roll because, they would have you believe, there is better wheel adhesion without the extra lift being developed with landing flap. If there is any braking improvement, I suspect it is more imaginary than real. I also suspect the technique of being one beloved of the local test pilot (who may never have faced the problems of training others to fly).

Most of the leading training establishments in Britain do not like the idea of raising the flaps on touchdown, for the following reasons:

1. It is doubtful if the gain in wheel adhesion (assuming it exists at all) is sufficient to balance the loss of aerodynamic braking that is provided by full application of flap.

2. The pilot should be concentrating on maintaining direction after landing, not groping for the flap control.

3. There is a real risk that the landing gear might be retracted in error.

Some years ago I wrote a hard-hitting article for *Flight International*, the well-known aviation weekly published in London. In it I expressed views similar to those outlined above, and letters poured in from all directions accusing me of being an old square and insisting that even if the wheels were selected UP in error, nothing would happen, because a safety switch or valve, operated when the weight of the aircraft was on the landing gear, would prevent it from retracting. Shortly afterwards in Britain we had a number of disappearing-wheel acts during the landing roll, and in Australia there were even more. One only has to hit a bump, and the safety device will cease to operate. The events that follow are always entertaining to those watching at a safe distance but very expensive in terms of mangled props, shock-loaded engines and so forth.

So, taking a hard look at the for-and-against of raising the flaps immediately after landing, my advice is: leave them alone until the aircraft has stopped, you are clear of the runway and post-landing checks are being carried out. 'Suppose my bird has a fixed set of wheels, can I not raise the flaps and improve braking?' is a question I am sometimes asked. Surely the answer is that fixed-gear aircraft land at a low speed anyway, so why mess about with the flaps at a time when you should be concentrating on the landing roll? And why develop potentially danger-ous habits for the future when you may well find yourself handling a retractable single or twin? In any case, I do not believe that raising the flaps will assist braking *when full flap has been used for the landing*.

Factors affecting the landing roll

In varying degrees the following factors will affect the length of roll after touchdown (as with all advice in this chapter, it is assumed that there is no crosswind):

1. Aircraft weight.

2. Touchdown speed, which depends on:
   (a) surface wind;
   (b) IAS at touchdown;
   (c) airfield temperature and elevation.

3. Amount of flap (full flap providing most braking drag).

4. Gradient of the runway.

5. Surface of the runway.

6. Braking technique.

Post-landing checks

Some of the major airports have a fast-departure lane, which allows even large, heavy passenger jets to clear the runway while rolling at a rate of knots. However, most airfields require a fairly abrupt turn while taxiing off the landing area, and it goes without saying that changing direction through, say, 60°, 90° or even more should be done at a fast walking pace. Having cleared the runway, carry out the post-landing checks as listed in the aircraft manual. These usually include most, if not all, of the following items, and sometimes one or two extras when the aircraft is a more complex design: Flaps UP; Fuel pump(s) OFF; Cooling flap(s) OPEN; Carb. air COLD.

The landing process summarized

Having explained each stage of the landing – in too much detail, some might complain, although this is a book dedicated to the subject of landing – it is now appropriate to summarize what has been said. No landing should ever be treated in a casual manner. If you watch a professional, even the skipper of a large passenger jet, he may make it all look easy. But there will be nothing off-hand in the way he goes about the task. Each landing is different, and the good pilot is always alert to departures from normal, however small. It is the slovenly pilot, sitting idly at the controls and watching an obvious overshoot go from bad to impossible, who ends up landing half-way into the airfield, pulling up in a cloud of smoke, a smell of burning rubber drifting on the breeze.

So to inject a little consistency into your landing performance, here are the golden rules to remember:

The approach

1. A good downwind leg is essential for a good base leg.

2. A good base leg is essential for a good approach.

3. On the base leg apply half-flap, adjust speed and power appropriately and retrim.

4. Make a *gradual* turn on to the initial approach, aiming to roll out in line with the runway at a height of not less than 400 ft.

5. Unless there are strong gusts or crosswinds, lower full flaps.

6. Co-ordinate elevator and power to achieve a steady glidepath at the correct initial approach speed. If the picture framed in the windscreen changes, indicating an overshoot or undershoot, it is no good sitting there, unmoved, in the hope that something may happen to improve the situation, because most likely it will get worse!

7. On short finals allow the aircraft to settle at target threshold speed, and be on guard for the effects of turbulence or wind gradient, instantly adding power if the rate of sink increases.

8. Aim for a landing area, which should remain fixed on the windscreen throughout the approach.

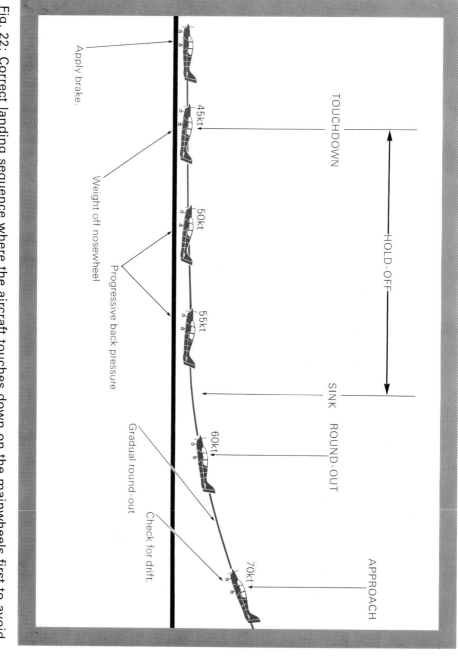

Fig. 22: Correct landing sequence where the aircraft touches down on the mainwheels first to avoid wheel-barrowing and excessive stress to the nosewheel.

The landing (Fig. 22)

1. As the ground comes up to meet you, look along the left of the nose for the correct round-out point. When it arrives, ease back on the elevators to check the descent.

2. When the level attitude has been attained, smoothly close the throttle(s). Keep straight down the runway centreline – that way there is room to swing left or right (whatever the reason) without departing from the runway.

3. Look along the left of the nose, shifting the gaze from relatively near the aircraft (but not so near that objects are blurred by speed) to the far end of the runway.

4. Be prepared for the aircraft to sink again, and regard this as the signal to hold off.

5. With your hand on the throttle, keep your eyes moving back and forth. Prevent the aircraft from touching down by progressive back pressure on the stick/wheel. If a balloon develops, resist the temptation to move the control forward. Hold the elevators where they are; add a little power to reduce the rate of sink; and then check further descent by back pressure on the elevator control. Close the throttle, and be prepared for the wheels to make contact soon afterwards (Fig. 23). Aim to touch down in a nose-high attitude, mainwheels first.

6. When the wheels touch, be prepared for the nose to pitch down. Prevent nosewheel contact by maintaining back pressure on the stick/wheel.

7. Allow the nosewheel to lower gently on to the runway as speed decreases. Then (and *only* then) apply the brakes, using short applications at first but longer pressures as the speed decreases.

8. Clear the runway, and carry out the post-landing checks.

Without doubt, one of the most satisfying aviation experiences is a really good landing, when the wheels grease on to the runway. The strange thing is that with experience, and using the techniques described in the preceding pages, one can climb aboard an unfamiliar aircraft,

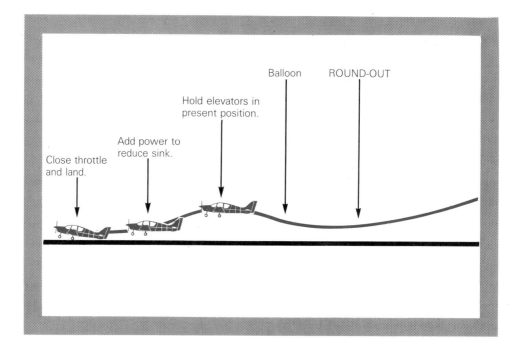

Fig. 23: Correcting ballooning with proper use of power.

totally different in size from the equipment usually flown, and pull off a decent landing. The fact that on the flight deck you might be sitting at twice the usual height above the ground seems to matter very little. With practice, a good pilot can register the picture while taxiing out for take-off and remember it during the landing, feeling for the ground, checking the rate of sink on the elevators during the final stages of the hold-off.

Missed-approach action

In the best of regulated worlds there may come a time when a pilot must break off the approach and try for another landing. Reasons for this are several. He could fail to see the lead-in lights in poor weather; the approach could be badly judged, making a safe landing impossible (too high, not in line with the runway, and so on); or some nut may have taxied on to the runway as he is about to pull off one of his faultless landings. Whatever the reason, a missed-approach action (sometimes called overshoot action) must be taken.

During a missed approach two main considerations apply:

(a) transition from approach to climbing configuration;
(b) avoidance of other circuit traffic.

Transition from approach to climb

Most aircraft that are in a stabilized approach, exhibit marked trim changes when full power is applied for the climb. Remember the flaps may be in the landing position (maximum extension) and since only moderate power will be in use prior to the go-round decision a fair amount of nose-up trim will have been applied. So when full power is added be prepared for the nose to come up. In some aircraft very considerable forward pressure will be required on the stick/wheel while the trim is wound forward. It is essential to maintain the correct flaps-down climbing speed; this will be slightly lower than that recommended for the flaps-up climb. It goes without saying that the aircraft must be kept straight as power is applied.

Most aircraft tend to sink when the flaps are raised, so raise them in stages, adjusting the trim as you do so. Usually the last 20° or so cause the most sink, consequently it is good practice to gain at least 300 ft before the final clean-up. If the aircraft has a constant-speed propeller this should be fully fine during the overshoot and, when applicable, the landing gear should be retracted without delay.

Avoiding other traffic

At most airfields a missed approach will be directed by ATC and the controller will give specific instructions regarding when to turn, and so forth. In the absence of ATC it is good practice to turn right and then line up with the runway in full view on your left. That way you can see other aircraft landing – and also keep an eye on the cowboy who took off without warning and caused you to take missed-approach action!

Landing at night

When all is black outside and there is a moonless sky above, disorientation can be caused by the reflection of ground or other lights on the cabin windows or canopy. Then again, stars and lights on the ground can merge in hazy conditions to give misleading impressions of aircraft attitude. All this sounds alarming and so it can be if use is not made of the flight panel. It is there to provide attitude and other references when normal visual cues are not available. So obviously pilots intent on night flying must first make themselves proficient on instruments.

When time comes to approach and the runway lights appear ahead like a giant Christmas tree a descent into that black void between you and the runway threshold must begin. This is the time when thinking pilots ask themselves 'What if I hit an unseen tree, building or powerline on the way in?', not a happy thought but a problem catered for by that pilot's friend, the angle of approach indicator

Angle of approach indicators

One of the earliest angle of approach indicators was a three-colour affair positioned near the runway threshold. To make it more distinguishable from the other lights it was sometimes arranged to flash on and off. When the aircraft was on the correct glideslope a green light could be seen but if it was too high this automatically changed to amber. Coming in below the glidepath caused the indicator to display a red light. It was a simple device consisting of three coloured strips of glass.

Some years after the war a more accurate system known as Visual Approach Slope Indicator (VASI) came into use. Like the earlier device VASIs are located near the threshold but in the form of a double row of three lights on each side of the runway. The two rows of lights are set at an angular difference to one another of about ½°. A pilot approaching too high sees two rows of white lights. On a correct glidepath the six lights nearest the aircraft glow white while the second row will be red, and if the approach is too low all lights will turn red. Other than a tendency for the lights to go pink during the transition from white to red or red to white, VASIs work well. Indeed we had all come to like them. But man is a discontented animal, never satisfied with his lot and a slave to perfection as a result. So now we are in the midst of another change.

The latest 'night-flyers' guiding hand' is known as Precision Approach Path Indicator (PAPI to its friends). It consists of a single row of four lights positioned on each side of the runway threshold. Starting from 'high', when all lights are white, a pilot descending to correct his approach path would first see the innermost lights (left and right of the runway) turn red leaving the outer lights white. That means 'slightly high'. On regaining the correct glidepath two lights on each side of the runway would be red and the two outer pairs (left and right of the runway) would remain white. But if he failed to arrest his increased rate of descent the next indication would be three reds on each side of the runway with the outermost lights showing white (described as 'slightly low'). Four reds on each side means 'low'. Such is the accuracy of PAPI that over the threshold the approach channel is only 2 m deep. There is no pink transition while changing colour.

With all types of approach indicator interpretation is much the same: never stay in the 'red' for a second longer than is necessary to open the throttle and get back on the glidepath. Conversely, avoid being persistently too high since this can demand a high descent rate at the end of the approach while nearing a surface that cannot be seen in the dark!

The night landing

There is little point in switching on the landing lights too early; even the most powerful ones will seem like a voice in the wilderness until the beams are able to make contact with the surface. Furthermore on a hazy night the landing lights will make it more difficult to see the lead-in lights and the runway lights themselves not to mention the angle of approach indicators. Use of the landing lights in dense haze can turn the surrounding air into what appears to be a sea of milk. Generally you should delay using the lights until short finals.

The act of landing is very similar to daytime practice. Some pilots prefer making the touchdown without landing lights, using the runway lights to indicate whereabouts of the surface. Personally I have always regarded this as doing things the hard way because the landing lights will illuminate the surface ahead and allow one to make a touchdown as if it is daytime. In consequence no special techniques are called for.

If for any reason the landing lights have failed, appreciation of ground proximity, while certainly aided by the runway lights, can be difficult to determine with accuracy. In such cases it is good practice to leave on a little power until the wheels make contact with the runway thus reducing sink rate to a minimum. Too much power could result in excessive float, something to avoid on a short runway.

So much for the engine-assisted approach and landing under normal conditions. The chapters that follow deal with the more difficult conditions that are the rule rather than the exception in day-to-day flying. For the perfect day (or night), offering ideal landing conditions, is rare indeed, at least in many parts of the world.

3. Glide, flapless and other abnormal landings

As the title of this chapter declares, it deals with abnormal situations: primarily, glide landings because of an engine failure, and flapless landings due to exceptional wind conditions or, perhaps, a mechanical malfunction. While some pilots will no doubt claim that all their landings are made flaps-up (because they like doing things the hard way) and that the glide approach and landing is their normal mode of arrival ('If it is good enough for the Space Shuttle, it is good enough for me'), viewed against the canvas of modern aviation, both techniques, flapless and powerless, are abnormal. The only reason why they occupy space in this book is that one day the reader might suffer a power failure while flying a single-engine aircraft, when, like it or not, a carefully judged glide approach and landing will be demanded; or there could be an electric, hydraulic or mechanical problem (according to aircraft system) which prevents the pilot from using his flaps for the landing. Both emergencies are rare these days, but the good pilot is prepared for all situations, and, at intervals, both glide and flapless landings should be practised. Regard such exercises as a form of insurance if you like, but *never* look upon any emergency training as a waste of time, a sop to the teachings of elderly pilots who have lost their nerve and who should give up flying and take up knitting. Periodic emergency training and check-rides are essential to good flying standards. Airline flight crews, with more time pushing back from the loading ramp than most readers are likely to amass flying, have six-monthly base checks, route checks, instrument-rating renewals, etc. Military pilots spend their lives checking one another, and, in Britain at least, flying instructors suffer a thorough biennial test on the ground and in the air before their ratings are renewed.

This chapter deals, in fact, with four abnormalities: the two already mentioned as well as wake turbulence and, for the benefit of multi-engine pilots, asymmetric landings. Exercises for the glide, flapless and asymmetric landings should be practised at, say, six-monthly intervals. Far from being a 'drag', they will make a change from the tedium of your usual perfectly judged, full-flap, engine-assisted 'greaser'.

The glide approach and landing

In the bad old days of biplanes, with their high drag and relatively steep descent path, the glide approach and landing was considered the normal way of doing things. Indeed, pilots regarded it as a point of honour not to touch the throttle once it was closed on the base leg. If the approach was too high, there was always the side-slip, but if you were too low, power had to be added – and the ridicule of friends watching from the ground usually followed. As transport flying developed, it was soon realized that if relatively large aircraft were to operate from the postage-stamp-sized airfields of the day, more accurate positioning of the touchdown point and a lower approach speed (as well as a smaller change of pitch angle from glide to hold-off) would result from motoring in. In some parts of the world the engine-assisted approach was known as 'rumbling'. To understand the difficulties posed by using the glide approach technique, it is first necessary to consider the disadvantages. In a glide approach and landing:

1. Stalling speed is higher than when power is used, and for reasons of safety a glide approach in a single-engine aircraft is usually flown at a speed 5–10 knots higher than that recommended for an engine-assisted approach.

The asymmetric landing-propeller feathered on the failed engine.

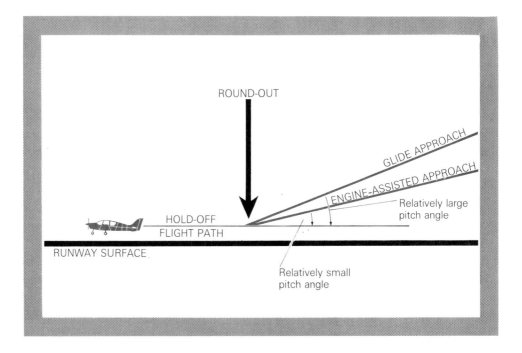

Fig. 24: Comparison between a powered approach and a glide approach. Note the relatively large pitch angle entailed while rounding-out from a glide approach.

2. Glide path, given equal flap settings, is steeper than that of an engine-assisted approach, and the transition from final approach to hold-off entails a large change in pitch angle during the round-out (Fig. 24). This demands of the pilot very accurate timing and precise control.

3. Although excess height during a glide approach may be adjusted by using flap or side-slipping, nothing can be done about being too low. As the wartime pilot of a troop-carrying glider once told me, 'If we are overshooting, we add more flap. If we are undershooting, it's a pity!'

4. Without an engine, speed control is particularly important. This will be discussed later in the chapter.

5. Generally, a higher standard of judgement on height, distance and positioning is necessary during a glide approach and landing than for a standard engine-assisted arrival.

In essence, the glide approach and landing is not one to adopt from choice; it is a difficulty thrust upon us following engine failure. So, really, we are back to our old friend the forced landing without power, an emergency procedure described in a companion volume, *Be a Better Pilot*, and in other books of mine. In this book the glide landing is treated as a variation on the standard theme, something to practise from time to time as a change from routine landings. For reasons of circuit traffic, it is not always possible to carry out glide approaches, but there are many occasions when one can. And the pilot who does develop skill in the art of landing without using power is far better equipped to deal with a real emergency, when the elastic breaks with a sound that proclaims, 'No more power today.' While one must accept that glide approach and landings are more difficult than the engine-assisted variety, that does not make them impossible, and the tricks of the trade that follow may be relied upon to defeat adversity by sheer pilot cunning (and there is none more cunning than a skilful pilot).

Planning the circuit

In the context of this chapter, everything that follows relates to a planned glide approach and landing, not a forced landing without power, where there may be circumstances demanding circuit patterns calculated to blow all fuses in the tower at a busy airfield. The aim of the game is to close the throttle on the base leg and glide in without using power again.

It is essential to plan the latter part of the circuit so that (a) judgement of height and distance is relatively easy, and (b) there are opportunities for adjustment if you get it wrong.

Fly downwind to the usual base-leg turning-point, and you will be faced with a long, straight glide towards the runway. That is probably one of the most difficult things to assess in aviation. Most experienced pilots avoid the trap whenever possible. For a glide approach, you should make the turn on to base leg *immediately* the runway threshold has passed your seat. The charms of doing it the right way are illustrated in Fig. 25. The top drawing shows that because of your distance from the runway threshold, the point at which you close the throttle must be absolutely correct. Chop the power too soon, and you will undershoot. Leave it too late, and touchdown will be half-way down the runway, if it is on the airfield at all. Take a look at the lower picture. This pilot is an ace. He has turned on to base leg as the runway threshold has drifted past his ear; as a result, the base leg is positioned close to the downwind boundary

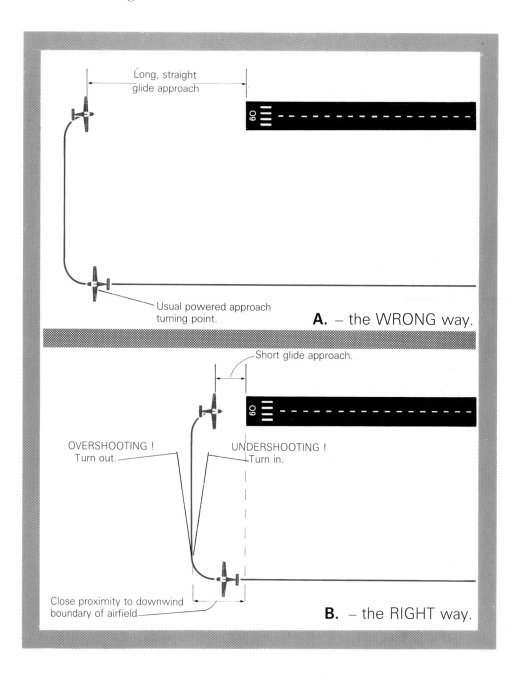

Fig. 25: Turning on to the base leg. (A) the wrong way in which the pilot must get it absolutely right first time, and (B) the right way where he may adjust the base leg to produce an ideal final approach.

of the airfield, close enough for him to assess the distance remaining with accuracy and therefore to close the throttle with confidence.

A word about closing the throttle. The majority of pilots tested by me seem committed to the technique of pulling back the throttle first and then applying carburettor heat. I know of at least one accident that resulted from this practice. It happened when a girl who was practising glide approaches found herself undershooting. The throttle was opened, 'No answer' came the loud reply from up front, and the hardware came to rest, more or less intact, in a field this side of a successful arrival on the intended runway. An examination revealed that the girl had, in error, pulled the mixture control (coloured yellow because the French manu- facturer liked the flavour). Had she applied carburettor heat *before* closing the throttle three things would have been established:

1. The presence or otherwise of carb. ice would have been determined.

2. A modest drop in **RPM** would have confirmed that the carb. heat system was working.

3. If, instead of 2 above, a dramatic silence had followed, the inescapable fact that all was not well would almost certainly have encouraged her to move the mixture back to where it belonged and to try a knob of different colour – the one that worked the carb. heat.

If I had my way *all* mixture controls, even French ones, would be coloured red. So, when closing the throttle, look before you leap. Apply carb. heat first, and only if the machinery keeps churning away should the throttle be closed.

Assessing and adjusting the glide

The plan is to roll out of the final turn, in line with the runway, at a height of around 400 ft and to be faced with a short glide aimed at reaching a touchdown point positioned 600 ft or so upwind of the threshold. The reason is that without power you can get rid of a tolerable amount of excess height, but remember the second half of that quote: if you're undershooting, 'it's a pity!'. Variables that can spoil this ideal situation are:

1. **Incorrect position for closing the throttle**. Only experience can illustrate where this should be, but the visual cue to take off power

is one of *aspect*, that is, the angular appearance of the runway as seen by the pilot. More about that later.

2. **Use of flap**. Before closing the throttle, one should be certain that it will then be safe to lower, say, 10–15° of flap. As a guiding principle, most manoeuvres or control actions in an aircraft are best taken on a step-by-step basis; that way sudden changes in performance or flight path are avoided. Only in an emergency should 'all-in-one-go' action be contemplated. In normal circumstances, such action – in this case, full flap selected in one application rather than in stages – may so disturb the flight path that you may feel moved to raise them again. Not all aircraft take kindly to having their flaps raised when the ground is not far below, so stick to the aims of the game. These are: a power-off glide, using part-flap, with a view to landing 600 ft into the runway, so ensuring there will be no undershoot problems. The remainder of the flap will be used later, but only when it is certain that the aircraft will reach the airfield.

3. **Wind conditions**. Obviously, a strong wind will tend to drift the aircraft away from the airfield and steepen the glidepath after turning on to finals. There are also the possibilities of wind-gradient effect (mentioned on page 43), so when the breeze is strong and perhaps gusty, the airspeed should be increased by 5–10 knots, according to wind conditions.

One of the advantages of adopting the base-leg position illustrated in Fig. 25b is that drift relative to the downwind boundary of the airfield allows good assessment of wind strength. And undershooting or over-shooting may easily be corrected by turning towards or away from the airfield accordingly. It is as simple as that. But how does one know if there is risk of an undershoot or an overshoot? Read on.

Recognizing aspect

In mentioning aspect what we are really talking about is glide angle, and this determines the undershoot and overshoot as discussed above. At this stage of the circuit, the aircraft will be gliding on the base leg with part-flap applied (10–15° would be typical), and an appreciation of aspect is essential for the success of the exercise. While aspect recognition is best learned from experience, in Fig. 26 I have attempted to illustrate

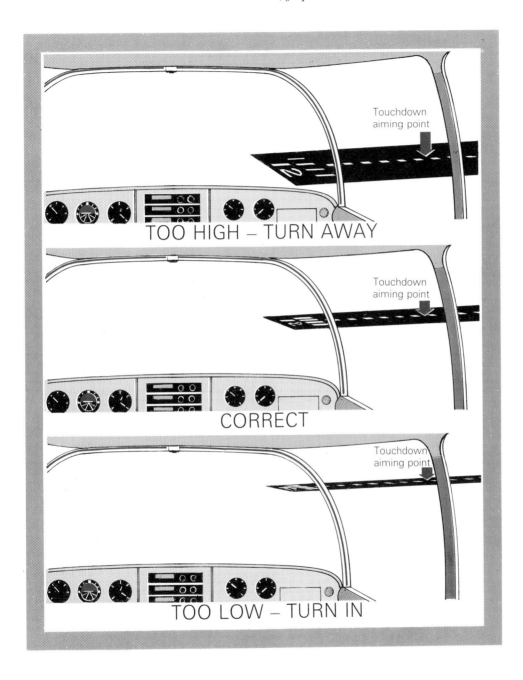

Fig. 26: Visual cues provided by runway aspect during a glide approach.

what a pilot should be looking for during a right-hand circuit.

The top picture shows the runway almost in plan view. Clearly, we are in for an overshoot, even taking into account that the initial touchdown aiming-point is well up the runway.

Remedy: Turn away from the runway threshold (in this case to the left) and so lengthen the approach. In extreme cases more (but not full) flap should be added.

The centre drawing is an 'all-systems-go' situation. Provided the pilot maintains that aiming-point and the windscreen in the same angular relationship throughout the base leg and final turn, we are in business.

The bottom picture shows trouble ahead, with the runway in flat aspect and high up the windscreen, unless in an effort to make the airfield the pilot has raised the nose to stretch the glide, but that must be avoided *at all costs.* Be in no doubt – we are not going to reach the threshold, let alone our touchdown aiming-point 600 ft upwind of it, unless decisive action is taken without delay.

Remedy: Turn towards the runway threshold (to the right in this case), and shorten the length of the approach. In extreme cases, be prepared to add power, and avoid a low-level final turn.

The importance of accurate speed

Best glide performance, and by that I mean greatest distance forward per unit of height loss, occurs when the aircraft is flown at its best lift/ drag (L/D) ratio angle of attack. For most aircraft we are talking about an angle of around 4–6°, but few aircraft carry angle-of-attack indicators. However, fortunately for those of us who fly, angle of attack is closely related to indicated airspeed, and the aircraft manual will give the speed for the best glide.

There is only one speed for best glide performance. Attempt to glide at a higher speed, or push your luck stretching the glide by raising the nose (reducing speed), and the rate of sink will increase in relation to forward speed. All this is elementary knowledge, the kind of information every student pilot should know. However, while even inexperienced pilots can usually quote these basic rules of aeronautics, few (in my experience) really understand what they are about. Consequently, when the chips are down and it has gone horribly silent up front, many a potentially attainable forced landing has ended in an untidy heap instead of on the intended field.

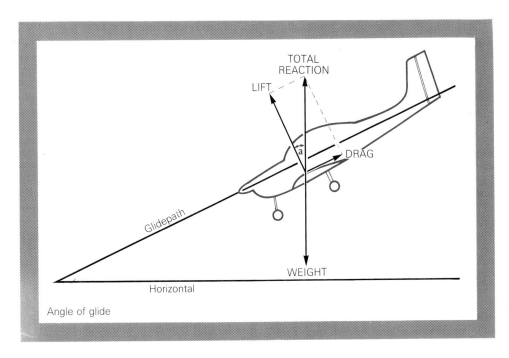

Fig. 27: The influence of Lift/Drag Ratio on glide performance.

So what about best gliding angle, and how do we obtain it? First, it should be clearly understood that when we talk about gliding at the best L/D ratio angle of attack we are interested in that which relates to the entire aircraft, not just the wing. Fig. 27 shows that if we draw to scale lift and drag, so that total reaction from both forces opposes the weight of the aircraft (as it would in a glide), the angle between lift and total reaction is equal to the angle of the glidepath relative to the horizontal. Put another way, if there is ten times as much lift as there is drag, an aircraft will glide forward ten units (feet, metres, nautical miles, etc.) for every unit of descent. Such an aircraft would be said to have a L/D ratio of 10. Disturb that ratio by any means, and you must affect the gliding angle.

It is often not realized how little change in angle of attack is required to affect the L/D ratio materially. The following figures are for an airfoil only (in fact, an NACA 23012), but they do illustrate the point I am making and show the importance of good speed control during a glide approach and landing.

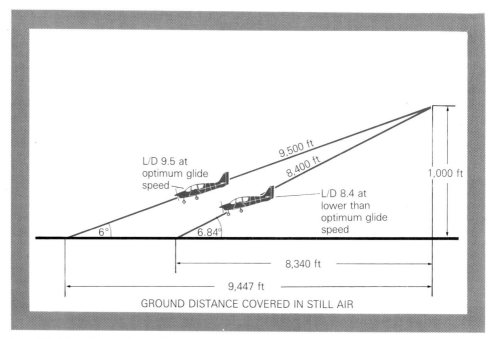

Fig. 28: The damaging effect on glidepath of incorrect approach speeds.

Angle of attack	Lift/drag ratio
0°	10.0
+2°	23.0
4°	24.6
6°	23.0
8°	18.9

From these figures it can be seen that over a pitch change of only 4°, L/D for this particular airfoil changes from 10 to its best value, which is 24.6. Any further increase in angle and the ratio reduces but, more important to the pilot, the glidepath becomes steeper. (Note that some of the more modern airfoils give very high L/D ratios over a wider range of angles, but the principle remains the same.)

Expressed in practical terms, this means that (taking a well-known, advanced, single-engine tourer as an example) when gliding at its wheels-and-flaps-up best L/D angle of attack, a glide from 1,000 ft will cover 9,500 ft along its flightpath, representing a L/D ratio of 9.5 for the complete aircraft. It would require only a small change in angle of attack to reduce the L/D to 8.4, when the same aircraft gliding from 1,000 ft would cover only 8,400 ft, which is 1,100 ft or 11.5 per cent less. Fig. 28 makes the point loud and clear. For practical purposes, flightpath distances may be regarded as ground distances.

The effects of weight

Contrary to popular belief, weight has no effect on glide performance in still air conditions, *provided* that the best L/D angle of attack is maintained. You get nothing for nothing in aeronautics, so if we want our wing of fixed area and shape to support more weight, two options are open to us:

1. We can increase the angle of attack.

2. We can glide faster.

We have already pinned our faith on gliding at best L/D angle of attack, so forget about option 1 and take a look at the alternative. The flight manual (certainly one relating to an aircraft more advanced than your common-or-garden trainer) will quote speeds against weight for best gliding performance. Let me give you a for instance:

Cessna P210 N Pressurized Centurion	
Weight	**IAS (knots)**
4,000 lb (1,816 kg)	87
3,350 lb (1,521 kg)	80
2,700 lb (1,226 kg)	72

Not all manuals give more than one speed for the glide, but on a do-it-yourself basis you can reduce gliding speed by about 5 knots for every 500 lb (227 kg) below maximum weight. So far it has been assumed that there is no wind, but, interestingly enough, a heavily loaded aircraft will glide further against a headwind than a lighter one of the same type, because although the ratio between feet per minute descent and feet per minute forward glide remains unchanged (i.e., best L/D ratio), the higher gliding speed of the heavier aircraft provides a better groundspeed. More distance is covered in the time taken to descend.

Here is a summary of what has been said about the glide:

1. The longest gliding distance per unit height loss (that is, the flattest glide path) will occur at the speed corresponding to best L/D ratio angle of attack.

2. Best L/D speed is usually shown in the aircraft's manual only for maximum weight conditions. To maintain the optimum angle for best glide, reduce the IAS by 5 knots per 500 lb (227 kg) decreased weight. This advice applies to four-seat and larger aircraft. In the case of two-seat trainers, variations in operating weight are not large enough to warrant more than one optimum gliding speed.

3. Any attempt to depart from optimum gliding speed (for a particular weight) must result in a reduction in gliding distance (in other words, a steeper glidepath).

4. In turbulent wind conditions, or when the effects of wind gradient are expected, it is important to increase the gliding speed by 5–10 knots according to wind strength. Allowance must be made for the reduction in gliding distance that will result.

The final turn

Imagine that you are nicely positioned on the base leg with 10–15° of flap lowered and that the aircraft is accurately trimmed to glide at optimum speed. To complete this picture of aviation at its best, your touchdown aiming-point has remained immovably glued to the same spot on your windscreen. The time has come to think about the final turn. By now you should be at a height above the runway of around 600 ft.

A common fault in all landing procedures, engine-assisted, glide or any other type of approach, is a tendency to delay the final turn until, even with the aid of a lot of bank, the runway extended centreline is flown through. To regain it, 'S' turns are then required, but at this stage of the procedure you have quite enough on your plate without adding unnecessary complications. So make the final turn a *gradual* one, with no more than 30° of bank. Fig. 4 (page 24) shows a problem of this kind, one caused by an incorrectly flown downwind leg. On this occasion, however, it is all going your way, so avoid spoiling everything by gliding up to the extended centreline and expecting your favourite plane to point itself at the runway *without radius*. It cannot be done in comfort.

In the old days, when the margin between flying and stalling was not all that wide and a stall almost invariably led to a spin, it was the practice at the start of a gliding turn to increase speed slightly by lowering the nose and adding another 5 knots or so. While modern planes are less twitchy in this respect, there is nevertheless a 7.5 per cent increase in stalling speed during a 30° bank – not a lot, you may consider, but the accident statistics reveal that most fatal spinning accidents occur while the pilot is under stress. Such a moment is the final turn towards the field in a real forced landing without power. Height may be running out; it looks as though the chosen landing area is beyond reach; instinctively, the pilot holds up the nose to stretch the glide and take his money's worth out of the rudder. The rest is a matter for the newspaper headlines.

On the basis that the human animal, like most others, is a creature of habit, why not take out a little insurance, allow for that 7.5 per cent increase in stalling speed and give yourself another 5 knots IAS for the gliding turn? By now you will be descending from around 600 to 400 ft – not a lot of room for spin recovery, even if you are good at it – so, at the risk of being called old-fashioned, just lower the nose a little before rolling on bank.

On the approach

Now is the moment of truth. If, on coming face to face with it, the wind proves to be stronger than anticipated, you are going to be thankful for having aimed at an arrival 600 ft or so up the runway. Wind has a profound effect on gliding performance, because although the rate of descent is unchanged, groundspeed is materially reduced.

Assuming we have rolled out of the turn at 400 ft above runway level with, say, 15° of flap, and the aircraft has a L/D ratio of 8 at its optimum gliding speed of 75 knots, how far will it travel before start of the hold-off? Fig. 29 compares the difference between still air conditions and a 20-knot wind, which causes a 2.5 per cent increase in gliding angle and an 862-ft decrease in gliding distance.

The touchdown aiming-point must now be watched carefully. If it starts to move up the windscreen and the runway begins to flatten, you will probably not make the original point, but remember – this is 600 or so ft into the runway. So leave the flaps where they are; check that your gliding speed is correct; and resist the temptation to stretch the glide by

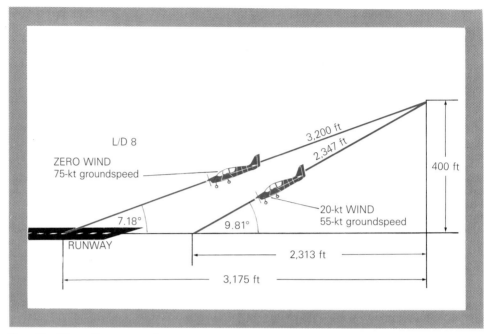

Fig. 29: The effects of wind on optimum glidepath angle.

holding up the nose. Be ready to add power if the aircraft seems unlikely to make the runway.

If the aiming-point starts moving down the windscreen and the runway begins to stand on end, this indicates that you are tending to overshoot. Add more flap, but delay lowering them fully until you are sure of making the runway. Then they should be used to bring back the original touchdown aiming-point to the runway threshold (Fig. 30).

As the runway threshold approaches again, check the gliding speed. If it is too low, there will be no hold-off and the aircraft will very probably sink heavily on to the ground, while a high-speed final approach will cause the aircraft to float for a considerable distance along the runway before it is ready to touch down. (This is dealt with in the next section.)

The glide landing

All the considerations applicable to the powered approach and landing, as described in the previous chapter, apply to the glide landing: the need to control speed; position in the centre of the runway and not to one side; the importance of starting the round-out early enough to take stock of the situation and to allow room for the sink that signals when to

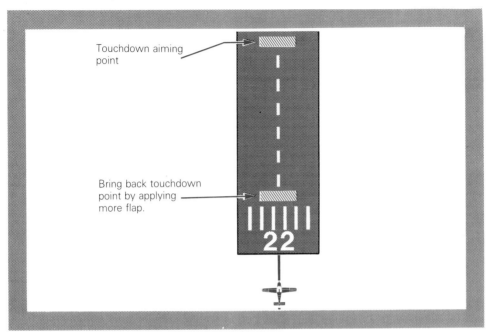

Fig. 30: Use of flap in moving back the touchdown aiming point to the required landing area.

commence the hold-off; the need to keep the eyes moving back and forth in order to appreciate aircraft attitude prior to landing and the proximity of the ground. To all those considerations must be added two more, which apply particularly during a glide landing:

1. During an engine-assisted approach the glidepath is usually 2.5–3° to the horizontal; consequently, there is a relatively small change in nose-up pitch while assuming the level attitude during the round-out. Fig. 29 shows that a glide approach may descend at an angle of 7–10° or more, according to wind conditions; remember that power is not being used to compensate for wind, as in an engine-assisted approach. So be prepared for a somewhat larger pitch-up while making the round-out. Another 4–7° may not sound much; in practice, it is enough to confuse those pilots who have not done a glide landing since Nelson lost his eye.

2. During the hold-off, if you do allow elevator back pressure to get ahead of reducing airspeed, and a balloon results, forget pride; space permitting, use power to ease the bird gently on to the runway. *Never*

tell yourself, 'This is a glide landing and, as a point of honour – no power', because the next enactment will probably be to ease forward on the wheel and have the landing gear through the roof.

Words of warning

● Never lower full flap unless you are certain of reaching the runway.

● Never attempt to stretch the glide by raising the nose. That *cannot* work.

● Never lower full flap if:
  (a) you have allowed your speed to become low;
  (b) there is a known risk of wind gradient;
  (c) there are strong winds, crosswinds or bad gusts;
  (d) you have descended below 200 ft.

● When lowering flap, be sure to maintain the recommended flaps-down gliding speed.

● Make full use of trim.

● Maintain the correct gliding speed until the round-out.

● Start the round-out early; make it gradual; and be prepared for a larger than usual change in pitch attitude while levelling the aircraft.

Earlier in this chapter I said that the glide approach and landing was more demanding than the standard power-assisted technique. Certainly, it requires skill, judgement and a nice touch – all of which makes it an ideal exercise to practise, one that can improve basic pilotage skills over the entire spectrum of the art. Sound pilot handling is the basis of all good flying. It is the foundation on which air safety is built.

The flapless approach and landing

On reading the title of this section, you could be forgiven for telling yourself, 'Loss of flaps is unlikely ever to affect me.' I had often told myself the same comforting story. Then one day I flew back from France in a high-powered, retractable tourer. Because of the usual stupid duty and tax laws most of us have to suffer, the owner, who had asked me to ferry his plane to England, particularly requested that I fill the tanks at Le Touquet, my point of departure. It so happens that there was a moderately full cabin, so ours was a heavy bird as it hopped across the English Channel and prepared to land. On selecting flap, all I could muster was 10°, although the ammeter showed that the electric motor was doing its bit. 'We have had trouble with the flaps,' announced the young French pilot in the right-hand seat, adding, 'The drive clutch slips,' as we crossed the threshold at 90 knots-plus, with the stall warner blowing its head off. I got him to hold down the spring-loaded flap-switch in the hope that as speed decreased during the hold-off, and pressure on the flaps became less, our anaemic drive clutch would have the muscle to give us those missing 35°. We needed them because the far end of the field was approaching the windscreen at an uncomfortable rate of knots. It worked. But suppose there had been total failure of the flap system – how would that have affected the approach and landing? When compared with the flaps-down configuration, a 'clean' aircraft will present these differences:

On the approach

1. Stalling speed will be 5–20 knots higher, according to aircraft type.

2. At any particular speed there will be a higher nose attitude, causing problems of reduced forward visibility.

3. The glidepath will be flatter.

During the landing

1. The flatter glidepath will require a smaller pitch change during the round-out.

2. Since touchdown speed is higher, the landing roll will be longer.

The net result of all this is that flapless approaches must be flown accurately to ensure that the full length of the runway is available for stopping the aircraft after landing. Let us examine in more detail the problems of landing without flaps.

Flaps-up stalling speed

Most light aircraft have a low stalling speed in the 'clean' configuration, and since even the best flaps can only reduce this speed by a percentage of the original, it follows that the difference in stalling speed between flaps up and fully down will normally amount to only 5–8 knots. More advanced single-engine designs might offer a 10–12 knot reduction, while the larger, general aviation propjets remove some 20 knots off the stalling speed when the flaps are lowered. Business jets (e.g., BAe 125/700) display a similar reduction, while the big passenger jets, with their leading-edge devices and multi-stage Fowler flaps, offer a massive reduction of 60 knots or so in this department.

In so far as light aircraft are concerned, the reduction in stalling speed is academic, because the lack of forward visibility when in the flaps-up condition discourages the pilot from pushing his luck and flying too slowly. In this class of aircraft the most important talent of flaps is their production of additional drag. Drag, the enemy of flight in most circumstances, is worth its weight in gold on the approach. It enables one to lower the nose and to see ahead without a build-up of speed; it encourages one to use more power for any particular speed and descent rate, which provides extra slipstream over the tail surfaces and better low-speed control (unless you are flying one of those 'T'-tail jobs, the designer of which has succumbed to fashion and received little back in return); and it provides the aircraft with a wide choice of glidepaths. These range from a steep, power-off descent to the flattest of flat approaches, according to the amount of power used.

It should always be remembered that without flap you are rather like those members of the public who, many years ago, bought Model T Fords. They could select one in any colour as long as it was black. You, in your flaps-up bird, can choose any approach as long as it is flat or very flat. We are back to the L/D ratio again. A typical light trainer would have a L/D of approximately 9.7, flaps-up (e.g., it would glide a distance of 9,700 ft or 1.6 nm from a height of 1,000 ft). With maximum flap, the additional drag could reduce the L/D ratio to 7.5 or less, when the glidepath would, of course, become steeper. This is shown opposite in Fig. 31.

The point is that without flap you are stuck with a decidedly flat glidepath, even without power, and there are only three actions open to you if you want to steepen the approach:

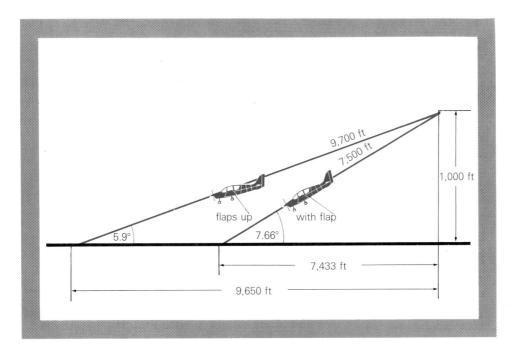

Fig. 31: Comparing the glide approach, with and without flap. Even without power a flapless approach is very flat and obstacle clearance is poor.

1. You can reduce speed to below that for best L/D ratio. The difficulty with this method is that in most aircraft forward visibility is badly compromised.

2. You could lower the nose. While that would certainly steepen the descent path, speed is bound to increase and to provoke the aircraft into floating down the runway like a ferret after a rabbit, a tantrum that could be embarrassing at a small airfield.

3. You could side-slip away surplus height.

In most cases only the last option will work satisfactorily, so on a flapless approach these are the golden rules:

● Remember that flat glidepath, and give yourself plenty of room by flying further downwind than usual before turning on to the base leg.

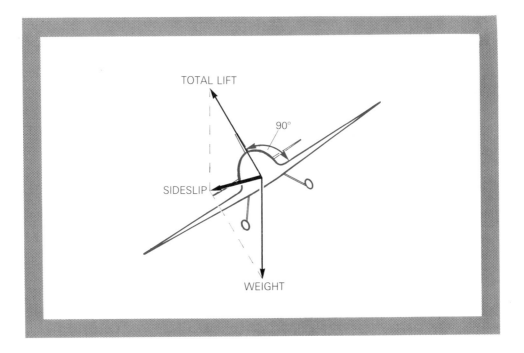

Fig. 32: Inclined lift in conjunction with weight causes a sideslip.

● Be mindful of the fact that without flap visibility ahead will be degraded because of the higher nose attitude. So be on your guard against flying into tall trees, telegraph wires or power cables on the way in to land.

● Because the aircraft is 'clean', make only small power changes, since a large increase in power will have a profound effect on your flight path.

● If you are very high, side-slip.

The side-slip

Since it is more or less a lost art, a word or two about the side-slip may not be out of place.

In a side-slip the aircraft has two speeds, the predominant one forward along the fore and aft axis, and a smaller but significant one in the direction of the lower wing, which is the result of inclining lift and upsetting its alignment with weight. Remembering basics, lift always acts at right angles to the lateral axis, and if that is inclined by rolling

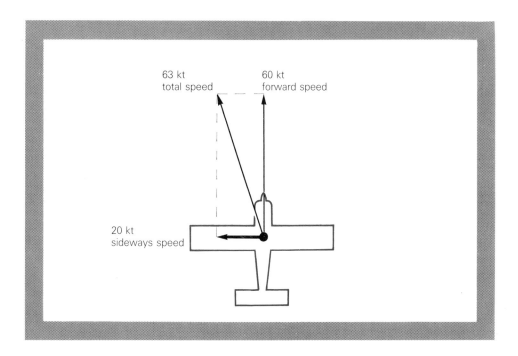

Fig. 33: Vectors in a side-slip. Actual descent path is between the nose and the lower wing (i.e. the 63-knot 'total speed' vector).

on bank, lift must be inclined by the same number of degrees (Fig. 32). Seen in plan form, the forward and sideways velocities result in the aircraft descending on a path that lies somewhere between the nose of the aircraft and the lower wing. In the example shown in Fig. 33, the aircraft is side-slipping to the left, and the descent path is about 18° to the left of the nose. Because the descent path is the resultant of two velocities, one forward, the other sideways, there is a tendency for the airspeed to increase slightly.

To prevent the aircraft from drifting away from the runway extended centreline at a rate which depends on the angle of bank in the side-slip (in Fig. 33 it is 20 knots), and to ensure that drift is not present while landing, the following procedure should be used when side-slipping to lose surplus height (it assumes that there is no crosswind element during the approach – that situation is explained in Chapter 4):

1. When the approach is high and it is decided that a side-slip is necessary, close the throttle and turn the aircraft to the right through 15–20°.

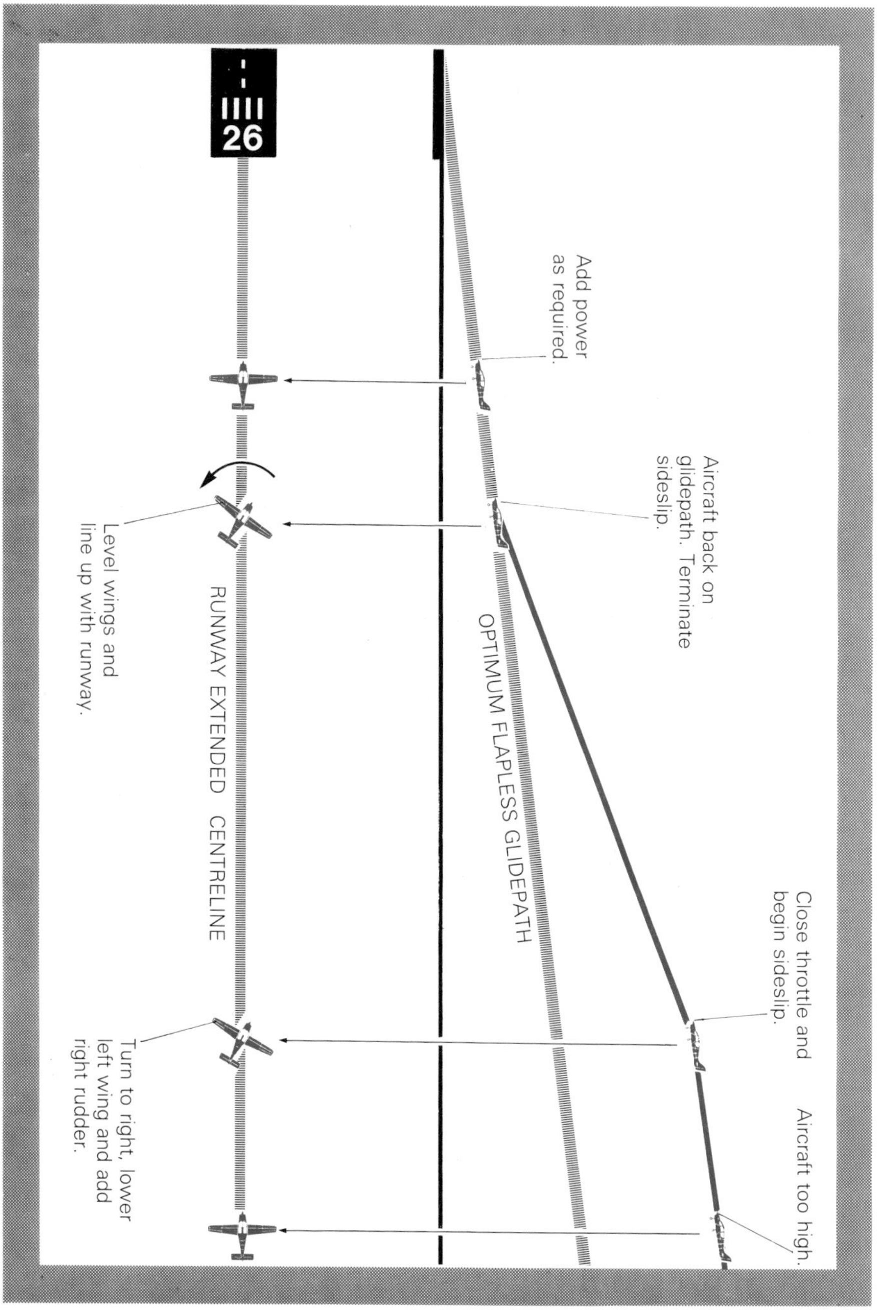

Fig. 34: Using the sideslip to correct a potential overshoot during a flapless approach.

2. Lower the left wing with aileron, and hold a bank angle of 20° or so.

3. Prevent the aircraft from turning to the left by applying right rudder. The aircraft is now side-slipping, with its descent path in line with the runway.

4. Maintain the descent along the runway extended centreline by turning the nose to the left or right as required.

5. Prevent the natural tendency for speed to increase by holding up the nose.

6. Increase or decrease the bank angle to obtain a corresponding change in rate of descent, at the same time increasing or decreasing the amount of opposite rudder to prevent a yaw from developing.

When the aircraft has regained the glidepath, it will be necessary to recover from the side-slip, but until you have had adequate practice at side-slips, they should not be continued below 100 ft. Sink rate can be quite high, and time will be required to settle into the final stages of the flapless approach. To regain straight gliding flight, the following actions are required:

1. Take off the bank, and simultaneously remove opposite rudder so that the nose lines up with the runway.

2. Allow the nose to return to its trimmed position, and maintain the correct flaps-up speed.

3. Add power as required to continue the flapless engine-assisted approach.

The sequence of events described, together with a profile view of the glidepath, is shown in Fig. 34.

Speed, power and the effects of wind

The clean aerodynamics of most modern aircraft result in a level gliding attitude, causing a restricted view ahead. Consequently, there is a tendency for pilots to glide at a faster speed than necessary when the flaps are up. Within reason, high-speed approaches are in themselves acceptable, but the problem with a 'clean' aircraft is that speed is difficult to dissipate when the time comes for the hold-off. Try this for yourself some time. You need a minimum distance of 800–900 m for comfort, preferably more. Try a flapless approach at 10–15 knots above the recommended gliding speed for that configuration. You will be surprised at the prolonged float, particularly on a windless day. It may even be necessary for you to overshoot unless there is plenty of runway ahead. So it is particularly important to settle at the correct flaps-up speed early in the approach and to make full use of the trim control. That way you will avoid floating across the airfield, through the far hedge and on to the front page of the local newspaper.

Because of the relatively low drag that is the result of your flapless predicament, make power adjustments sparingly. Only when an overshoot is called for or a potentially dangerous undershoot becomes obvious should more than a minor power increase be contemplated. Remember also that the more power that has to be used, the flatter the approach, the higher the nose attitude and the more restricted the forward visibility (Fig. 35). Furthermore, a 'clean' aircraft is a lively aircraft.

The effects of wind are as already described for the engine-assisted approach (pages 41–44), but in the context of this chapter strong winds, with or even without gusts, rather than mechanical failure of the flaps, may be the reason for making a flapless approach (and, in exceptional circumstances, a flapless landing). And when there are strong crosswinds, most flight/owners' manuals recommend landing with the minimum amount of flap that can be used for the available runway length.

Winds of up to 20 or 30 knots (according to aircraft type), particularly when they blow in line with the runway, are of assistance during a flapless landing because:

(a) they allow a higher approach speed to be used and consequently provide better forward visibility;
(b) there will be a steeper glidepath and better obstacle clearance as a result;
(c) groundspeed, and therefore touchdown speed, are both lower.

The problems of flat approach and poor forward visibility should not be regarded lightly. So restricted was the view ahead from some World War II fighters, even when the flaps were down, that pilots developed

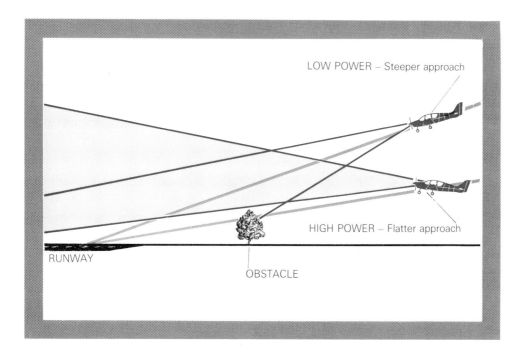

Fig. 35: Damaging effect on forward visibility when using excessive power during a flapless approach.

a curved 'fighter approach' to ensure that the runway remained in view out of the side window until the threshold was crossed. From then on the landing was completed by instinct!

Final approach without flaps

Since the hold-off period without flap is bound to be prolonged, and because the higher touchdown speed will produce a longer post-landing roll, it is essential during the final approach to aim for a landing at the beginning of the runway, particularly when the airfield is small. In a real emergency, loss of flap could mean diverting to a larger airfield if the intended destination is inadequate for a flapless arrival. The trouble with most aircraft manuals, even those compiled by the leading general aviation manufacturers, is that so much space is devoted to trespassing on the territory of flying training manuals that important information about their aircraft is often omitted. In most manuals you will look in vain for a table of flapless landing distances, or even a simple statement like 'When the flaps refuse to go down, add X per cent to the landing performance figures we have provided for a normal arrival.'

The trouble is that aircraft vary quite considerably in this respect, but for their larger, twin-engine designs, which have a 12–16 knots higher approach speed without flap, Cessna advise pilots to allow for a 35 per cent increase in landing distance. In so far as light, single-engine aircraft are concerned, these usually have a flaps-up approach speed some 5–10 knots higher than normal, and a 25 per cent increase in landing distance can be used as a working rule.

The flapless landing

All the considerations for a normal landing apply at this stage. While the approach speed is higher without flap, it is only when flying larger, high-performance aircraft that there is any noticeable difference. Because of the flatter glidepath, change in pitch attitude during the round-out will be less pronounced, so avoid overrotating while checking the descent prior to the hold-off.

During the round-out the throttle should be closed, otherwise the presence of even a little power at this stage will lengthen what is any case likely to be a longer than usual hold-off float, particularly when there is no wind.

Aim to reduce speed and attain a nose-up attitude in the normal way, touching down on the mainwheels first and lowering the nosewheel before applying brake. Much depends on length of runway and type of surface, but in a light, single-engine aircraft touchdown speed is usually 5–10 knots higher than usual during a flapless landing (and up to 20 knots higher in some of the larger general aviation multis), so be prepared for a longer ground roll.

Maximum braking effect will be obtained on a hard, dry runway, but unless the ground is soft, causing an increase in rolling friction, landing roll will be increased by 25–45 per cent on dry grass (according to aircraft type), while wet grass will undermine braking efficiency even more seriously.

So, if you must make a flapless landing on a hard but wet grass airfield, be quite sure that there is adequate distance for stopping. The accident statistics are punctuated with incidents that have occurred when a pilot was taken by surprise because the flaps refused to work.

Running out of airfield

These days most airfields are adequate for light aircraft, although some of the privately owned strips may be relied upon to concentrate the mind. But if, due to poor speed control or a badly positioned touchdown point, the upwind end of the field begins to dominate the vision at an alarming rate, there is little point in sitting by and taking bets with your passengers about whether you will stop on the airfield boundary or across the road outside. At the first sign of a delayed touchdown well into the field, execute an overshoot and have another try, this time placing the aircraft over the right position at the correct speed. If you have made a perfect approach to the hold-off stage and there is any risk of running into the upwind boundary, then clearly there can be only one decision to take: open up power, climb out and head for the nearest airfield capable of offering sufficient runway length for a flapless landing. There is no shame in giving up and making other arrangements. But you *will* be in the hot seat if, through lack of airmanship, a flapless landing has been attempted at a totally unsuitable airfield.

Taking the worst case, when it has been left too late to open up power and overshoot, you will be committed to making the best of a bad situation. The following actions will help to reduce damage to the aircraft and may prevent it entirely:

1. Pull back the idle cut-off; turn off the ignition; and, if possible, select fuel OFF. That way you will stop the engine, help to shorten the post-landing roll and avoid the risk of fire if you do run into anything.

2. On a hard, dry runway, brake hard but avoid locking the wheels, since a skid will develop and will prove counter-productive.

3. On wet grass be prepared for the wheels to lock when the brakes are applied. To prevent a skid from developing, apply the brakes in a series of pressures, releasing the pedals between applications.

4. Be prepared to take violent avoiding action if there is any risk of hitting something.

The flapless landing is at worst a minor emergency and, under certain conditions, a necessity. But it demands skill: and skill requires practice.

To conclude this chapter dealing with abnormal circumstances here are two additional problems that demand airmanship of a high order.

Wake turbulence

With the introduction of large transport aircraft general aviation has had to face an additional hazard – wake turbulence. There is nothing new about this particular nasty; it has been with us since the dawn of powered flight. However the problem has become serious because large aircraft, particularly the wide-bodied jets now in common use, are capable of disturbing the air in a way that can persist over a period of three or four minutes.

The wingtip vortex

Cast your mind back to basic aerodynamics and remember that in flight there is high pressure under the wing and lower pressure above. Since nature objects to uncontained pressure differences, high pressure air will flow from under the wing, around the tips and over the top where it tends to equalize the low pressure over the outer portions of the wing. As a result a helix or vortex is generated at each wingtip. Imagined from behind the aircraft, rotation is clockwise around the left-hand wingtip and anticlockwise around the right. Since these wingtip vortices are a function of differences in pressure it follows that they will be at their most intense development when the greatest pressure difference exists between lower and upper wing surfaces.

We are, of course, talking of our old *bête noire*, induced drag. May I therefore remind you that this attains its maximum at high angles of attack. In other words, while rotating during the take-off or flogging in, nose-up on the approach, big pressure differences generate powerful vortices and when the aircraft is a DC10 or a Boeing 747 there is enough disturbance to roll inverted any medium-size aircraft that might be following a little too closely for its own good. Furthermore a medium-size aircraft can have the same effect on a light plane. What do we mean by 'heavy', 'medium' or 'light'? As usual the various state authorities differ but here are the ICAO definitions.

Classification	Weight
Heavy	136,000 lb (61,740 kg) or greater
Medium	Less than 136,000 lb (61,740 kg) and more than 7,000 lb (3,180 kg)
Light	7,000 lb (3,180 kg) or less

Experiments using a smoke tower to one side of the runway have shown that wake turbulence can persist for three to four minutes after a heavy aircraft has churned up the surrounding air and that a crosswind will drift the revolving disturbance over areas imagined to be turbulence-free.

Dealing with wake turbulence

The consequences of flying into wake turbulence during the take-off or landing can be very serious and some fatal accidents have resulted. A number of variables (aircraft weight, wing span, speed, configuration, aircraft attitude and ambient temperature) affect the intensity of wake turbulence so in order to simplify what can be a complex subject here are a few rules for use when flying a smaller class of aircraft into or out of an airport handling big jets.

During take-off

1. **Same runway** Since the vortex system behind a large aircraft is formed at point of lift-off (when the aircraft rotates and adopts a high angle of attack) aircraft following should take-off well before that point and avoid flying through the vortex pattern.

2. **Different runway** Avoid flying through the wake of a larger aircraft that has just departed from another runway.

When these steps cannot be taken here are the recommended time separations to be used:

Leading aircraft	Following aircraft	Minimum spacing at airborne time
Heavy	Medium or Light (departing from same position)	2 minutes
Heavy (making full length take-off)	Medium or Light (taking off from an intermediate part of the same runway)	3 minutes

During landing

1. **Same runway**   The vortex system from a large aircraft will continue until touchdown. One is therefore at risk any time the wake turbulence is entered. This can be avoided by approaching to land above the large aircraft's flight path and touching down well after its landing point.

2. **Different runway**   On a parallel runway be prepared for wake disturbances to drift, particularly in a crosswind blowing the turbulence in your direction. It is better to treat the landing as though the heavier aircraft has used your intended runway and select a touchdown accordingly.

When these steps cannot be taken here are the ICAO recommended separations. I have also shown those listed by the UK Civil Aviation Authority:

Leading aircraft	Following aircraft	Separation minimums (distance and time)			
		ICAO		UK CAA	
		nm	min	nm	min
Heavy	Heavy	4	–	4	2
Heavy	Medium	5	2	6	3
Heavy	Light	6	3	8	4
Medium	Heavy	3	–	–	–
Medium	Medium	3	–	3	2
Medium	Light	4	–	6	3
Light	Heavy	3	–	–	
Light	Medium	3	–	–	–
Light	Light	3	–	–	–

These minimums apply to aircraft operating directly behind another aircraft or when crossing behind at the same level or less than 1,000 ft below.

Separation of aircraft is usually an airfield control responsibility but that does not absolve the pilot from understanding the problem, 'seeing' the invisible turbulence and avoiding it like any other obstruction.

The asymmetric approach and landing

For the benefit of twin-engine pilots here are a few words about landing when it has been necessary to shut down one motor. Engine failure may occur during any phase of flight – take-off, climb, cruise, turns or during the descent. I even had an engine stop after landing on one of the busiest runways in Europe. It was an aircraft type that would only taxi in tight circles on one engine and, as you can imagine, the event did not exactly make me pilot of the week at that particular airport. If I may refresh your memory as a twin pilot, when an engine fails in flight you must:

1. Check the yaw.

2. Attain the correct engine-out speed.

3. Identify the failed engine, try to rectify the cause and, assuming the problem cannot be rectified–

4. Feather the propeller and shut down the dead motor.

5. Safeguard the fuel, electric and other systems.

6. Clean up the airframe (trim, cowl flaps etc.).

7. Revise the flight plan.

Little of this has to do with the landing although the success or otherwise of an engine-out arrival is dependent upon these procedures which have been devised to make the aircraft safe during what can only be regarded as an emergency.

My earlier display of dogma ('a good landing requires a good approach requires a good etc., etc.') is particularly true when an engine has been shut down on a twin. So here are a few hints for happy pilots who, through no fault of their own, find themselves carrying an additional passenger in the form of an inert engine:

1. While flying towards the destination monitor the live engine instruments. Be sure it is not about to blow a fuse; a double engine failure is double bad news.

2. Advise ATC of your problem so that the circuit will be kept free of other traffic.

3. Join the circuit at a convenient point but at all costs avoid crowding the airfield, a common fault among pilots often caused through anxiety not to undershoot.

4. If the aircraft has marginal engine-out capabilities delay the pre-landing vital actions until just before turning on to base leg. On no account split the checks with thoughts of lowering the wheels later in the circuit – that way they can be forgotten with interesting results!

5. Lower part flap on the base leg then make a gentle turn on to finals.

6. On finals correct drift (if any) and maintain at least V_{mcl} (minimum control speed, landing) so that directional control is assured in the event of overshoot action being required.

7. Control the glidepath with the live engine but delay using more flap until the aircraft has descended below committal height, that is, the minimum height at which it is safe to initiate missed-approach action (see page 64). Then add flap as required.

8. Cross the airfield boundary and prepare for the landing.

The engine-out landing

It will be remembered that during the subsequent actions following engine failure rudder trim will have been used to counter yaw from the live engine. Now we are about to round out and close the live throttle so be prepared for rudder trim to cause a swing towards the live motor as power is reduced.

Some pilots like to take off a little of the rudder trim during the final approach but personally I have never cared for the practice. You should be concentrating on the last part of the deal, not messing about with the rudder trim. In any case, rudder loads on a light twin are not very demanding.

The act of landing is no different from that described in Chapter 2.

A final word of warning. Not all twins will taxi safely on one engine. So having pulled off a masterly asymmetric landing do not push your luck trying the impossible. Better by far to await help rather than cause untold expensive damage to your favourite machinery.

4. Crosswind landings

Whereas the previous chapter dealt with abnormal types of landing, this one explains what is likely to be the most normal type of landing in the book. Unfortunately for pilots at large, despite careful scrutiny of local prevailing winds, sometimes taken over a period of many years, airfield constructors have yet to build runways that are truly into wind except on a relatively few days of the month. This is hardly surprising, for, if you think about it, in most locations it is not possible to lay down a runway (or even two, three or more) so that perfect wind alignment is always assured. The best one can hope for is that runways will offer take-off and landing conditions that are never beyond the limits of the aircraft or the skill of an average pilot.

The crosswind problem

A basic principle of flying is that wind from ahead reduces groundspeed; a tailwind donates an increase while crosswinds create drift. In the air this presents no more than a navigation exercise that has become less demanding since the introduction of radio navaids. However, during the approach and landing phase, wind has a direct effect on the conduct of the procedure and, indeed, its very safety.

An aircraft's main landing gear is designed to absorb the shock of quite firm arrivals (that is, vertical loads), as well as the not inconsiderable effects of heavy braking, but no landing gear of conventional design can be expected to withstand the severe loads that would result from an uncorrected landing with drift. When the wind blows at 90° to the landing direction, sideways drift of the aircraft will, of course, be equal to wind speed. Taking as an example a modest 5-knot crosswind and an aircraft approaching at 80 knots, rounding out at 75 knots and touching down at 48 knots, if no steps were taken to correct drift, the landing would occur some 130 ft distant from runway centreline. While a 5-knot drift would probably not entail any damage to the aircraft on touchdown (unless the arrival took place in rough ground or among, for example, the angle-of-approach indicators), think of the consequences following

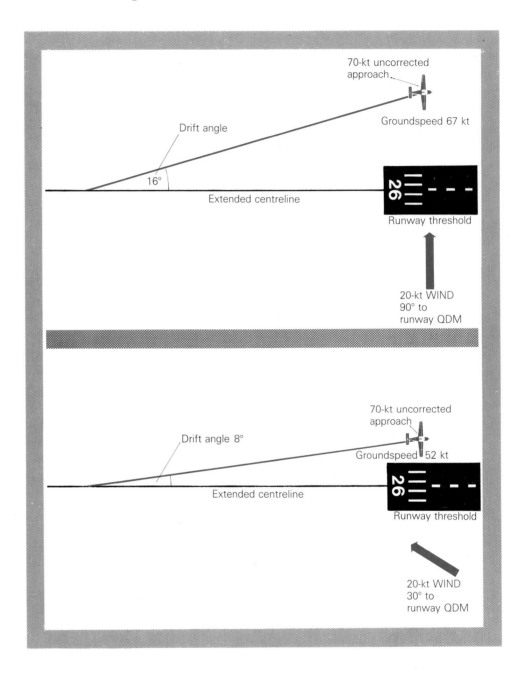

Fig. 36: The effect on drift of wind angle relative to the approach.

an uncorrected landing with your favourite plane drifting sideways at 10, 15 or 20 knots. No landing gear will tolerate that.

To some extent, the severity of drift effect depends on the touchdown speed of the aircraft, in so far as the higher the landing speed, the less drift angle there will be with any particular crosswind component. But it should be emphasized that all aircraft, whatever their size or speed, are sensitive to drift during the approach and landing, although after touchdown, during the landing roll, heavy aircraft with high landing speed are less affected by crosswinds.

Wind will obviously provoke maximum drift when it approaches an aircraft at 90° to its flight path. Fig. 36 illustrates a comparison between a 20-knot wind blowing at 90° to the approach and a similar one acting at 30°. This is elementary navigation, but mention is made of it here because it is sometimes forgotten that what happens at cruising levels also affects an aircraft while it is coming in to land. In fact, the effects of a crosswind are not confined to the approach and landing; they can also distort the circuit. And since we have already established that a good crosswind leg means a good base leg, means a good approach, means a good landing, now is perhaps the time to discuss crosswind circuits.

Crosswinds and the circuit pattern

Although pilots are more likely than not to find themselves having to cope with a crosswind during the landing, it is astonishing how few of them have a real understanding of the problems involved. Usually the difficulty starts long before the approach because, as is the case with any other type of landing, the foundations go deep and start at the beginning of the circuit.

Imagine you have taken off, and a 20-knot wind is blowing at 30° to the left of the nose. How will that affect the circuit? The following text should be read in conjunction with Fig. 37.

During climb-out
The aircraft will want to drift to the right, so turn slightly left. Frankly, in these wind conditions you would be well advised to climb straight ahead and delay turning crosswind until circuit height has been reached (see 'Around the circuit' on page 19).

On the crosswind leg

In addition to the usual need to maintain 90° to the runway by turning slightly into wind when flying under the conditions depicted in Figure 37, there will be a tailwind component. So be prepared for a slightly higher groundspeed. You will arrive at your downwind turning-point a little earlier than usual.

On the downwind leg

Drift will be the reverse of that during the climb-out, and it will be necessary to prevent a drift to the left by turning slightly towards the field. To safeguard the forthcoming base leg, it is essential that the wingtip should be made to trace your landing path down the runway, as explained on page 22 and illustrated in Fig. 3 (page 23).

While flying downwind in a crosswind some instructors advise using the DG (DI in Britain) as an aid to making the correct allowance for drift, but provided the wingtip continues to track correctly down the runway, there should be no need to engage in the mental gymnastics of remembering the drift angle while climbing away from the airfield and applying it in the opposite sense on the downwind leg.

Think ahead about the approach. You will have some trial-and-error adjustments to make while descending on the centreline, so give yourself a little more room by extending the downwind leg in order to ensure a *slightly* longer approach. I stress the word 'slightly' – there is no need to turn the approach into a minor cross-country.

On page 25 you were advised to turn on to base leg when the runway threshold lay at an angle of 45° behind your shoulders. On this occasion, because the aircraft is tracking perhaps 10° to the right of track (course in the United States), that must be taken into account while deciding when to turn. In this case, the same 45° would place the aircraft nicely for an extended downwind leg, but in the presence of right drift, when the nose would be to the left of track, the 45° rule would have the effect of shortening the downwind leg and subsequent approach. So, in these circumstances I am afraid you will have to use other methods. Try lining up with the runway reciprocal for a few seconds, so that you can assess the position of the runway relative to your shoulders, the seat backs or anything else that runs across the cabin. Better still, learn the correct turning-point through experience born of practice.

The circuit from climb-out to the base leg, as shown in Fig. 37, relates to a 20-knot wind from 060°, in other words, at 30° to the left of the

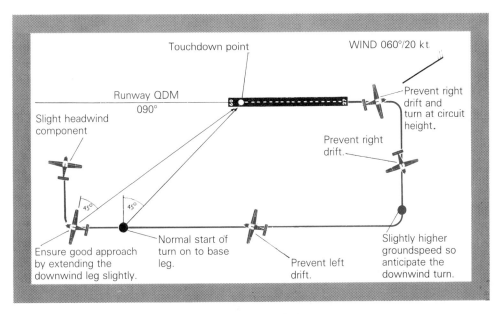

Fig. 37: Crosswind circuit, wind from the left.

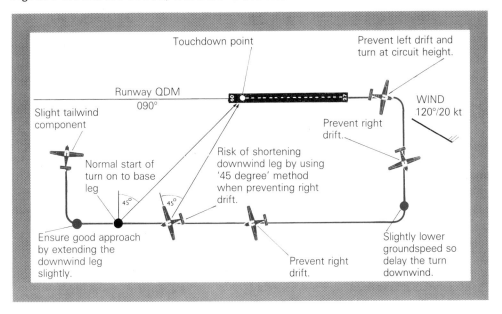

Fig. 38: Crosswind circuit, wind from the right.

runway. To make this part of the chapter absolutely clear, I have drawn
another circuit, in which the same 20-knot wind is blowing at 30° to the
right of the approach QDM (Fig. 38).

The base leg

Whenever there is a wind, it is necessary to head in towards the runway
and so prevent the aircraft from being drifted away from the threshold.
This is another way of saying: maintain the base leg at 90° to runway
QDM by turning slightly into wind. But in a crosswind there can be
either a headwind or a tailwind component while on this leg. This is
shown in Figs. 37 and 38. At this stage of the circuit the aim is to:

(a) reduce speed;
(b) lower part-flap;
(c) set the correct power for the required descent rate;
(d) turn on to the approach, rolling out in line with the runway at about
     400–500 ft agl.

Because item (d) seems to present the most difficulty, it is honoured with
a section of its own, which now follows.

The final turn in a crosswind

Because of the importance of establishing a good approach as a prelude
to one of your usual immaculate landings, it follows that this part of the
circuit should be as tranquil as good planning can make it. At all costs,
we should avoid spending most of our time on the approach putting right
the previous error of flying through the centreline or turning too soon for
the prevailing conditions. Unless the final turn is handled correctly, the
runway will probably be approached at an angle, and the aircraft may
end the trip being thumped down hard to one side of the dotted line.

I have seen tyres burst, wingtips touched and landing gears collapsed
because the pilots concerned never settled into the approach, failed to
appreciate that the situation was getting out of hand and sat back in the
hope that something would happen to put it all right, when missed-
approach action would have been more appropriate. We could all do
without this sort of clowning about; it does nothing for the image of
aviation.

Take a look at Fig. 39a (the left-hand drawing), and imagine the
situation. You are on a left-hand circuit, and there is a crosswind com-

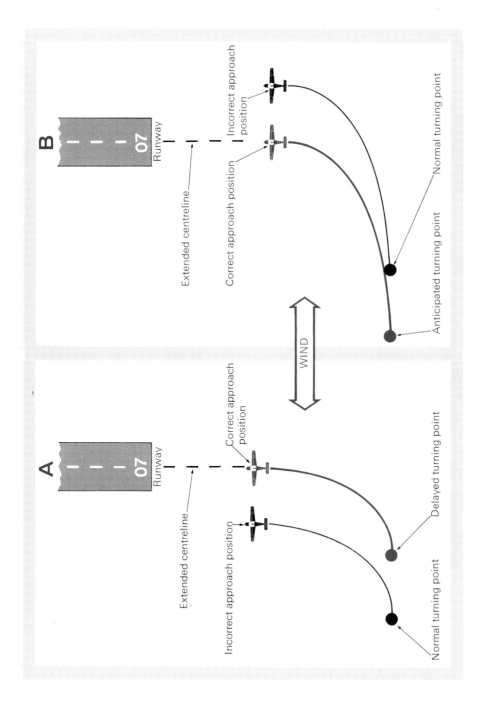

Fig. 39: The final turn in a crosswind, (A) from the right and (B) from the left.

ponent from the right. Given a chance, such a wind will tighten the radius of the final turn and place the aircraft to the left of runway extended centreline.

Remedy: Delay the final turn and, if necessary, widen its radius by decreasing the angle of bank slightly to reduce the rate of turn.

Fig. 39b shows the same circuit, but this time with a wind component from the left, which threatens to increase the radius of turn and to displace the aircraft to the right of runway extended centreline.

Remedy: Anticipate the final turn and, if necessary, tighten its radius by increasing the bank angle slightly and increasing the rate of turn.

At this stage the aircraft will be flying at reduced airspeed, so bank angle should not be increased beyond 30–40°, bearing in mind that stalling speeds become progressively higher as bank is added.

By a process of sound airmanship and good management, you are now in line with the runway, at the correct height and airspeed, and therefore ideally placed to maintain the aircraft on the centreline despite the presence of a crosswind.

The crosswind approach and landing

Two techniques of crosswind approach and landing are in common use:

1. The crabbing method.   2. The wing-down method.

Like most subjects in aviation, both crosswind landing techniques have their supporters, each camp being equally certain that its own method is best. Personally, I have no particularly strong preferences, as long as the technique, whichever it is, is executed in a competent manner. Some pilots profess to using a combination of both methods, but that seems like turning the exercise into something of juggling act. It reminds me of Jimmy Durante's famous song about finding the Lost Chord: 'My right hand was playing Rachmaninoff's 'Prelude', my left hand was playing Rubenstein's 'Melody in F' and at the same time I was peeling a banana – you see, I had to eat too!' To avoid that kind of nimble footwork, I give you the two methods separately.

The crabbing method (Fig. 40)

At this stage we are back to pictures through the windscreen, but in the presence of a crosswind, other considerations apply apart from those

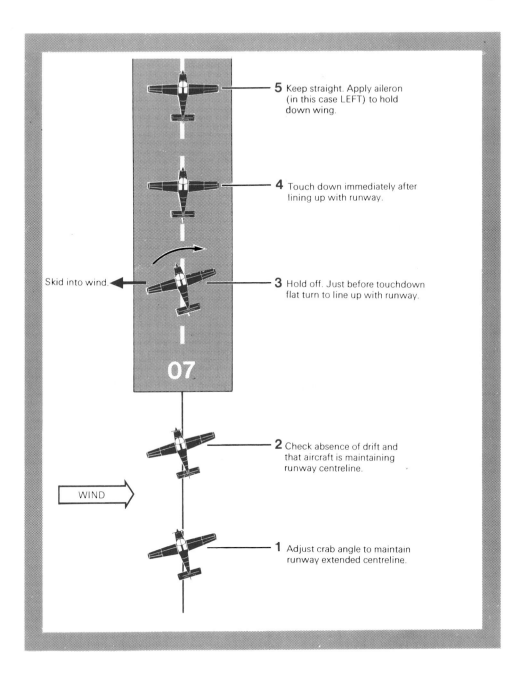

Fig. 40: Crosswind landing, crabbing method.

illustrated in Fig. 10 (page 36). Picture the situation. The runway is beginning to slide to the left, indicating the presence of starboard drift caused by a wind from the left. Here is the procedure to adopt:

1. Turn to the left, and regain the runway extended centreline.

2. Maintain the centreline by keeping the aircraft nose slightly left of centre – into wind. If the picture alters, turn away from the direction of drift: aircraft drifting right, turn slightly *left*; aircraft drifting left, turn slightly *right*.

3. Adjust power and attitude to maintain the glidepath.

4. Over the runway threshold, check that there is no drift. Remember, the wind will change in speed and direction during the descent, and if a windsock is present, use it as a guide to assess surface wind. It is essential that you position over the runway centreline to ensure room either side of the aircraft – somewhere to go if a swing develops!

5. At the usual height, round out and take off power, but counter drift by maintaining the nose left of centreline.

6. Continue the hold-off; then, just before touchdown, hold the wings level by means of aileron and apply right rudder to flat-turn the aircraft in line with the runway. *This must happen immediately prior to the landing.* Time it correctly, and the skid generated by flat-turning will balance drift. Align with the runway too soon, and drift will begin. Touch down without flat-turning, and the aircraft will attempt to run off to the left (see positions 3 and 4 in Fig. 40).

7. After the aircraft touches down, apply left aileron to prevent the left (into-wind) wing from rising. Sometimes the nosewheel will snatch as it lowers to the runway, so be prepared but not alarmed – it is quite normal.

8. During the landing roll, keep straight, with the nosewheel steering, if necessary assisted by brake. When flying twin-engine aircraft under extreme crosswind conditions, it may be necessary to use asymmetric power to assist in preventing a swing:

swing to the left, open *left* throttle;

swing to the right, open *right* throttle

9. Brake to a halt; clear the runway; and complete the post-landing checks before taxiing in.

I have explained the crabbing method in some detail because it is the most widely used. Consequently, the various steps do not conform exactly with the five stages shown in Fig. 40. They are, however, in the same order, and the illustration should be used in conjunction with the text.

Having laid the foundations, I can now explain the alternative crosswind procedure on a step-by-step basis that relates to the numbers on Fig. 41.

The wing-down method (Fig. 41)

The preamble to the crabbing method applies equally to the wing-down technique, but whereas the former procedure makes use of the standard navigational ritual of heading into wind and away from drift, the wing-down method is based on the side-slip. So imagine that having lined up with the runway in the presence of a crosswind, you are ready to juggle with the elements:

1. Look for drift. Check its direction (in this case to the right) and intensity.

2. Bank the aircraft in the opposite direction to drift (in this case to the left) by lowering the into-wind mainplane.

3. Prevent the aircraft from turning to the left by applying sufficient right rudder to maintain alignment with the runway.

4. Hold the aircraft on the runway extended centreline by adjusting the side-slip. In the example illustrated, if the aircraft moves to the right, drift is more powerful than side-slip. So increase the bank and add more opposite rudder to maintain direction. Conversely, should the aircraft move to the left of runway centre, there is too much side-slip for the prevailing crosswind. Therefore reduce the bank angle slightly, at the same time taking off a little rudder. While maintaining runway

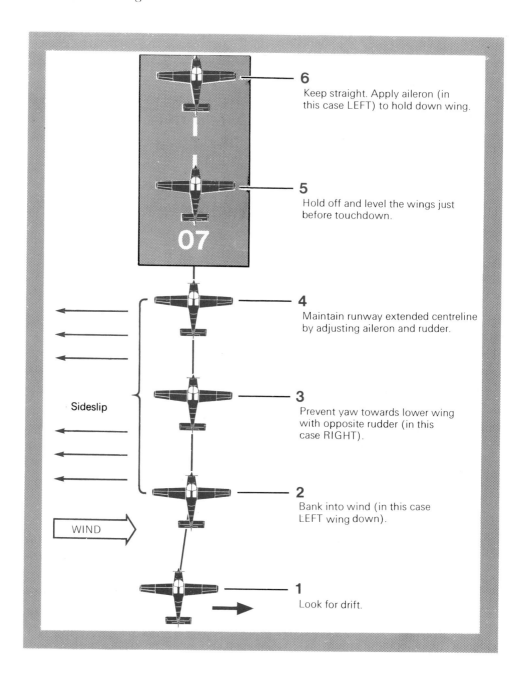

Fig. 41: Crosswind landing, wing-down method.

extended centreline, the usual power/attitude adjustments must be made to conform with the glidepath.

5. Cross the threshold; check that you are over the runway centreline; then round out, close the throttle(s) and hold off in the usual way. In conditions of light crosswind, level the wings just before touch-down; when drift is more pronounced, land on the into-wind main-wheel only, allow the other mainwheel to lower as speed increases, and then let the nosewheel make contact.

6. Hold on into-wind aileron (in this case, left aileron) during the landing roll, and keep straight, using the nosewheel steering and, if necessary, brake. Multi-engine aircraft should be handled as de-scribed in paragraph 8 (page 110).

So there are the two established methods. The wing-down procedure had its origins in the day of biplanes. Then it went out of fashion. Now even the idea of landing on one wheel, at one time calculated to get you drummed out of the Brownies, is back in favour. Each technique has its advantages and disadvantages. For example, although the approach down to the hold-off is simple enough using the crabbing method, the final enactment just prior to touchdown demands a nice degree of antici-pation. The two possibilities – too early and too late – have already been described (paragraph 6 on page 110). Likewise, the wing-down procedure expects of the pilot that he maintain the glidepath with elevator/power adjustments while flying with crossed controls (rudder against aileron). Odd as it may sound, that part of the deal is not too difficult, but the thought of landing on one wheel is not every pilot's idea of light enter-tainment. However, it is surprising what a little practice can do, and both methods, correctly executed, produce the right results in the face of a crosswind.

Whichever method is used, it is important to apply into-wind aileron during the landing roll. In a strong crosswind even quite heavy aircraft are not beyond lifting a wing to show who is boss when the going is a little rough.

Use of flap in a crosswind
Aircraft behaviour in a crosswind differs from one design to another. While the use of maximum flap under these conditions is permitted for

some designs, manufacturers recommend reduced settings for most air-craft, usually in such vague terms as 'Use the minimum amount of flap for the runway length available.' That could mean anything.

Furthermore, there are arguments in support of using full- as opposed to part-flap in a crosswind. However, we pilots, like most other folk, are creatures of fashion, so in deference to the 'Use part-flap in a crosswind' lobby, and in the absence of specific advice in the aircraft's manual, use half the maximum setting. In fairness to supporters of limiting flap, many pilots are of the opinion that during a crosswind aircraft handle better in that configuration.

Aircraft crosswind limits

Strange as it may seem, an aircraft's size does not in itself determine its tolerance of crosswinds during the take-off or landing. There are, in fact, some light single-engine types in common use that will cope with more adverse out-of-wind conditions than a few of the much larger and heavier twins. Reasons for this are many: disposition of keel area and degree of weathercock stability, landing gear width, distance from nosewheel to mainwheels and, very important, effectiveness of the flying controls (elevator, ailerons and rudder) at low airspeeds.

As far as pilots are concerned, it is important that they should under-stand that there is a limit to the amount of crosswind an aircraft can accept. The two factors that apply are: (1) wind speed and (2) wind direction *relative to aircraft landing path.*

Reference to Fig. 36 (page 102) will serve as a reminder that, in itself, wind speed is only part of the story, the other important factor being how it connects with the aircraft. That is why I have emphasized the words 'relative to aircraft landing path'.

While most of the flight manuals provide you with a pompous defi-nition of the term 'demonstrated crosswind velocity', one or two of the manufacturers are not exactly forthcoming about volunteering a figure for their wonderplane. Some provide no limit figure at all; others quote one in the 'Normal Procedures: Landing' section for some (but not all) of their models; while Beech print it where it should be – with the wind component diagram which, in good flight manuals, is included in the 'Performance' section.

The purpose of wind component diagrams, such as the typical example shown in Fig. 42, is to resolve the prevailing wind into two components relative to the aircraft:

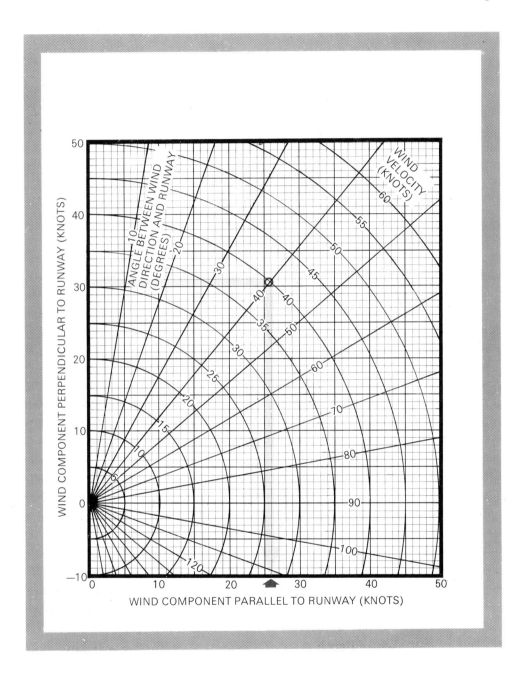

Fig. 42: Typical wind component graph. Blue arrows in this illustration give the following example; Wind 40 knots blowing at 40° to landing path. Wind at 90° to the aircraft will be 26 knots. The aircraft manual will advise if this is within limits.

(a) that part which acts down the runway and affects the take-off or landing distance;
(b) the component acting at 90° to the aircraft.

Here we are mainly interested in component (b) because that is the one causing drift during the landing.

Reference to Fig. 42 shows that the crosswind element is provided with a scale entitled 'wind component perpendicular to runway' (some manuals call it 'crosswind component', which says what it means). The other scale relates to the headwind component. The example shown in blue arrows on the graph relates to an aircraft landing (or taking off) with a 40-knot wind blowing at an angle of 40° to its take-off or landing direction, say, a wind velocity of 310°/40 knots and a runway QDM of 270°. Reference to the chart shows that the actual wind at 90° to the aircraft is 26 knots (with 31-knot headwind).

When the aircraft manual quotes a demonstrated crosswind velocity, the figure assumes it to be at 90° to the aircraft. So if the aircraft in the example shown in Fig. 42 has a limit of 15 knots, better taxi back to the hangar; you may think yourself able to cope with the situation, but the hardware will have other ideas.

While acknowledging that all landings are different, none is quite so different as the one that occurs in a strong crosswind. The variables are many; the demands on pilot and aircraft can be quite severe; and the fact that pilots tend to gloss over the problems involved is borne out by the accident statistics. Yet there is really no reason why airframe drivers should get themselves into a knot just because the wind will not oblige by conforming with the runway. Those who mess about with boats are constantly having to contend with changing winds and shifting currents. At least pilots are not plagued with shifting runways. To sailors it is all a matter of seamanship, a matter of great pride to mariners. For some reason, there is a breed of post-war pilot that never thinks in terms of the aviation equivalent – airmanship. Be in no doubt: without airmanship, during a crosswind landing the opportunities for mishap are endless. On the other hand, think of the satisfaction to be derived from pulling off a splendid landing when the going is rough.

Go out and practise crosswind landings with a good instructor – and why not read this chapter again in a few weeks' time?

5. Short-field landings

In the good old biplane days of 1920–30, when landing speeds of around 45 mph (72 kph) were considered quite fast enough, the short strip of today would have been regarded as adequate for a busy airfield. This is easy to understand when it is remembered that airliners of the period cruised at around 85 knots, while some of the faster single-engine tourers of the 1980s approach at that speed. At one time, approach speeds were going up and up, and many of us wondered when they would reach the unacceptable. Fortunately for us all, the latest generation of passenger jets is actually a little slower on the approach than some of the earlier breed, and light planes have now stabilized at around 70 knots for trainers and not a lot more for tourers. In itself, a relatively high landing speed does not present the pilot with any particular problems; on the contrary, most of the modern light planes are easier to land than their grandfathers were, while in many respects the bigger, heavier aircraft which approach at 110–130 knots are even less demanding. Here is a representative list of approach speeds and ground rolls. They assume that standard, engine-assisted landing techniques have been used on a sea-level runway in zero wind conditions when the temperature is 15° C.

Aircraft type	Approach speed (knots)	Landing roll (ft)
Cessna 152	60	475
Robin R2112 Alpha	60	590
Piper Tomahawk	62	650
Cessna P210 Centurion	75	770
Piper Archer II	75	900
Robin Aiglon	70	1,100
Cessna 340A	94	790
Cessna 421 Golden Eagle	100	730
Beech Super King Air 200	103	1,100
BAe 125/700	119	3,500
Douglas DC10–30	125–145*	5,000–6,100*
	* according to landing weight	

No doubt there will be a few surprises here. For example, who would have thought that a Beech Super King Air 200, at the top of the so-called light-aeroplane limit with a maximum authorized take-off weight of 12,500 lb (5,700 kg), would have the same ground roll as the Robin Aiglon, a light, single-engine tourer? But the King Air has reverse thrust. Note also that certain larger, heavier and faster piston twins – for example, the Cessna 340A and the Cessna 421 Golden Eagle – require less ground roll than some of the singles. Why? There are various reasons – extra drag from two windmilling propeller discs and more powerful brakes, to mention two of the more important considerations. A short comparison of this kind illustrates that approach speed alone does not determine the length of the landing roll. But having made the point, it is important to qualify it with another fact: given the same landing conditions (runway surface, aircraft weight, surface wind), length of landing roll or landing distance over a 50-ft screen *for any particular aircraft type* is directly influenced by approach speed. Judging from the number of accidents that occur while pilots are trying to land at private strips or small airfields, this is an obvious fact that needs repeating. Furthermore, it is the corner-stone of uneventful short landings.

The need for short landings

Like most terms used in connection with practically every activity, be it fishing, golf, flying or even the pursuit of amassing money, the word 'short', as applied to the landing, is of only relative value. Take another look at the table of landing ground rolls on page 117. Ask the pilot of a Robin Aiglon to land on a 900-ft strip, and he will think it is rather short, although another airframe driver of moderate skill flying a Cessna 152 would probably be reasonably happy with the challenge. Likewise, pilots of the piston and turboprop aircraft mentioned, even that stately giant among light planes, the Beech Super King Air 200, would probably look at the field requirements of the British Aerospace 125/700 with some respect, while to the pilot of a DC10–30, this largest of the medium-size business jets is no more than a light plane (although it weighs practically as much as the old DC3). The point is that with the possible exception of those aircraft employed on airline duties, all the others (private light singles and twins, air-taxi piston-engine and turboprop equipment and even the business jets) may be called upon to make a landing at an airfield that is smaller than usual.

Possible causes are several: the business meeting at a place served by a smaller than average airfield; a training flight in which the student pilot on a solo cross-country gets himself low on fuel and a little bit lost; the private pilot who ought to know better but runs out of suitable weather and, like the student, has to land in a suitable field. Then there is the most common situation, the pilot who, for one reason or another, wishes to land at a private strip.

While this chapter is directed primarily at the last-named, purely voluntary landing, much of the advice reads across to both the business trip terminating at a small airfield and the emergency situations already mentioned. Although in those cases there could be a bad-weather element; and, of course, there is the added hazard of landing in the best field available – *surface unknown*. This book is devoted to landings, not emergency procedures, so I shall confine myself to describing those situations in which a planned landing is to be made on an airfield that is smaller than usual or even a private strip.

Aircraft landing performance

The figures shown in the table on page 117 are for a standard, engine-assisted approach followed by a landing on a hard, dry runway. Any one of the aircraft mentioned, or for that matter any aircraft quoted on the same basis, could be made to land with a considerably shorter ground roll, given the correct technique. The quality of flight manuals differs quite considerably, not just from one manufacturer to another but also between manuals for aircraft types by the same manufacturer. For example, 'Section 5: Performance' in these manuals gives landing distances in one of the following ways:

(a) graphs showing landing distances over a 50-ft screen (i.e., barrier) with adjustments for aircraft weight, wind conditions, airfield elevation, temperature and, in some cases, incline or decline;
(b) as for (a) but with an additional scale for ground run;
(c) tables of figures in columns, one each for 0° C, 10° C, 20° C, 30° C and 40° C. The columns give ground roll followed by landing distance over a 50-ft screen, and they are listed at 1,000-ft intervals from sea-level to 8,000 ft. For single-engine aircraft figures are only given for landings at maximum weight, but multi-engine types have a set of tables to cater for various weights.

Usually, but not always, the information provided is confined to the normal engine-assisted landing, but some manuals also provide landing distances that will result from using the short-field technique. As I mentioned earlier, there is little uniformity among these manuals, and it obviously pays to know what information is available in the book of words for the aircraft you intend to ease into that cosy little airstrip.

In the absence of specific information on the short-field performance of your aircraft, write to the manufacturers, tell them their manual is incomplete and ask for a table of landing distances using the short-field technique. In the not unlikely event that no such tests have been made during the certification programme, you must find out for yourself. Pick a day of zero or light wind; approach at the recommended short-field speed (you should find that in 'Section 4: Normal Procedures'); cross the threshold at about 50 ft; land; stop with decisive but not harsh use of the brakes; and check the distance involved. Make a note of this and the wind strength at the time, but to be on the safe side do the test with the aircraft at or near its maximum weight. If you can repeat the exercise several times under different wind conditions, even better, because you will then be able to make up a list of landing distances against wind speeds.

Other factors affecting landing distance

If, in the absence of published information, you have to compile your own table of landing distances using the short-field technique, here are some simple, rule-of-thumb corrections to apply, which will allow for the other factors affecting landing distance. They are approximate but based nevertheless on information extracted from flight manuals of aircraft ranging in size from the Cessna 152 to the pressurized twin-engine Golden Eagle.

Temperature

A study of the manuals reveals increased landing distances of 20–40 ft for each 10° C above ISA (i.e., 15° C at sea-level, 13° C at 1,000 ft, 11° C at 2,000 ft, and so forth, in steps of 2° C per 1,000 ft). So to provide a safety margin, add 50 ft to the landing distance for each 10° C increase in temperature above ISA.

Airfield elevation

The flight manuals for the same group of varied aircraft indicate a 25–

45-ft increase in landing distance per 1,000 ft airfield elevation above mean sea-level. In the interests of safety add 50 ft to the landing distance for each 1,000 ft above the sea-level airfield figure.

To quote an example: if, during short-field trials at a near-sea-level airfield where the temperature is +15° C, your wonderplane has a landing distance of 1,200 ft, and you propose to land at a strip on a 1,500-ft plateau when the temperature is 5° C above ISA, your revised landing distance will be 1,200 + 75 + 25 = 1,300 ft.

Airfield surface

One would imagine that a grass field might provide more rolling friction than a hard runway. So it does. But these days modern brakes play an important part in reducing the landing roll, and grass, particularly if it is damp, acts as a skid-pan when the anchors are used with enthusiasm. A scan of the flight manuals for a wide variety of aircraft reveals that most of the light singles up to Cessna Centurion weight should have about 20 per cent added to the landing distance when using a dry grass airfield, while those light twins that are cleared for such landings require 10 per cent. So when landing on dry grass, add 20 per cent to the landing distance for singles; add 10 per cent to the landing distance for light twins.

Airfield suitability

In the Republic of Ireland there is a profusion of tiny airstrips, many of them the homes of enthusiastic flying schools, like the one at Coonagh, near Limerick, that has a Mickey Mouse tarmac runway only 1,300 ft long and 20 ft wide. Every approach must be right down the slot, and every arrival is like an aircraft-carrier landing. Consequently, the boys and girls at the Limerick Flying Club have no trouble dealing with small fields. To them it is an everyday experience. The great majority of pilots are not brought up to do things the hard way from the start, partially because most flying schools enjoy the use of runways big enough to accommodate much larger aircraft.

Spend a little time watching landings at a normal-length busy training airfield, and most likely you will become aware of the following pattern among pilots, some of them experienced enough to know better:

1. The airfield boundary is crossed too high.

2. Approach speed is too fast.

3. Many pilots do not select full flap, although there is no crosswind.

4. Because of points 1, 2 and 3 above, these aircraft touch down a quarter to a half of the distance along the runway.

5. Most of the pilots making these errors land on all three wheels simultaneously, possibly in an effort to get on to the ground and jump on the brakes before the aircraft runs out of runway (Fig. 43).

When pilots, through sheer bad handling skills, find it difficult to land in comfort at a moderately large airfield, what chance have they of arriving safely on a small grass airstrip? Very little chance, I would suggest, because the all-too-common behaviour described in points 1 to 5 is a sure recipe for disaster during a short landing. Techniques to be adopted will be described as the chapter develops, but now it is appropriate to talk about airfield suitability.

Aim for any established airport, airfield or even private airstrip for which published information is available, and there will be no difficulty in deciding whether or not it is long enough for you. Runway or grass-strip lengths are there in black and white, together with such useful warnings as 'Be prepared to avoid the sheep' or 'In the event of missed-approach action becoming necessary, a steep climbing turn to the right is required to avoid the mountain that starts at the end of the runway.' (I fool you not; such a runway, surrounded by mountains left, right and straight ahead, exists at La Mole, a private airfield near St Tropez on the French Mediterranean coast.) The problem arises when, for whatever reason, an invitation is accepted to visit some hospitable soul with a *private* private strip, so private that no details are published in the Aerad supplements, Pooley Guides or Jeppesen plates – not even a duplicated sheet. 'Will it be long enough for my plane?' you ask. Back comes a voice confident in the certain knowledge that his neck will remain intact even if you do leave your wonderplane in a heap. 'Long enough? My dear chap, you could get a Jumbo Jet in there. During the war they operated fighters out of my private airfield.' Unfortunately, he does not say which war or what fighters, but herein lies a trap born of potentially dangerous circumstances. You want to land there, and he would enjoy a visit from a flying friend. But no one is sure about field

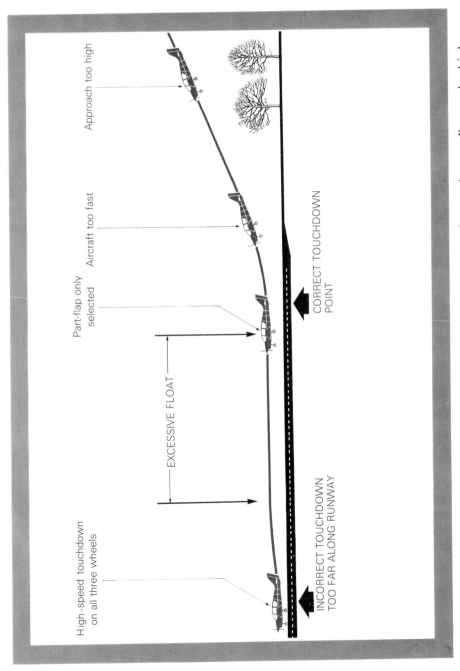

Fig. 43: An everyday picture at the training airfields – too high, too fast, only part-flap and a high-speed landing on all wheels that is well down the runway.

length or even the state of the surface. The airstrip may never have been measured properly. Even worse, someone may have paced out the field. The trouble with that method is that most adult males firmly believe that each of their manly paces spans 3 ft, whereas in practice it has been found an average pace is only 2.5 to 2.7 ft (or rather less if you are wearing tight jeans). So measured, an airstrip believed to offer 1,500 ft may only be 1,250 ft long, which is 17 per cent less, and that is enough to be significant. Obviously, you want to know how much room there will be for the touchdown and roll *before* attempting the landing, but for your own use it is well worth pacing out a known distance using normal steps to determine your stride length. This should be done over a distance of at least 100 ft. Having established the average length of your stride (by dividing the number of paces into the known distance), it could prove of value if ever the need arose to advise others wishing to land in a large field.

Before deciding to land at any airstrip or private airfield about which little information is available, this is what you must know:

1. The length of unobstructed grass, sand, gravel, etc., available for the touchdown and landing roll. Ask the owner if the figure he is offering is based on proper measurements or inspired guesswork. If you are told it is 'about 500 yards', deduct 20 per cent and buy yourself a little insurance.

2. Ask if there are any power lines, tall structures or massive trees on the approaches, and note down all information of this kind.

3. Ask about the surface. You want to know the answers to these questions:
   (a) Are there any rabbit holes? (These can have the wheels off in no time at all.)
   (b) Is the ground firm? If not, where are the soft patches? (These must be avoided.)
   (c) Is there a risk of hitting unexpected rocks, low wire fences or other hazards?
   (d) Is there a hedge or high fence to cross when flying into the airstrip?
   (e) Is the grass cut? (Very long grass will have the paint off your wheel spats.)
   (f) If it is a beach airstrip, when is the next high tide?

4. Relate the landing run to your aircraft requirements, remembering that you must also be able to fly out of the airstrip when time comes to leave.

5. Check whether there are any noise-sensitive areas to avoid while flying on the circuit. Properly planned, your arrival need upset no one. On the other hand, a sudden low-level fly-over in your private airliner might upset the local population, particularly those who might be sunbathing in their birthday suits.

6. Obtain a weather report and ask the owner of the airstrip to confirm landing direction. Not all strips display a windsock or a 'T'.

The short-field landing procedure

Assuming you are satisfied that the proposed landing area will be long enough for your arrival and subsequent departure, that the weather is suitable and that you have noted such local conditions as areas to avoid, obstructions, and so forth, the procedure may be regarded under these headings:

1. Circuit planning.

2. Low-speed approach.

3. Short-field landing.

When no published information is available, these three stages should be *preceded* by airstrip inspection. To keep the various stages in correct order, the following text is for a landing at an airstrip about which little is known.

Airstrip inspection

What does the pilot with ambitions to age gracefully need to know before attempting a landing at a private airstrip?

1. Are there any obstacles on the approach or within the climb-out area?

2. Is the strip long enough?

3. Is it into-wind, or would it be better to select an alternative landing direction (if there is one), free of obstacles, even if this entails coping

with a crosswind?

4. Is the surface fit for a landing, or does a close inspection reveal craters, ruts, ditches, etc.?

Unless one has had the advantage of a previous visit on foot, the first fly-in must be preceded by an inspection from the air. And that must be conducted in the correct order because clearly there is little merit in descending to take a close look at the grass only to hit a large tree in the process. The procedures that follow are, blow for blow, similar to those that a pilot would undertake when stuck with an emergency landing with power.

1. Fly to the field; determine the wind direction; decide on the approach path; and position the aircraft for an inspection run.

2. Reduce speed; lower part-flap; and retrim. *This is very important.*

3. Line up with the airstrip for an inspection run, with the purpose of checking the position of obstacles in the approach and overshoot areas (high trees, power lines, and buildings, for example). Lower the aircraft to a height of 150–200 ft asl, and fly at approach speed to the right of your intended landing path. That way you will be able to look out to the left in the normal way and will be able to see the final approach path clearly (Fig. 44).

4. While conducting the inspection run, check that wind conditions are within limits by assessing the amount of drift. At the same time, decide whether or not there is sufficient room for a landing and the subsequent take-off when you depart. There are no short-cuts to making this assessment. It is a matter of experience.

5. Climb away; fly another circuit at low safe cruising speed (with 10–15° of flap); and position for the next inspection run. Like the previous one, it should be flown to the right of your intended landing path.

6. At approach speed, head in for the second run, this time descending to hold-off height so that the surface can be inspected. (You can do this with confidence, having previously made an approach to ensure there are no hazards on the approach and overshoot.) Look for small wire fences that may not have been spotted before, soft patches, ruts, holes, rocks or other debris, and plan to avoid these during the

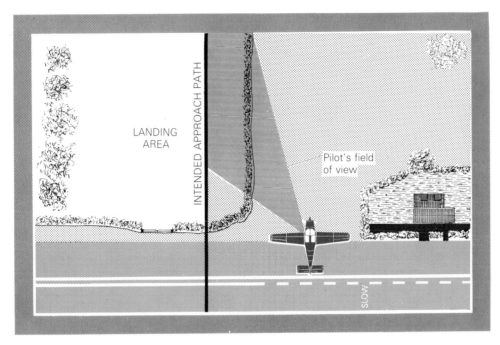

Fig. 44: Flying the inspection runs prior to landing.

touchdown and landing roll. The position of animals should be noted, although usually the two inspection runs will have chased them away.

7. Climb away and, if satisfied with what you have seen during the two inspection runs, prepare for a short-field landing.

Procedures 1 to 7 will not be necessary when proper information is available for the airstrip, but the approach and landing are the same whether or not prior inspection of the field is necessary.

Planning a low-speed approach

At one time the 'creeper' approach was the in thing, but these days it is rarely used. When there is a fence or hedge to cross on entering the airstrip, the 'creeper' type of approach can end in a frantic scramble, with power poured on at the last second, and that is bound to carry you well into the field. Furthermore, by its very nature the 'creeper', flown at low speed in a nose-high attitude, seriously limits the view ahead and brings with it the risk of hitting something on the approach.

Better by far is the descending-path method. Visibility ahead is accept-able, and because the aircraft is flown down an incline, better clearance

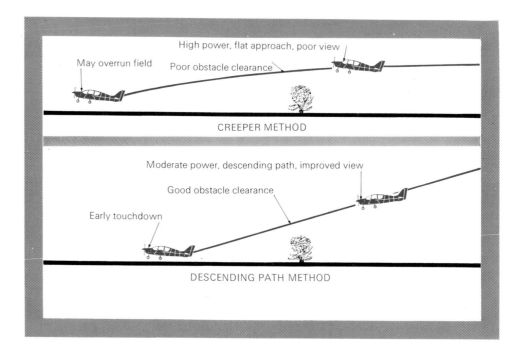

High power, flat approach, poor view

May overrun field   Poor obstacle clearance

CREEPER METHOD

Moderate power, descending path, improved view

Good obstacle clearance

Early touchdown

DESCENDING PATH METHOD

Fig. 45: Short-field approach and the disadvantages of the creeper method (upper picture).

is provided as you cross the hedge, fence or wall, and point of touchdown is brought nearer to it. Fig. 45 shows the advantages of the descending-path technique.

Since you are required to settle into an accurately controlled final approach at a lower than usual airspeed, adequate room to manoeuvre should be allowed by flying a little further downwind than is usual for an engine-assisted landing before turning on to base leg. Having said this, I am at pains not to create the impression that you should indulge in a long drag in, with the aircraft hanging on the prop. There is no need to extend the downwind leg by more than, say, another 15–20 seconds' flying. The turn on to base leg now follows, and everything is handled in exactly the same way as for an engine-assisted approach (see pages 31–44).

Make a gradual turn to line up with the approach; check the picture in your windscreen (see Fig. 10, page 36); and fix within it a touchdown point that will provide the maximum landing roll. Lower full flap unless there is a significant crosswind, and adjust the throttle to maintain the touchdown point in a steady position within the windscreen area.

Approach speeds

On page 76 it was explained that the flattest glide occurs at the speed which relates to best L/D ratio angle of attack. Any attempt to glide at a faster or slower speed must result in a steeper glidepath. A flat glidepath is, on occasions, an embarrassment rather than a blessing, particularly when you are trying to land in the shortest possible distance. The ideal situation is one in which the aircraft is in a state of high drag, speed is low and a relatively high power setting is required to prevent an excessive rate of sink, the advantages being:

1. The pilot can enjoy the widest possible range of descent paths, from high-power and relatively flat to low-power and steep.

2. The relatively high engine power ensures that plenty of slipstream is available to enhance the effectiveness of the rudder and elevators or stabilator.

3. Touchdown point can be controlled to within fine limits.

Fig. 46 shows a comparison of glidepaths at various airspeeds. These relate to a typical light single in the approach configuration, assuming zero wind conditions.

Like the standard, engine-assisted approach, that for a short-field landing is flown by maintaining the correct speed with the elevators while adjusting power to conform with the glidepath; the throttle is moved in response to displacement up or down of the touchdown point relative to the windscreen.

Drift, if it is present, should be contained by using either of the methods explained in Chapter 4, and at the first hint of wind-gradient effect, power must be added to arrest excessive sink. The flight manual should recommend a speed for short-field landings, but regrettably not all manu-facturers provide this important information either (although page after page is often devoted to such matters as 'Definitions', 'How lucky you are to be the proud owner of our wonderplane' and 'How to give it a wash'). Some manuals and training books advise pilots making a short-field landing to approach 'at the lowest speed consistent with safety', a cosy if meaningless piece of enlightenment when it comes to hard num-bers, the kind we want to set up on the ASI. In essence, we do want to approach at the lowest possible safe speed, but in the absence of rec-ommended flight-manual figures, the inexperienced pilot is at a disad-

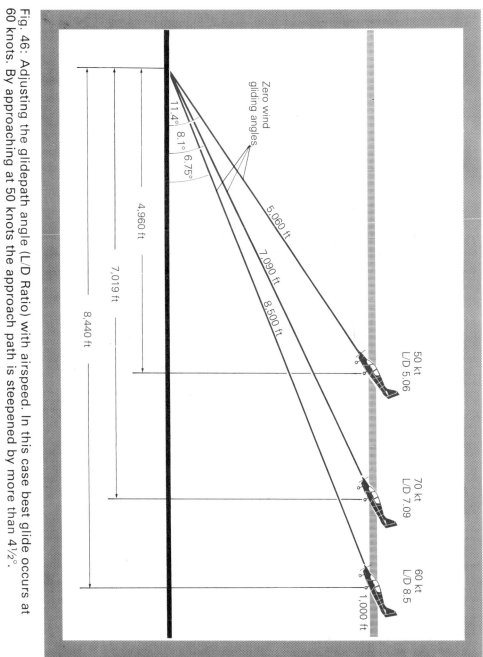

Fig. 46: Adjusting the glidepath angle (L/D Ratio) with airspeed. In this case best glide occurs at 60 knots. By approaching at 50 knots the approach path is steepened by more than 4½°.

vantage. So how do we know what speed to adopt? As a guide here are a few short-field approach speeds compared with those for best glide performance and the standard, engine-assisted landing.

Aircraft type	Stall (knots)	Best glide (knots)	Engine-assisted approach (knots)	Short-field approach (knots)
Cessna Cardinal RG	50	75	70	63
Cessna Pressurized Centurion	58	87	80	72
Robin Alpha	48	65	65	59
Robin Aiglon	52	75	70	67

In studying these figures, it should be understood that the stalling speeds quoted are with full flap, engine off. This is important because there is a significant reduction in stalling speed when the aircraft is under power, partly because of the additional airflow caused by slipstream over those parts of the wings within its flow, but also as a result of the upward-inclined thrust line that occurs when a low-speed/nose-high attitude is adopted during a short-field approach (Fig. 47). Other than those for the Robin Alpha, speeds recommended for an engine-assisted approach are 5–7 knots lower than those for best glide (I suspect the Robin Alpha manual is wrong), but in each case the speed quoted is about 1.35 times the stalling figure, whereas the short-field approach is flown at 1.23 to 1.28 times stalling speed. Frankly, that is a quite considerable safety margin, having regard to the fact that the stalling-speed figure, used as a starting-point, is measured power-off, although during an approach for a short-field landing, the not inconsiderable power used will materially reduce the stalling speed and will provide a corresponding increase in safety margin as a result. So, in the absence of specific recommendations in the aircraft's manual, you may compute short-field approach speed as follows: flaps-down stalling speed (wings level) × 1.25.

The speed found by this method is applicable to an approach in wind conditions of zero to, say, 20 knots. In gusty conditions or when crosswind is involved 5–10 knots should be added, according to experience and ability; less accomplished pilots would be prudent to allow themselves an extra 10 knots.

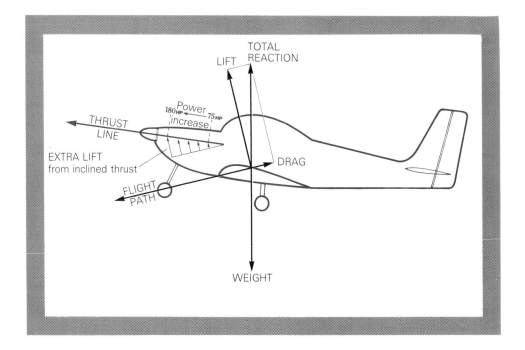

Fig. 47: Thrust contributing to lift when an appreciable angle exists between the glidepath and thrust line. As power is increased so does the vertical component of thrust.

Flying the short-field approach

The technique to be adopted is very similar to that outlined for engine-assisted approaches (page 61). All the aims and corrections in response to visual cues apply, as does the procedure of considering the approach in two sections, initial and final. If, for example, you have calculated a short-field approach speed of 60 knots, there is little point in battling in, mile after mile, control wheel gripped in white-knuckled fists, sweat pouring from the brow, while the airstrip refuses to come any nearer. Fly the initial approach 5 or even 10 knots faster; then, as short finals are reached, reduce power (to prevent yourself from climbing above the glidepath as speed is reduced); adopt a slightly higher nose attitude; and, as speed reduces to 60 knots, open the throttle again and retrim (Fig. 48).

Here are some of the traps to avoid:

1. Avoid chasing the airspeed. Accurate trim is vital; incorrect or inaccurate use of the trim control can wreck the exercise.

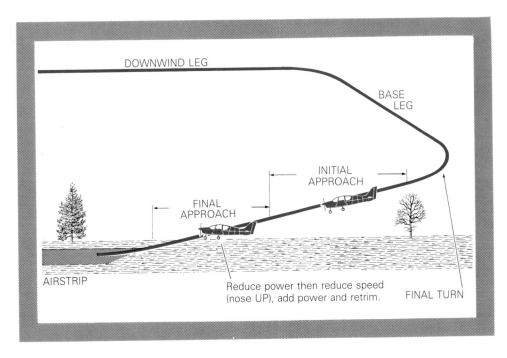

Fig. 48: Setting up the final approach.

2. On no account allow the aircraft to descend below the glidepath so that the approach degenerates into a low-flying exercise with the nose held high, obscuring the view ahead. In that kind of situation, pilots usually find themselves adding more and more power in an effort to make the field.

3. Keep the touchdown point in a constant position within the windscreen frame by correct power/attitude adjustments.

4. Guard against allowing the aircraft to climb above the glidepath as a result of the incorrect use of power. Such a situation, which is the reverse of item 2, is bound to entail reducing power in an effort to avoid overshooting, and the exercise will probably turn into a glide approach at low speed, bringing with it the following risks:
    (a) a high sink rate at low speed, which cannot be arrested unless considerable power is added (Fig. 49);
    (b) an insufficient safety margin between gliding and stalling speeds;

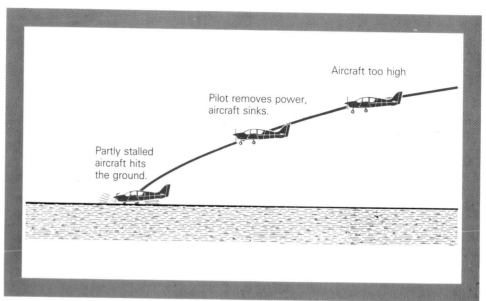

Fig. 49: Danger of allowing a high sink rate to develop as a result of taking off power while approaching at a low speed.

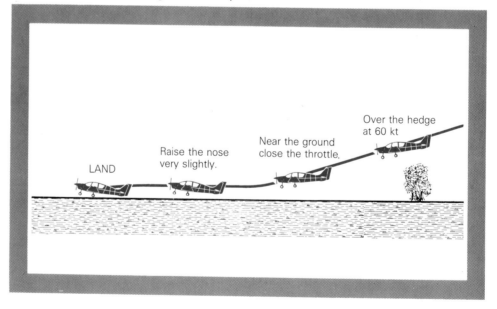

Fig. 50: Completing the short-field landing. Note that power is left on until the aircraft is ready to touch down.

(c) the possibility of poor pitch and yaw control, due to low air-speed and lack of slipstream;

(d) difficulty in controlling the approach and touchdown point with precision.

5. Ensure that the aircraft is aligned with the landing area *before* short finals have been reached. During short finals, when the airspeed is lower than for a normal, engine-assisted approach, heading corrections must be kept to a minimum, using moderate angles of bank. (Remember, stalling speed increases with bank angle.)

Crossing the airstrip boundary

Some private airstrips are not exactly overendowed with ideal approaches; however, the first inspection run will have revealed the presence of large trees and other obstacles. There may be a low wall, hedge or fence to cross, and while the lower the overflight of the boundary the better (in so far as full use of the landing run will be available), never cut this part of the procedure so fine that there is no margin for error. Like all functions calling for judgement, crossing a fence or hedge with minimum safe clearance must be handled with caution. Only with experience is it possible to shave the wheels across whatever it is that marks the boundary of the airstrip with no more than a few diameters to spare. Cut it too close, and at best you will collect some twigs and leaves in your landing gear. Make the same mistake when the airstrip boundary is a stone or brick wall, and you will make your shortest landing ever.

Of prime importance is the flightpath adopted while crossing the hedge or fence. The aim should be to fly a descending path, so that an early touchdown can be made after crossing whatever it is that must be crossed (see Fig. 45, page 128).

The short-field landing

If you have set up the aircraft correctly, it will be descending, power-on, at (in this case) 60 knots. Because the speed is lower than usual (and the angle of attack is relatively high), the removal of power would cause the aircraft to sink heavily on to the ground (see Fig. 49). Therefore it is essential that power be left on until the wheels are near the surface.

Round out in the normal way, remembering that the aircraft is already in a semi-landing attitude and that very little back pressure will be needed on the elevator control (Fig. 50). At the required touchdown point, close the throttle, and the aircraft should land almost immediately. If, on the other hand, there is a tendency to float, then the final approach speed was too high.

After touchdown, allow the nosewheel to make contact with the surface, then apply the brakes.

Use of brakes on a grass surface

Grass, particularly when it is wet, can be anything but ideal when a short-field landing encourages the pilot to make firm use of the brakes. The technique of using short periods of pedal pressure rather than applying the brakes in a single, prolonged onslaught will usually prevent locking of the wheels, but if at any time the wheels stop rotating, the skid that follows will increase the landing run and may cause the very fracas with the far hedge that you have tried to avoid by adopting the techniques previously explained.

If the wheels do lock, and you can feel it even when the landing gear cannot be seen from the pilot's seat, release the brakes, and then reapply them in a series of short jabs.

The often-recommended practice of raising the flaps in the belief that braking effect will improve was given less than enthusiastic mention on page 59. All the risks and disadvantages of this dubious technique were explained, and they certainly apply during a short-field landing at a time when the aircraft can take full advantage of the drag created by use of maximum flap. In any case, the pilot would be better employed in maintaining direction and avoiding rough ground than in switching his attention to the flap control. Brake effectiveness is best assured during the landing roll by holding the stick or yoke hard back, thus planting the mainwheels firmly on the ground.

Taxiing to the parking area

The owner of a private airstrip, if he uses it himself, will be aware of its warts and blemishes. Not so the visiting pilot, who lands at his or her own risk. There may be no ground markings indicating rough or soft areas, and nothing more than a cryptic note on the airfield plan (if one exists at all) to the effect that 'North-east corner is liable to flooding' or a warning to the pilot to 'Avoid taxiing across a point bounded by the public footpath and the barn on the northern perimeter'.

Often the only safe place for an aircraft to manoeuvre on these private airstrips is the landing area itself. Having made a skilful approach and landing on a small field, it would be a pity to spoil the achievement by taxiing into a ditch or getting stuck in the mud. So when the time comes to make for the parking area, check where you are taking your expensive aircraft. Avoid long grass if at all possible; look out for any hazards on the ground; and taxi slowly.

Minimum-distance short landings

The short-field landings so far described have been based on an approach at manufacturers' recommended speeds or, in their absence, a speed calculated by the pilot on a basis of 1.25 times the flaps-down, power-off, wings-level stalling speed. Because these approach speeds – manufacturers' or pilot-calculated – are based upon applying a safety margin to the power-off stalling speed, there remains a little 'fat' because, power-on, most aircraft will continue flying 5, 10 or even more knots below their published stalling speeds. (This was illustrated in Fig. 47, page 132.) Pilots who, for one reason or another, must earn their keep flying into very short airstrips – and there are many such operations being conducted on a day-to-day basis in various parts of the world – have good reason to appreciate the value of this quirk of aerodynamics. Manufacturers' recommended short-field approach speeds would have these pilots off the strip and into the bush in no time at all. Then there are those little strips in Borneo where an overshoot is followed by an uncontrolled plummet down the side of a mountain, and others in Switzerland where the consequences of similar misjudgement are covered in snow. Pilots having to contend with such landing conditions as routine must develop the ability to fly the final approach at the 'lowest possible speed consistent with safety', as those flight manuals say that are too coy to put a number on it. In some respects one must excuse the manufacturers concerned, because they are at least leaving the door open for pilots to find their own personal lowest possible speed.

Is approach speed all that important? you are entitled to ask. After all, most light planes have modest enough ground rolls, so why the fuss about low speeds for short landings? The following figures relate to three light singles – a low-powered trainer, a 180-hp tourer and a pressurized six-seat, top-of-its-class design, which probably has the most powerful flaps in this category of aircraft. Middle approach speed in each case is for a normal, engine-assisted landing.

Cessna 152		Robin Aiglon		Cessna P210 Centurion	
Approach speed (knots)	**Ground roll (ft)**	**Approach speed (knots)**	**Ground roll (ft)**	**Approach speed (knots)**	**Ground roll (ft)**
45	330	60	843	62	567
54	475	70	1,148	72	765
60	586	80	1,498	82	993

So the answer to the question is that a mere 6-knot increase in approach speed on a windless day will add more than 23 per cent to the landing roll of a little Cessna 152.

Factors affecting the lowest safe approach IAS for any particular aircraft are:

1. Aircraft weight at time of landing.

2. Pilot skill – *a very important factor*.

3. Wind conditions.

On the basis that the reader may one day earn a living flying into the bush or landing on mountain airstrips, the following exercises will help to develop the required technique of arriving over the airstrip threshold at the lowest possible safe approach speed:

1. At a safe height (4,000 ft agl would be ideal) decelerate to normal, engine-assisted approach speed; lower full flap; add sufficient power to maintain height; and retrim.

2. Allow the aircraft to settle, if necessary making small power adjustments to hold a constant height.

3. Gradually hold up the nose until the airspeed decreases to around the published flaps-down, power-off stalling speed. At first there will be a tendency for the aircraft to gain height, but when the ASI has settled, a gentle sink will begin. At that stage the aircraft will be flying on the 'back of the drag curve' (see Fig. 51), and to maintain height the throttle must be opened as speed is decreased.

4. Continue raising the nose and adding power to maintain height, retrimming at each stage. By now the stall warner will probably be

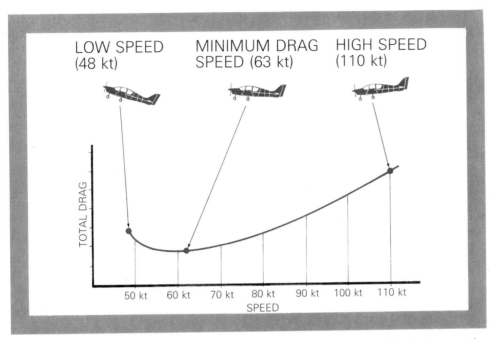

Fig. 51: The effect of airspeed on total drag. Left-hand aircraft is flying on the back of the drag curve, a useful condition when approaching for a minimum distance short landing.

sounding intermittently. The point will be reached at which the aircraft stalls (a pre-stall buffet will occur with most low-wing aircraft). Note the ASI reading, which will be considerably lower than the published stalling speed, and recover from the stall by lowering the nose, if necessary adding power (although considerable power will be on just before the stall) and checking the yaw with opposite rudder.

This exercise will demonstrate how to set up an aircraft so that it maintains height at the lowest possible speed and show how to recover from a power-on stall if you push things too far. With practice, recovery can be made with minimal height loss.

Unfortunately, this is only part of the story, because we land off a descent, not straight and level flight, and in a descent the airflow comes up to meet the wing, increasing the angle of attack in the process. Fig. 52 illustrates the important and sometimes forgotten fact of stalling during a descent. So, having practised flying at low airspeeds, it now only remains to apply your newly acquired skill to a descent at controlled rate. At a safe height:

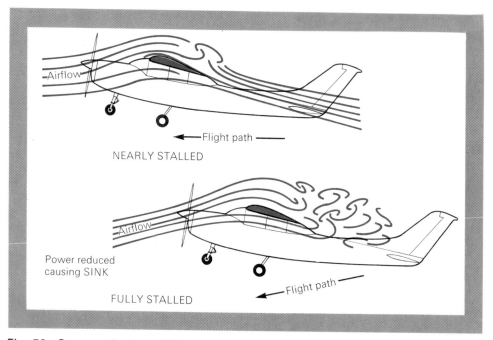

Fig. 52: *Same attitude – different flight condition.* Upper aircraft is flying level at just above stalling speed. Lower aircraft is sinking, the airflow approaches from below, angle of attack increases and a stall results.

1. Set up the aircraft with full flap and sufficient power to maintain height at about 10 knots above the previously found power-on stalling speed.

2. Reduce power slightly, and maintain the required airspeed. Note both the RPM and the rate of descent.

3. Adjust the power to provide a 300 ft/minute descent rate, which would be typical for a short-field landing.

4. Practise gradually reducing speed until the onset of the stall. Note the speed, and note also that recovery is almost instantaneous when back pressure on the elevators is relaxed and the throttle opened slightly.

5. While descending at low speed and with power on, close the throttle. Note the rapidly increasing sink rate, which may be followed by a stall. Recover in the usual way.

The two exercises should be practised until the aircraft can be set up with confidence and then flown with precision. However, a word of warning is appropriate here. While flying with a lot of power at speeds just above the stall, coarse use of the rudder can provoke a spin. So treat it kindly, and remember that slipstream increases its effectiveness.

It is one thing to practise low-speed descents at a safe height, but quite another to continue into an approach as trees drift past and the ground fills the vision. However, the aim is to make the initial approach at or just below normal, engine-assisted landing speed, progressively decreasing speed on short finals until, as the hedge is crossed, the aircraft arrives just short of the threshold in a tail-down attitude and at a speed just above the stall. With the wheels near the ground, the throttle is closed and the control wheel brought back slightly to reduce the rate of sink that will follow. Almost immediately the aircraft will settle to the ground, mainwheels first.

During the procedure (Fig. 50, page 134), speed must be added in gusty conditions, and when wind gradient causes excessive sink, the throttle should be opened accordingly.

Short-field landings, particularly those flown to the limit in the manner described at the end of this chapter, demand skill, exceptional judgement and a fine touch. This is an interesting and rewarding exercise, one that with a little practice should improve general handling, because the pilot who can land at a small airstrip in comfort will find that his normal, engine-assisted approaches have taken on a new shine. No longer does he land half-way along the runway, leaving behind a smell of burning rubber and overheated brakes. His landings reflect a degree of professionalism – a touch of class.

6. Tailwheel techniques

Although there was a time when all aircraft were of tailwheel design, the gradual move towards the 'tricycle' landing gear was in fact no more than a return to the days of the pioneers. As early as 1908 the French boat and aero-engine designer, Léon Levavasseur, had built a large monoplane for Jules Gastambide (head of the Antoinette firm named after his daughter) and his partner Mengin. This aircraft, the *Gastambide–Mengin 1*, the forerunner of those elegant and highly successful Antoinette monoplanes that were to grace the skies of Europe until the start of World War I, sported a four-wheel landing gear, which, like that of a modern aircraft, supported the airframe on the ground in a near-level attitude. The following year Glenn Curtiss in the United States was flying his *Gold Bug*, a biplane fitted with what we would even today recognize as a nosewheel undercarriage. (The Americans do not use the term 'undercarriage', preferring 'landing gear', although the equipment is equally important while taxiing and during the take-off.)

For some reason best discovered by aviation historians, the nosewheel idea rapidly went out of favour. Tailwheels were fitted almost without exception, and it was not until the mid- to late 1930s that the 'tricycle' landing gear came back on the scene. In many respects, this turn of events is surprising because, for the most part, the tailwheel arrangement offers few advantages over the nosewheel and quite a number of disadvantages. Here are the pros and cons of both types of undercarriage.

Nosewheel	
Advantages	**Disadvantages**
Directionally stable.	Creates more drag than tailwheel landing gear
Brakes can be used firmly.	
Visibility good while taxiing.	More vulnerable to damage on rough ground or through poor handling than tailwheel gear.
Less affected by wind while taxiing than tailwheel types.	
Easy to handle during take-off and landing.	Heavier than tailwheel gear.

Tailwheel	
Advantages	**Disadvantages**
Less drag than nosewheel landing gear.	Directionally unstable; prone to ground-loops during landing and swinging while taking off.
Less prone to damage on rough ground or through poor handling than nosewheel gear.	Firm braking may cause nose-over.
Lighter than nosewheel gear.	Visibility poor while taxiing.
	Can be badly affected by wind while on the ground.
	Landing and take-off require more judgement than with nosewheel aircraft.

Most World War II pilots were trained on tailwheel aircraft. Then peace brought with it a new breed of easy-to-fly, light planes. Tailwheels were out, nosewheels were in, and by now several generations of post-war pilots, great numbers of them all over the world, have probably never flown a 'tail-dragger'. Why, then, should they bother with mastering tailwheels now that the great majority of aircraft, big and small, have the third wheel up front? There are various reasons:

1. Most Ag-planes are tail-draggers because they are more usually suited to operating from rough fields than are nosewheel types.

2. Some of the modern STOL aircraft, which have been purpose-built for bush operations, have tailwheels for the same reasons.

3. From time to time the lucky ones among us are given an opportunity to fly vintage aircraft. These are almost invariably of tailwheel design, and it would be unforgivable to bend a priceless piece of living aeronautical history through ignorance of the special techniques demanded when the little wheel is at the back.

The table above shows in brief the pros and cons of tailwheel design; I want now to examine in detail what makes tail-draggers more difficult to handle than a nosewheel aircraft.

The special demands of tailwheel design

Stability on the ground

No matter what kind of vehicle you are dealing with, the relationship between point-of-wheel contact and centre of gravity is vital to its directional stability. You have only to watch the customers at any airport fight a losing battle with their baggage trolleys, and you will know what I mean. These masterpieces of bad design are prepared to go in any direction other than the one you chose.

Take a look at the left-hand aircraft in Fig. 53. As it is a nosewheel design, its centre of gravity is ahead of the mainwheels. While taxiing, a strong gust of wind tries to weathercock the aircraft to the left (right-hand picture). Other than an easily corrected deviation from the original rolling direction, there is no tendency to ground-loop because:

(a) the nosewheel, acting through its moment arm some distance ahead of the centre of gravity, resists weathercock action caused by the wind;

(b) the distance between the right wheel and the centre of gravity (B), is now greater than distance A which is trying to ground-loop the aircraft; consequently moment B is more powerful than moment A, and there is a natural tendency to correct a swing in the early stages and run straight.

Fig. 54 examines the behaviour of a tailwheel landing gear in similar circumstances. The left-hand drawing shows that in tailwheel designs the centre of gravity is located *behind* the mainwheels. It has to be, otherwise the hardware would threaten to stand on its nose at the slightest provocation – but more about that later.

Along comes a gust of wind from the left, and unless the tailwheel can be locked in the straight-ahead position (few aircraft have tailwheel locks, by the way), the events that follow can be interesting if allowed to get out of hand because:

1. On most tailwheel aircraft an arrangement is provided which gives limited steering capabilities via spring linkage to the rudder pedals. After about 25° or so (according to aircraft type) a spring-loaded cam disengages, allowing the tailwheel freedom to caster – a useful facility while parking, but the cause of endless anguish when a crosswind

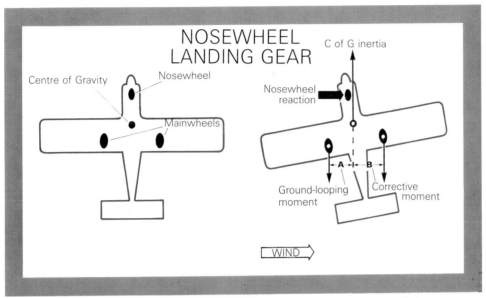

Fig. 53: Nosewheel stability during a swing. Corrective moment B is greater than ground-looping moment A.

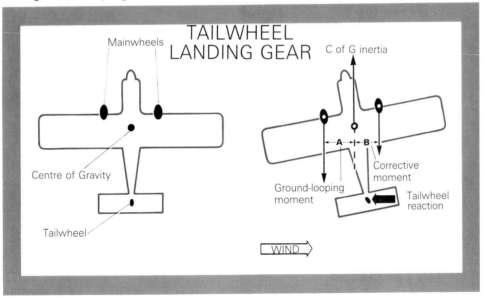

Fig. 54: Tailwheel instability during a swing. Corrective moment B is less than ground-looping moment A.

threatens to have the tail meet the nose. Once the tailwheel kicks out of linkage with the rudder pedals, it is incapable of controlling a swing. In this respect the steerable nosewheel is greatly superior.

2. Distance between the right wheel and the centre of gravity B is now less than distance A, which is trying to ground-loop the aircraft. In other words, moment A is more powerful than moment B, and the centre of gravity will rapidly swing ahead of the left wheel, which then becomes the pivot point for a classic ground-loop.

A little thought will reveal that the further we position the mainwheels ahead of the centre of gravity, the more unstable a tailwheel design becomes while on the ground, since the difference between moments A and B is accentuated. Many of the stability problems associated with tailwheel designs would be overcome if it were possible to arrange the centre of gravity in line with, or preferably slightly ahead of, the main-wheel – but, as the next section will explain, such an aircraft would be unmanageable on the ground.

The effect of braking

The right-hand picture in Fig. 55 shows the relationship between the centre of gravity and a nosewheel undercarriage (or landing gear, if you insist). The pilot of the aircraft is taxiing without a care in the world, having resigned himself to the fact that he is number 19 to take off, when without warning, and for no apparent reason, aircraft number 18 suddenly decides to stop. Naturally, our pilot applies the brake firmly and decisively. The left-hand picture shows that the centre of gravity has a mind to continue on its way, producing an inertia force equal to the retarding action of the brakes. Whether the aircraft is moving or at a stand-still, its weight must act vertically in a downward direction; consequently, a combination of these two forces (known in the best textbooks as the 'resultant') acts in a direction that ensures that the weight is behind the nosewheel – and we can all be thankful for that. Other than allowing the plane to make a gentle nod of disapproval, the nosewheel ensures that the tail will not rise to the point where the propeller can make contact with the ground.

Consider the situation as it applies to a tailwheel aircraft (Fig. 56). The same pilot taxiing one of these would have perhaps just a few cares in the world, because it is difficult to see ahead (a topic to be dealt with

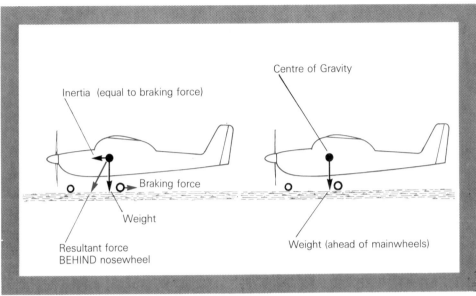

Fig. 55: Nosewheel stability while braking. Resultant force trying to cause a nose-over is restrained by the nosewheel.

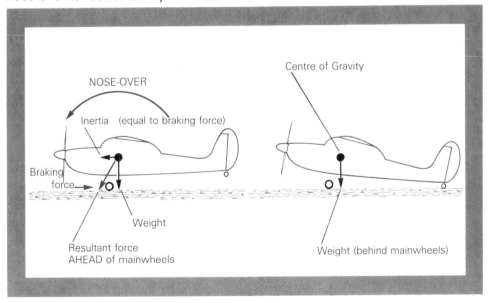

Fig. 56: Tailwheel instability while braking. Resultant force will move ahead of the mainwheels, and, if powerful enough raise the tail and possibly cause damage to the propeller.

later), and he must exercise care not to allow a swing to develop; as already explained, the centre of gravity is behind the mainwheels and, given an opportunity, will try to get ahead.

The same emergency stop is called for, bringing with it the previously mentioned resultant (a combination of aircraft weight and centre of gravity inertia). This time the resultant is ahead of the mainwheels – the distance being dependent upon the amount of braking force. The centre of gravity tries to throw itself over the cliffs; the tail raises; and, since it is firmly glued to the rest of the airframe, the propeller will strike the ground.

Naturally, designers of tailwheel aircraft (and such aircraft are still being made) do their best to avoid the kind of situation just described. But even the best designer has to face the conflicting requirements of providing directional stability by not placing the mainwheels too far forward, yet not risking a nose-over through positioning them too far back. Of course, other factors have an influence on directional stability and resistance to nosing-over – for example, length of mainwheel struts, landing-gear track, wheelbase (distance between mainwheels and the tailwheel), type of tailwheel (with full castering, fully retained to the rudder pedals, with spring linkage, lockable, and so on) – but as practising pilots we need not concern ourselves with those here. Better for us to leave these problems to the designers, in the knowledge that we are free to be rude about their efforts later!

Having described some of the problems associated with tailwheel designs, it is now appropriate to explain the operating techniques required. Although this book is confined to landings, tailwheel aircraft are an unknown quantity to the majority of modern pilots. In fairness to them, I feel unable adequately to explain the return to earth without first describing, if only briefly, how to get off the ground.

Handling techniques

General
When becoming acquainted with tailwheel aircraft for the first time, pilots should remember these important differences between tailwheel and nosewheel practice:

1. The view ahead is, in most cases, poor.

2. Harsh use of brake may cause the tail to rise and may even allow the propeller to strike the ground.

3. On the ground, tailwheel types are sensitive to wind, and a swing can easily develop into a ground-loop.

While starting

One can never be sure exactly how an engine is going to light up. It may putter gently into a rhythmic tick-over or, following prolonged use of the starter and a little pumping of the throttle, the animal may roar into life. It is therefore essential that the elevator control be held fully back while starting to ensure that if the engine does burst into song, the slipstream that comes with the RPM will hold down the tail. Down elevator, or even neutral elevator, could provoke the tail to lift as the engine starts – and the results could be expensive in terms of damaged propeller blades and a shock-loaded motor.

While taxiing

There are two main problems here:

1. Control of direction and preventing a swing when the wind is strong.

2. Seeing directly ahead of the aircraft.

When the wind is light, direction is easily maintained in a modern tailwheel design, but some of the older types have tailskids, and these are the only brakes fitted to the aircraft. Consequently, you will need willing help on one or both wingtips while taxiing in a moderate to fresh breeze and at all times when hard taxiways must be used. Tailskids tend to skate over tarmac or concrete.

When brakes are fitted to pre-war tail-draggers, these are likely to be of the cable-operated drum type, and they can be relied upon to fade at the very moment when they are most needed – for example, while fighting off a crosswind that is determined to weathercock the aircraft. Rather better are the hydraulic drum brakes that were in use until discs took over, but all drum brakes are prone to fading, and they must be applied sparingly.

If at any time the brakes prove incapable of turning in the required direction, reverse the turn and go round the long way. As an aid to turning older aircraft with indifferent brakes, the use of slipstream over the rudder can be of value. There is, of course, the risk of building up excessive speed, so it is essential that such a turn (using brake, rudder and slipstream combined) should be started at no more than a walking pace.

Being fitted with disc brakes, modern tailwheel aircraft are easier to control on the ground than earlier designs; nevertheless, even when the tail-dragger is of recent concept, more skill is required while taxiing than in nosewheel types. It goes without saying that all light aircraft benefit from the correct use of aileron while taxiing on a windy day, and this is particularly true of tailwheel designs. When the situation warrants a blast of slipstream before adding a lot of power, the stick/wheel must be held fully back to keep the tail on the ground.

Other than some of the last of the French Jodel designs, which sat on the ground in an almost level attitude, most tailwheel aircraft have a moderately steep nose-up stance, which effectively blocks forward visibility. It is therefore of vital importance to clear the path ahead by tacking left and right of the intended direction. Fig. 57 shows that you should turn to the left while looking along the right of the nose, then

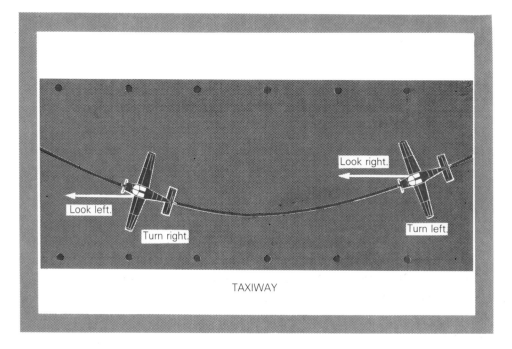

Fig. 57: Improving the view ahead by swinging the nose from side to side and looking the other way.

turn to the right and look along the left of the nose; a tiresome zigzag, but an essential part of the tail-dragging ritual – unless you enjoy the risk of taxiing into unexpected solid objects, that is.

The advent of modern brakes, good visibility and nosewheels that steer like a family car have encouraged pilots to taxi like drivers in the Monte Carlo Rally. Such behaviour in a tailwheel aircraft, particularly one of older design, is certain to end in trouble. Above all else, while taxiing a tail-dragger the golden rule is MOVE SLOWLY.

During take-off

It should be remembered that a tailwheel aircraft sits on the ground in the three-point attitude, with its propeller shaft inclined upwards. Because of this the take-off is affected by various factors which, if allowed to take over, will cause a swing. First, there are the two forces that affect all aircraft, nosewheel or tailwheel.

1. **Slipstream effect.** The efflux from the propeller rotates around the fuselage like a giant coilspring as it moves back towards the tail, striking one side of the fin and rudder (vertical stabilizer, if you live in the United States), pushing it to one side and encouraging a swing.

2. **Torque effect.** As a result of this, the aircraft has ambitions to rotate in the opposite direction to the propeller, pushing one wheel on the ground harder than the other and, into the bargain, producing a braking effect on that side. This too endeavours to swing the aircraft while taking off.

To these propeller-induced tendencies to depart from the straight and narrow during take-off must be added another pair that are peculiar to aircraft of tailwheel design.

3. **Asymmetric blade effect.** While the tail is on the ground during the early part of the take-off run, the propeller shaft is inclined upwards, and the top of the propeller disc is therefore tilted back towards the pilot. A little thought will reveal that because of this tilt the down-going blade will enjoy a larger angle of attack than its up-going neighbour, the difference in angle being related to the steepness of the aircraft's tail-down attitude at this stage of the take-off run. The net result of this unequal or asymmetric relationship in

blade angle is that more thrust is developed by the down-going half of the propeller disc (the right-hand half as seen by the pilot when propeller rotation is clockwise) than by the up-going half. The resultant swing, which is in the same direction as the two already mentioned, will obviously disappear when the tail is raised prior to lift-off, because the propeller disc will then rotate in a vertical plane, each blade taking an equal bite from the air. But in raising the tail, as asymmetric blade effect disappears, another takes its place:

4. **Gyroscopic effect.** What can you remember about gyroscopes? They possess rigidity; they will maintain a fixed position in space; they may be air-, vacuum- or electrically-driven, but they may also take the form of any rotating body – a cycle wheel, for example, or (more important to readers of this book) a propeller. Another property of gyroscopes is precession, a perverse little idiosyncracy if ever there was one. Imagine yourself looking ahead during take-off in a tailwheel aircraft. Before you is the propeller, spinning in a clockwise direction and adopting the properties of a large gyroscope in the process. The time comes for the tail to be raised and then the fun starts, because as the propeller disc is tilted forward to the upright position, it is as though a forward force has been applied to the top of the arc described by the blades. At this point precession occurs. The propeller, behaving as an out-sized gyroscope, resists the force trying to tilt it upright, and a reaction is generated acting at 90° in the direction of rotation. In other words, while you are raising the tail and forcing the top half of the propeller disc forward, a reaction, pushing on the right-hand half of the disc, contributes to the left swing generated by the other three propeller forces already described. Naturally, since it is a gyroscopic phenomenon, the power of this effect is influenced by rate of tail lift during take-off, engine RPM and the weight of the propeller. So metal propellers are better at causing a swing than wooden ones.

How does all this influence the tailwheel take-off? It means that tail-draggers, unlike nosewheel aircraft, will not run straight unless made to tear along the dotted line by a vigilant pilot. The technique to adopt is the following:

1. Line up on the centre of the runway, and allow the aircraft to roll forward a short distance to ensure that the tailwheel is straight.

2. Look along the left of the nose, and select a distant point on which to keep straight.

3. Open the throttle slowly but fully in one movement, while holding the stick/wheel just aft of neutral. Keep straight with rudder, using the aiming-point for reference.

4. As the speed increases, ease forward on the stick/wheel and bring the aircraft to the level attitude. Be prepared for an additional tendency to swing as the tail rises and gyroscopic effect occurs. When propeller rotation is clockwise, there will be a need for right rudder pressure.

5. As speed increases, there will be a tendency for the tail to rise. Prevent this by progressive back pressure on the stick/wheel until the aircraft leaves the ground.

Not quite as simple as a take-off in your usual winged tricycle, but certainly more interesting.

Having outlined the various techniques involved in getting a tailwheel aircraft safely into the air, it now remains to explain the business of getting it back on to the ground.

Landing a tailwheel aircraft

Everything related to the climb-out, circuit and approach in a tailwheel aircraft is exactly the same as usual practice in a nosewheel type. The landing, on the other hand, demands rather different treatment. Two techniques are in use:

1. The wheel landing. Often known as a 'wheeler' and usually favoured when there is a crosswind, this method is also adopted for larger designs such as the DC3.

2. The three-point landing. This technique is so called because in a perfect example the aircraft touches down on all three wheels simultaneously.

The wheel landing

Having approached in the usual way and having arrived over the threshold at the normal speed for an engine-assisted landing, the aircraft is allowed to descend, wheels near the runway, and the landing is made as follows (reference to Fig. 58 will assist in following the text):

1. Round out over the runway centreline.

2. Progressively reduce power, without lowering the tail, and allow the mainwheels to make contact.

3. Prevent any tendency for the aircraft to lower the tail or bounce into a nose-up attitude by applying *slight* forward pressure on the stick/wheel. The technique to adopt is similar to that for raising the tail during take-off. On no account must the tail be forced down with elevator control, since this would cause the aircraft to lift off again.

4. Keep straight with rudder and, as the speed decreases, allow the tail to lower naturally to the ground. There may be a slight tendency to swing to the right (when propeller rotation is clockwise) due to gyroscopic precession following the tilting back of the propeller disc (see page 152).

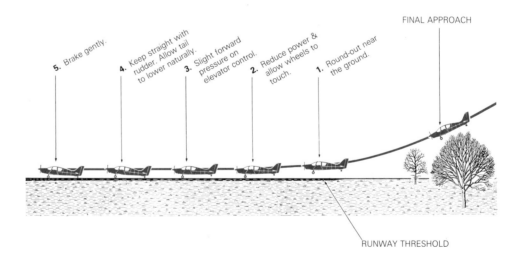

Fig. 58: The wheel landing.

5. Apply the brakes sparingly, and bring the aircraft to a halt.

Unlike nosewheel aircraft, on which the mainwheels are behind the centre of gravity, tail-draggers have a natural tendency for the angle of attack to increase when a touchdown is made on the mainwheels alone (Fig. 59). Since a wheel landing entails making contact with the ground in the near-level attitude, and consequently at a higher than usual speed, the aircraft will need little encouragement to leap off the ground again unless the following elements are handled with care:

1. Touchdown *must* be gentle. Drop the aircraft on to the ground and a bounce, caused by wheel-strut recoil and the increased angle of attack (middle aircraft in Fig. 59), will entice it to lift off the ground in a low-speed/nose-high condition that needs immediate correction – the addition of engine power followed by a second landing.

2. The aircraft is flown on to the ground by making a lower than usual round-out, controlling the final sink on to the mainwheels by gradually closing the throttle. Take off the power too suddenly and you

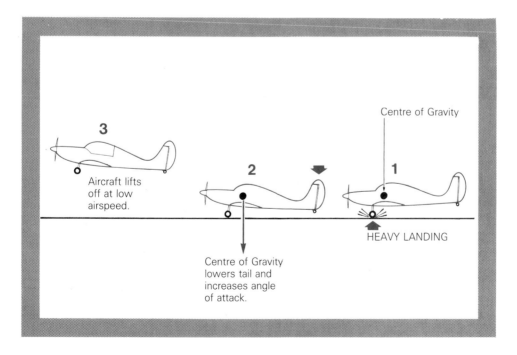

Fig. 59: Mechanics of a bounce while landing a tailwheel aircraft.

risk dropping the aircraft on to its wheels. Leave on the power too long and it will continue floating until you run out of airfield.

3. If, having made the round-out and closed the throttle, the aircraft does continue to float just above the runway, resist the temptation to move the stick/wheel forward – that is a recipe for controlled disaster because a bad case of Fig. 59 is bound to follow. Instead make sure the throttle is fully closed. If it is, and the aircraft finally touches down too far along the runway for comfort, then your approach speed was probably excessive.

A 'wheeler' should 'grease' on to the runway with a gentle squeal of tyres. As stationary rubber accelerates to 50 knots (or whatever is the touchdown speed for your favourite plane), there will be a slight retarding effect at wheel level which, without assistance from the pilot, will cause a modest nose-down/tail-up pitch. In a really good arrival this will reduce the angle of attack sufficiently to hold the aircraft on the ground.

The three-point landing

We have now arrived at the one that divides the nobs from the peasants, the three-point landing, one of aviation's hurdles and frustrations that can at the same time be a pilot's pride and joy. For nothing can be more satisfying than a smooth-as-silk three-pointer, so gentle that the transition from air to ground is marked only by a change in noise as the swish of airflow gives way to the rumble of wheels on concrete.

The three-point landing is enacted at the lowest touchdown speed possible (that is, unless the aircraft is made to arrive tailwheel first – but that is not a perfect three-pointer). Indeed, while the manufacturers of one or two tailwheel aircraft based on the French Jodel design actually recommended landing tailwheel first, the technique is not without its hazards, and I would never recommend it to my best friends. In the first place, an arrival tailwheel first can so easily be followed by heavy ground contact with the main landing gear. But the prime risk is that in trying to attain the necessary tail-down attitude for this 'blunt end first' caper, there is every possibility that you will stall.

Which brings me to the popular belief that in a properly executed three-point landing the aircraft is stalled on to the ground. The myth dies hard, and even to this day Piper talk about a 'full stall touchdown' in the manuals for their Tomahawk and Dakota light planes. They even use the term in their manuals for the quite massive Saratoga and the even heavier Turbo Seminole light twin. In the first place, all these aircraft are nosewheel designs, but even if they had tailwheels, Piper would be incorrect in talking about stalled landings.

In the days when most people learned to fly on tailwheel aircraft it was fashionable for the instructor to conclude his landing demonstration with the words 'Come back on the stick until she stalls on to the ground on all three points.' It was wrong then, and it is equally wrong now. Following the usual debate among instructors on this very subject, a number of us went around the large hangar where I was employed at the time and measured the angle of attack of everything in sight. In those days they were all tail-draggers, yet the only aircraft which actually assumed a larger than stalling angle while resting on its wheels was the old de Havilland Rapide, a quite large, twin-engined biplane of 1935 design. There may be others, but the Rapide is the only one known to me that stalls in the three-point attitude. It is also almost impossible to do a good three-point landing in the old 'bamboo bomber' for reasons that are obvious if you think about it.

'What happens when a gentle aircraft stalls?'
'The nose drops.'
'And what happens when a not-so-gentle aircraft stalls?'
'The nose drops, and so does a wing.'

This imaginary conversation explains why few tail-draggers have been designed with long enough legs to permit a 'full-stall' landing in the three-point attitude. Such aircraft would be unmanageable unless a pilot was brilliant enough to place the wheels, with consistency, no more than a few inches above the runway when the pre-landing stall occurred. Ask anyone who has tried to three-point a Rapide, and I am sure you will be told the same.

So what does happen in the final stages of a three-point landing? The aircraft *sinks* to the ground, unstalled – and, in a good landing, under control.

Like the wheel landing, all circuit and approach procedures applicable to a nosewheel aircraft apply to the three-point arrival, which in many respects may be regarded as an extension of the normal, nose-wheel type of touchdown, even if a little more judgement and skill are demanded of the pilot. The three-point landing (see Fig. 60) is handled as follows:

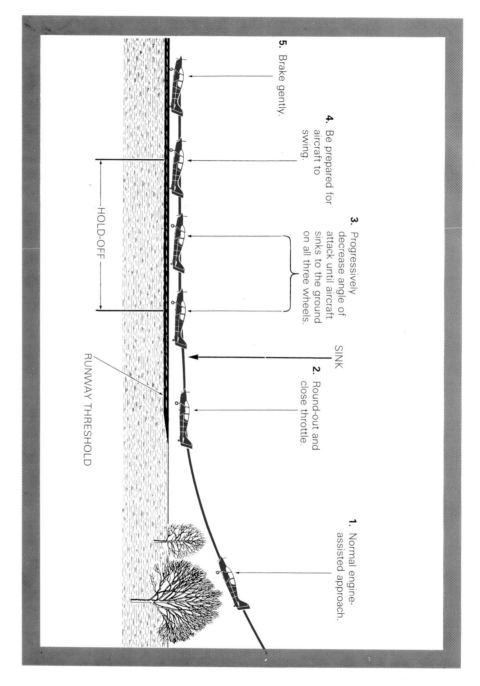

5. Brake gently.

4. Be prepared for aircraft to swing.

HOLD-OFF

3. Progressively decrease angle of attack until aircraft sinks to the ground on all three wheels.

SINK

2. Round-out and close throttle.

RUNWAY THRESHOLD

1. Normal engine-assisted approach.

1. Fly the initial and final approach as described for the engine-assisted landing (pages 31–44), adjusting the glidepath with reference to the visual cues illustrated in Fig. 10 (page 36).

2. Cross the airfield boundary at the correct speed; arrive over the runway threshold; round out; and progressively close the throttle (see page 46).

3. As the aircraft begins to sink from the initial round-out position, come back on the stick/wheel to prevent the mainwheels from touching the ground. Keep the eyes moving back and forth as described on page 53; guard against ballooning (page 46); and continue coming back on the control until the three-point attitude is reached, when the aircraft will sink to the ground. This is explained after point 5.

4. Once down, be prepared for a swing to develop, and control direction on the rudder, if necessary assisted with brake. Keep the stick/wheel fully back to prevent the tail from lifting.

5. Use the brakes sparingly, and bring the aircraft to a halt.

Whereas a nosewheel aircraft can be landed in a number of different attitudes, from nearly level to a tail-down angle that is almost as steep as the landing just described, tailwheel aircraft are not as forgiving if you are intent on a three-pointer in which all wheels make simultaneous contact with the runway. Obviously, this can occur only at one angle or, to be more correct, in one attitude. Unfortunately, not all aircraft tell the pilot when he has arrived at the magic three-point stance by demanding that the stick or wheel be moved fully back prior to touchdown. Some do require full up-elevator; others do not. So you are left with learning how the outside world should look from the pilot's seat when all wheels are on the ground – something, as was suggested in Chapter 2, that can be learned simply by spending a little time (and no money) sitting in the aircraft. Here are some of the traps that may be encountered during a three-point landing.

Holding off too high

If, after the round-out, you start the hold-off immediately, without awaiting the sink that tells you when the energy is winding down, the three-point attitude may be reached several feet above the runway. Consequently, the aircraft will drop heavily on to its wheels. It is surprising how much punishment an aircraft can take, provided the shock of such a landing is distributed through all three wheels, but there is a limit to everything, so do not cultivate the habit.

Landing mainwheels first

If you have not reached the three-point attitude prior to touchdown, either through making the initial round-out too low or through not continuing the backward movement required on the elevator control:

(a) the aircraft will touch down at a higher than ideal speed;
(b) there will be a tendency for the mainwheels to raise the nose, increase the angle of attack and cause an embarrassing lift-off (see Fig. 59).

When this happens, the aircraft will be in a potentially dangerous situation – nose high, speed low, near the ground. Most pilots' natural reaction is to push forward on the stick/wheel, but this can produce a heavy landing on the mainwheels. Some pilots faced with the situation illustrated in Fig. 59 tend to pull back fully on the elevator control, but this can provoke a stall and culminate in a different kind of three-point landing, the kind in which you arrive on one wheel, a wingtip and the prop!

Correct recovery action following the tail-down 'wheeler' shown in the illustration or a balloon of the kind depicted in Fig. 15 (page 47) is the same as that for a nosewheel aircraft: add power; keep the wings level; prevent yaw; and ease the aircraft back on to the ground.

Landing tail first

While in moderation a tailwheel-first arrival need be no more than untidy, carried to excess the mainwheels can be thumped hard on the runway – and that is certainly not to the betterment of pilot or aircraft. The tendency to land tailwheel first is caused by: (a) moving the elevator control fully back in an aircraft that attains the three-point attitude with the stick/wheel only partly retarded; and (b) a sharp, backward movement of the stick/wheel at a time when sufficient airspeed remains to provide active elevator response.

The problem can be avoided only by learning from experience the proper rate at which to ease back on the elevator control so that the aircraft gradually assumes the three-point attitude with its wheels just above the runway. We are back to our old friend practice again.

The effects of wind on handling tailwheel aircraft

Ground manoeuvring

In the table of pros and cons on page 143, one black mark against tailwheel aircraft was that they can be badly affected by wind while on the ground. To the problems of visibility when taxiing and the difficulty that can be experienced while trying to steer down a narrow taxiway in a crosswind must be added another – the risk of putting a wingtip into the ground. This primarily affects aircraft of light weight, but in extreme cases it has been known for an aircraft to blow over while being taxied in winds that obviously demanded the assistance of willing hands on the wingtips. Tailwheel aircraft are more vulnerable in this respect than nosewheel designs (although even these have their wind limits while manoeuvring on the ground) because, being in the tail-down attitude, the wing is at a high angle of attack. Depending on its direction and timing, a 25-knot wind can very easily lift one wing or possibly the tail. To avoid the risk of catching a wind fit to stand the hardware on its nose, it is important that pilots of tailwheel aircraft should park them facing either downwind or into wind. In the latter case the stick/wheel must be tied fully back with the safety harness, thus raising the elevators and helping to keep the tail on the ground. If the wind is strong, the aircraft must be securely tied down. And never park an untied tail-dragger across a wind of any consequence. Which brings me to the last part of this chapter.

Landing tailwheel aircraft in a crosswind

Because of the large angle of attack presented when a tailwheel aircraft is in the three-point attitude, and following on the risk of lifting a wing under certain conditions (explained in the previous section), it is self-evident that when landing in a crosswind the 'wheeler' technique (page 154) is preferable to the three-point arrival.

All the preliminaries explained in Chapter 4 apply to making a cross-wind landing in a tailwheel aircraft, and either the wing-down or the crabbing method may be used. However, unless you are very good at tailwheel flying, the three-point landing in anything other than a modest crosswind can be difficult to execute in a tidy fashion and may easily cause a wingtip to touch the ground. It is not uncommon for the tail to rise, allowing the propeller to strike the ground.

Whatever method of landing is used (wing-down or crab approach), when *strong* crosswind conditions exist, a wheel landing should be made. After touchdown remember to execute the following procedures:

1. Keep the mainwheel firmly on the ground by slight forward pressure on the stick/wheel.

2. Move the stick/wheel towards the wind to prevent the into-wind mainplane from lifting. The into-wind aileron must be held ON throughout the landing and while taxiing across wind.

3. As the aircraft decelerates, there will be a marked tendency for it to swing into wind. This must be prevented at all costs – a swing at this stage can easily develop into an uncontrollable ground-loop. Use coarse application of rudder, assisted by brake, to curtail the swing. In bad cases a burst of power can contribute to the recovery by increasing the effectiveness of the rudder.

You may by now have formed the opinion that flying tailwheel aircraft is too much like acting the one-armed paper-hanger. However, there was a time when all the aircraft were tail-draggers, and the war years inspired the biggest pilot-training effort the world is ever likely to witness. The Americans trained on Stearmans, Cornells, BT13s and AT6s; the British, Canadians, Australians, South Africans and New Zealanders flew Tiger Moths (9,000 of them were built); while the Germans used Bucker Jungmann biplanes. All of these aircraft were of tailwheel design, yet on average, cadet pilots went solo after 7–12 hours dual.

If I have stressed the hazards presented by tailwheel aircraft, it is because too many Spam-can trained drivers approach tailwheel aircraft for the first time in a lighthearted manner, never having received any conversion training whatsoever. The result? Too often a ground-loop causing serious damage to what may be a valuable aircraft of historic interest. Handling tailwheel designs is as different from nosewheel flying as multis are from singles, landplanes are from seaplanes and jets are from piston-engine aircraft. So, before leaping into that priceless Stampe, Tiger Moth or Ryan monoplane (or even a modern, replaceable Pitts Special), get yourself checked out on tailwheel techniques.

7. Landing turboprop aircraft

This chapter is written for the benefit of pilots about to make the transition from light, single and multi-engined piston-powered aircraft to the gas-turbine fraternity. Obviously, the transition from piston-powered aircraft to turboprops entails proper conversion training. The engines and their management are different; the systems are usually more complex than those of most piston equipment; handling techniques can be a new experience (though not necessarily more difficult than those of piston-engine aircraft); and a new set of limitations must be observed – even taxiing is different. Consequently, the transition from, say, your Piper Seneca to a Beech King Air or the like is not something you undertake by sitting on the flight deck and reading a textbook. Formal ground school and a professional instructor are essential.

I want first to clarify the mechanical differences between piston-engine and turboprop aircraft as far as is necessary to comprehend the second part of the chapter, which explains why certain techniques and procedures for landing turboprops are as they are – because make no mistake: some of these techniques will appear strange to the majority of piston-engine pilots.

Turboprop engines

In the main, there is little difference between a turboprop airframe and a piston-engine airframe. Both types of aircraft may or may not have a pressurized cabin, and in general the aerodynamic design of both is identical. Indeed, some of the most widely used light turboprops have been developed from piston-powered ancestors, the Beech King Air range (grandma was a Queen Air) and the Piper Cheyenne (grandpa was a Navajo) being obvious examples.

The only turboprop known to me that departs from the conventional in any significant way is the Mitsubishi MU-2 series, which has no ailerons. Instead, when the control yoke is moved to the left, for example, a spoiler raises itself from the top of the port wing, disturbing the airflow, reducing lift and provoking a bank to the left. This excellent arrangement allows the manufacturers to fit a tiny wing to the MU-2, which, being small in area and producing low drag, is ideal for fast cruising. Naturally, in a conventional airframe this would result in an unacceptably high landing speed, but by dispensing with ailerons it has been possible to equip the MU-2 with full-span, double-slotted Fowler flaps that roll out to add some 25 per cent to the wing area and provide a quite modest stalling speed into the bargain.

All this is by the way and no more than a little chat about the exception that proves the rule already mentioned, namely, that turboprop airframes are very similar to your genuine cooking-type piston plane, and such differences as exist are mainly in the engine department.

Differences between piston and turboprop engines

In broad terms, both types of engine, piston and turbine, are of the internal combustion variety. A mixture of fuel and air is compressed and ignited to generate power through expansion. However, while induction, compression, ignition and exhaust take place on an intermittent basis in a piston engine, all functions being performed within the same cylinders, a gas turbine (propeller-driving or jet) enacts the four functions on a continuous basis but in different parts of the engine.

A gas-turbine engine, particularly of the jet variety (not a turboprop), is a very simple animal compared with a modern high-performance piston engine. It is only the automatic systems or refinements that are in themselves complex. The basic jet engine, which we shall consider first as it forms the basis of turboprop power units, consists of a compressor, which may be of the axial flow type (shaped very much like a multi-blade propeller disc) or might be a centrifugal compressor.

The compressor supplies air to a combustion chamber, where a series of spray nozzles introduces atomizer fuel, which is ignited to expand the air and to provide gas energy. The hot gases are directed to one or more turbines, and these are coupled to the compressor by a drive shaft. Such an engine as the one just described is, in fact, a straight turbojet. Propulsive thrust is provided in the form of reaction to the weight of high-speed gases departing from the tailpipe of the engine in much the same way as a rubber balloon will fly around the room if you inflate and release it without tying a knot in the little tube – hence the term 'reaction propulsion'.

The simple engine described above is illustrated in Fig. 61, and in fact forms the basis of *all* gas-turbine units, propjets and fanjets. In principle,

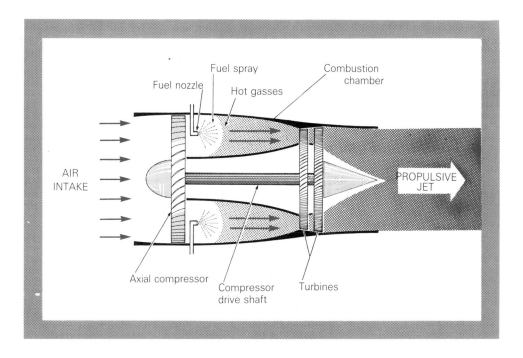

Fig. 61: Simple turbojet engine (fixed guide vanes have been omitted for clarity). This basic motor forms the core or gas generator of turboprop and fanjet engines (illustrated in Figs. 62, 63 and 68).

the lower-powered (and smaller) the gas-turbine engine, the higher its RPM, and speeds in excess of 40,000 are not uncommon. Since propeller speeds are usually within the range of 1,550–2,200 RPM (according to propeller size), it follows that a reduction gear will be necessary if the compressor/turbine assembly is to be harnessed to the airscrew. Propeller-turbine, or (to use the more popular name) turboprop engines, are of two dissimilar breeds:

1. Fixed-shaft engines.   2. Free-turbine engines.

Fixed-shaft engines (Fig. 62)

If you think back to the simple turbojet illustrated in Fig. 61, extend the shaft forward, add a reduction gear and fit a propeller, there is your fixed-shaft turboprop. The engine is simplicity itself, there being only one major rotating part, the compressor/turbine assembly. In the process of driving the propeller (and, of course, the compressor), most of the gas energy is removed by the time it has passed the turbine section, but a

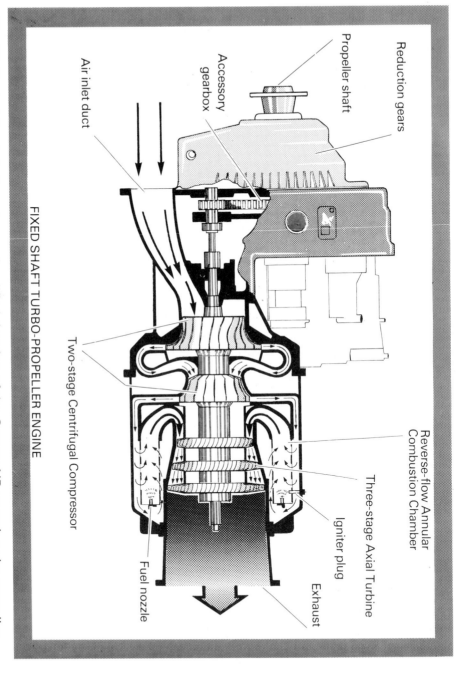

FIXED SHAFT TURBO-PROPELLER ENGINE

Reduction gears

Propeller shaft

Accessory gearbox

Air inlet duct

Reverse-flow Annular Combustion Chamber

Three-stage Axial Turbine

Igniter plug

Exhaust

Two-stage Centrifugal Compressor

Fuel nozzle

Fig. 62: Typical fixed-shaft engine, a simplified drawing of the Garrett AiResearch turbo-propeller engine (fixed guide vanes omitted for clarity).

useful amount of thrust is still provided via the engine tailpipe, and this is added to the shaft horsepower (SHP) delivered at the propeller to arrive at a total or equivalent shaft horsepower (ESHP). Here are some figures for three typical turboprop engines in common use:

Shaft horsepower (SHP)	Thrust (lb)	Equivalent shaft horsepower (ESHP)
575	75	605
715	102	755
1,040	115	1,086

Once the propeller lever has been set to any particular position, a fixed-shaft engine will rotate at a constant speed, irrespective of the power selected by the pilot. During take-off, for example, the power lever is moved forward like a piston-engine throttle; more fuel is introduced to the combustion chamber; and the propeller blades automatically increase pitch to absorb the additional power. Conversely, while landing, the power lever is eventually moved back to the idle stop; fuel flow is reduced; and the propeller blades take up a fine pitch in response to the decrease in power. There is no reduction in engine speed and little change in engine note, an eccentricity that is often disconcerting to pilots under turboprop conversion training, who are used to things becoming quieter when engine power is reduced.

The most widely used fixed-shaft engines are the TPE 331 series, manufactured by Garrett AiResearch. They are available in power outputs of from around 700 to more than 1,000 SHP.

Free-turbine engines (Fig. 63)

The rather odd name of these engines derives from the fact that although the power-producing compressor/turbine core of the unit is very similar to the basic turbojet shown in Fig. 61, there is no direct linkage between it and the propeller. Instead a second shaft is provided, with a power turbine on one end (so positioned that it absorbs most of the gas energy that would otherwise be ejected from the tailpipe) and a reduction gear/propeller assembly on the other. Because there are two shafts in these engines, the pilot is provided with two RPM indicators, one for the compressor/turbine assembly (which is known as the gas generator) and

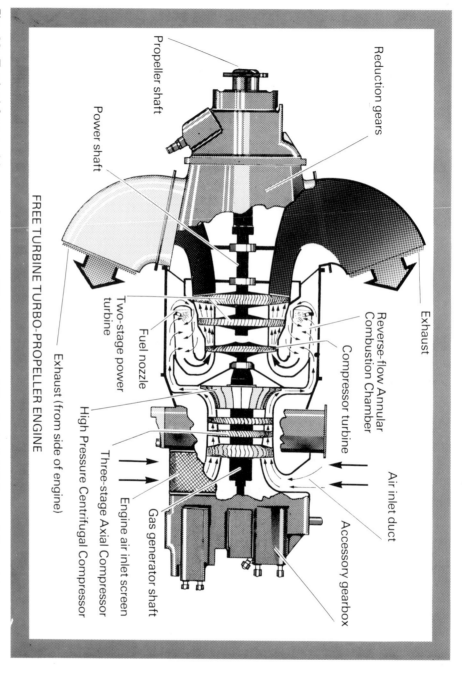

Reduction gears

Propeller shaft

Power shaft

Exhaust

FREE TURBINE TURBO-PROPELLER ENGINE

Reverse-flow Annular Combustion Chamber

Two-stage power turbine

Fuel nozzle

Compressor turbine

Air inlet duct

Exhaust (from side of engine)

High Pressure Centrifugal Compressor

Three-stage Axial Compressor

Engine air inlet screen

Gas generator shaft

Accessory gearbox

Fig. 63: Typical free-turbine engine, a simplified drawing of the Pratt & Whitney of Canada PT6 series of turbo-propeller engines (fixed guide vanes omitted for clarity).

another for the propeller. Aircraft manufacturers have yet to agree on terminology, but it is usual for the gas-generator turbines to be known as N_1 and the power turbines to be referred to as N_2. Their respective RPM indicators are usually labelled accordingly.

It is the practice to start and shut down these engines with their propellers feathered. When the gas generator is running at ground idle speed, little power is transmitted, and the still-feathered propeller wafts slowly around until its blades are moved towards the flight range.

Supporters of the free-turbine concept (sometimes known as the two-shaft engine) claim that the arrangement allows the gas generator to operate at its most efficient speed whatever selection is made on the propeller pitch control. The most widely used free-turbine engines in general aviation are the PT6 turboprops, manufactured by Pratt & Whitney Aircraft of Canada. They range in size from about 500 to 1,200 SHP.

Having described very briefly the two main types of turboprop engine, it now remains to explain their method of control.

Handling turboprop engines

Engine controls

While flight-deck arrangements vary a little according to the whims of designers, most turboprop aircraft are provided with the following engine controls.

Starter/generator

Very considerable energy is required to spin up the gas generator, particularly when it is coupled directly to the propeller (as would be the case in a single-shaft engine). Consequently, a larger-than-usual starter motor is fitted to turboprop engines. To save weight, the starter, having wound up the engine, is arranged to take on the role of generator. A rocker switch is usually provided to bring the generator on line.

Ignition

When the engine is running, it becomes self-sustaining and, unlike a piston engine, there is no need for constant ignition under normal flight conditions. However, like any fire, that of a gas turbine must be ignited in the first instance, and a number of spark-plugs are fitted around the combustion chamber. It is also the practice to switch on the ignition while flying in conditions that might provoke a 'flame-out' (during heavy rain, for instance). Ignition is selected on a switch in some aircraft, but it may be automatic in others.

Power lever

From the idle stop to fully advanced, the power lever performs a function similar to that of a piston-engine throttle. Open the tap: more fuel becomes available and the power increases. Close the tap, and the reverse happens.

Because of their high residual thrust while idling (a combination of jet efflux and slipstream), turboprop aircraft are inclined to taxi like racing cars going down the straight. To cater for the problem, which could also prolong the landing roll, ingenious design features are incorporated in the propeller-control system. The power levers may be lifted and moved back behind the normal idle stops (some power levers have latches which may be hooked upwards by the fingers while the palm of the hand operates the lever proper). In this range of movement the power lever takes over manual control of the propeller. It is then said to be operating in the 'Beta' range.

First movement behind the idle stops places the propeller blades in a near-zero pitch, when little or no thrust will be generated by the propeller. In this position speed while taxiing can be kept within reasonable bounds without the need for excessive use of the brakes. Further backward movement of the power lever moves the blades into reverse pitch, progressively adding power to provide reverse thrust for use after landing. Appropriately, this is called the 'reverse pitch' range. The power lever and its effect on the propeller is shown in Fig. 64.

Propeller lever

This lever performs the same function as the propeller lever on a piston engine, except that its quadrant is usually placarded LOW RPM (used while taxiing) and HIGH RPM (fully forward for take-off, slightly retarded for cruise). It is common practice for turboprop aircraft to be fitted with a synchrophaser which, as the term implies, synchronizes the propellers.

Feathering is usually selected by lifting the propeller lever out of an indent and moving it back behind the LOW RPM stop. However, some aircraft (the Swearingen Merlin 111B, for example) have a separate feathering knob, which also cuts off the fuel to the engine.

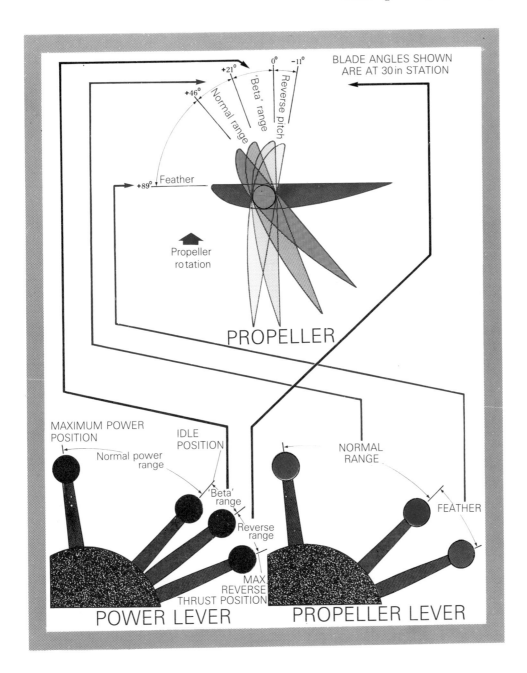

BLADE ANGLES SHOWN
ARE AT 30 in STATION

Fig. 64: Relationship between power lever movement, propeller lever
adjustment and propeller behaviour.

Condition lever

In addition to the power and propeller levers, free-turbine engines are provided with a condition lever, which is usually capable of selecting these engine conditions:

HIGH IDLE (lever fully forward) when the N_1 or gas generator will idle at 70 per cent maximum RPM (that is, with the power lever on the idle stops). The condition lever is placed in this position for take-off, the climb, cruising flight and during the landing.

LOW IDLE (lever moved back against the stop) when the gas generator will idle at 52 per cent N_1 RPM with the power lever on the idle stop. Condition levers should be set to LOW IDLE while taxiing.

FUEL CUT-OFF (lever lifted out of its indent and moved fully back behind the LOW IDLE stop). In this position fuel is cut off from the engine. PT6 engines are started in this position, and the condition lever is moved forward to the LOW IDLE setting only after the electric starter has spooled up the gas generator (N_1) to 12 per cent RPM. The engine is shut down by moving the propeller lever into feather and placing the condition lever in FUEL CUT-OFF position.

Engine instruments

In a twin-engine aircraft it is the practice to fit the engine instruments in two vertical columns, one for each engine. Turboprop engine read-outs tend to be rather small (some of us think a little too small), but a typical instrument presentation would be as described below, although there can be differences from one aircraft type to another in terms of the calibration of instruments and the order in which they appear on the flight panel.

Interstage turbine temperature (ITT)

This important instrument, more conveniently known as the engine temperature gauge, warns the pilot if the engine is running too hot for its own good, and usually two red lines are marked on the dial. One, at around 650–750° C (according to engine type) represents the maximum temperature for flight; the other, at 750–1,000° C, is the maximum allowed for a period of no more than five seconds while starting. If the ITT needle shows an inclination towards exceeding the red line during light-up, you must shut down immediately to avoid cooking the engine and causing the most expensive damage next to flying into a mountain.

Torque meter
This will be a new instrument to piston-engine pilots. In essence, it tells you how much power is being delivered by the turbine to the propeller. The instrument may be calibrated in percentage (100 per cent being the normal maximum, more than that being time limited) or, alternatively, the dial will be marked in foot. pounds. Some aircraft also give horse-power. To prevent overloading the propeller drive, the torque meter will be red-lined at the maximum permitted figure. This instrument is used for setting up the required flight performance (e.g., cruising speed, rate of climb, rate of descent).

Propeller RPM indicator
This instrument may be calibrated in hundreds and thousands when two-finger presentation is usual, or it can be of the percentage type, 100 per cent being the normal maximum, 96–98 per cent being usual for turboprop cruising. These may seem high RPM by piston-engine stan-dards, but it should be remembered that some turboprop aircraft have very slow-turning propellers – less than 1,600 RPM in one case, when the propeller lever is set to achieve 100 per cent and rather less than that in the cruise. Propeller RPM are selected with the propeller lever in much the same way as one would set up a piston engine. When the engine is of the single-shaft type, this is the only RPM indicator provided. Free-turbine engines with their two shafts and two sets of turbines require a second tachometer (see next paragraph).

N_1 RPM indicator
This instrument, which is sometimes known as the gas generator RPM indicator, is calibrated in percentages. While there is no need for a pilot to know the actual turbine speed of his engine, as it is much easier to remember such figures as 85 per cent or 98 per cent, as a matter of interest 100 per cent N_1 on a PT6A-41 engine (the type fitted in a Beech King Air 200) represents 37,500 turbine RPM. Some manufacturers refer to gas generator RPM as N_g.

Fuel flow
These meters are calibrated in pounds per hour and they provide the pilot with an instant indication of the rate at which fuel is being con-sumed. When setting up the aircraft for, say, long-range cruise, the aircraft manual will give the torque and fuel flow related to flight level,

outside air temperature and aircraft weight. Some manuals present these figures in a separate table for each of the various recommended propeller settings; for example, the King Air 200 manual gives power settings and the cruise performance to be expected for 1,700 RPM, 1,800 RPM and 1,900 RPM. The fuel-flow meter is an important aid to accurate engine setting.

Oil temperature/oil pressure

These two read-outs are usually incorporated within the same instrument case, and their purpose needs no further explanation.

Automatic safeguards

Turboprop engines are remarkably small for their power, and they are also very expensive. This is hardly surprising, in view of the perfection of construction demanded by their exceptionally high rotational speeds and the high working temperature of the turbine assembly. To offset their initial cost, turbine fuel is considerably cheaper than AVGAS (less than half the price in some countries); it is more universally available throughout the world; and engine life at between 3,000 and 3,500 hours is very much better than even the best piston engine can achieve. In terms of engine costs per hour, a turboprop can be cheaper than a large, complex piston engine of only half the power.

Turboprop engines are of small size and relatively low weight because they are based upon small turbines that produce a little energy fast, so fast that it cannot be used directly. If you look at some turboprop units, the reduction gearbox is almost as large as the rest of the engine – hardly surprising when it is remembered that almost 42,000 turbine RPM are in some engines reduced to 1,590 propeller RPM, a gear ratio of 26.4 to 1. If fuel efficiency is to be achieved with these engines, turbine speed and engine temperature are critical, and the dividing line between peak running conditions and an overextended power unit is thin by piston-engine standards. To safeguard the engine the following safety devices are fitted (some engines have them all, others just a few).

Negative torque sensor

If the engine fails for any reason, we are faced with a situation in which the propeller will windmill and thus start to drive the engine through a massive gear ratio which steps up the turbine speed by more than 20 times propeller RPM. Think of the strain imposed on the engine transmission and the drag of that big propeller when it tries to spin the engine at 37,000–42,000 RPM. To guard against this situation, a negative torque sensor reacts to reverse transmission loads and automatically moves the propeller blades towards feather. Some engines have full autofeather.

Torque limiter
Particularly at low levels, when the engine is able to develop a lot of power (for example, during take-off), the turbine is capable of inflicting damage on the propeller drive. Torque meters are red-lined at the 'never exceed' figure, but as an added safeguard some engines are fitted with torque limiters, which prevent a pilot from straining the engines by overzealous use of the power levers.

Temperature limiters
At the higher cruising levels in particular, it is possible to run the engine at too high a temperature and to inflict very serious damage on the hot sections of the motor. Interstage turbine temperature or engine temperature gauges have the red lines already mentioned, but as an added safeguard an automatic temperature limiter may be fitted. Some of the Garrett engines have an ingenious device called a single red line (SRL) computer which, acting on information from various parts of the engine (compressor and inlet temperature, exhaust temperature, airspeed and altitude), automatically trims the amount of fuel entering the combustion chamber and prevents overcooking of the engine.

Ice protection
The air inlet on Garrett engines is heated by bleed air from the compressor which, due to adiabatic heating, will be above freezing temperature at all flight levels. The PT6 engines use exhaust-heated air for the same purpose.

Starting locks (Garrett engines only)
Being single-shaft engines with the propeller coupled via its reduction gear to the compressor/turbine assembly, a positive or reverse blade pitch would impose additional loads on the electric starter during spin-up. To prevent pitch displacement during starting, the propeller blades are held in a minimum-drag position by centrifugal locks. After starting, these are released by first selecting reverse pitch and then moving the power lever back to the idle stop.

The description of turboprop engines has, I hope, set the scene, so that the following sections can be fully understood by piston-engine pilots.

The approach

Fuel weight and approach speed

Although the point has already been made about the close similarity between piston-engine and turboprop airframes, there is one important difference that should not be overlooked. Turboprop engines burn quite a lot of fuel, and most turbine-powered aircraft, particularly the larger ones intended for flights in excess of 1,000 nm, carry a greater proportion of their maximum weight in fuel than the bigger, general-aviation piston twins, as the following table reveals.

Aircraft type	Max. weight	Max. fuel weight	Fuel as percentage of max. weight
PISTON-ENGINE			
Piper Navajo PA31	6,500 lb (2,951 kg)	1,116 lb (507 kg)	17.17
Navajo Chieftain	7,000 lb (3,178 kg)	1,411 lb (641 kg)	20.16
Cessna 421	7,450 lb (3,382 kg)	1,670 lb (758 kg)	22.42
TURBOPROP			
Piper Cheyenne I	8,700 lb (3,950 kg)	2,560 lb (1,162 kg)	29.42
Piper Cheyenne III	11,000 lb (4,994 kg)	3,600 lb (1,634 kg)	32.72
Beech King Air 200	12,500 lb (5,700 kg)	3,640 lb (1,653 kg)	29.12
Swearingen Merlin IIIB	12,500 lb (5,700 kg)	4,320 lb (1,961 kg)	34.56

Because fuel weight represents so large a proportion of the take-off and landing weights of a turboprop, it is the practice to calibrate fuel-content gauges in pounds or kilogrammes rather than in Imperial or US gallons, a convention shared by some piston-engine multis. As far as turboprop aircraft are concerned, they may approach the airfield at their maximum landing weight at the end of one trip and be several thousands of pounds lighter during the next arrival; consequently, there is no such thing as a single recommended approach speed for this class of aircraft. The flight manual will provide final approach speeds against landing weights.

Embraer Bandeirante (max. take-off weight 12,500 lb/5,700 kg)	
Weight	**Approach speed (knots)**
11,680 lb (5,303 kg) (max. landing)	91
11,000 lb (4,994 kg)	88
10,000 lb (4,540 kg)	84
Beech Super King Air 200 (max. take-off weight 12,500 lb/5,700 kg)	
Weight	**Approach speed (knots)**
12,500 lb (5,700 kg) (max. landing)	103
12,000 lb (5,448 kg)	102
11,000 lb (4,994 kg)	99
10,000 lb (4,540 kg)	96
9,000 lb (4,086 kg)	93
Swearingen Merlin 111B (max. take-off weight 12,500 lb/5,700 kg)	
Weight	**Approach speed (knots)**
12,500 lb (5,700 kg) (max. landing)	114
11,500 lb (5,221 kg)	110
10,500 lb (4,767 kg)	104
9,500 lb (4,313 kg)	97
8,500 lb (3,859 kg)	91

The Swearingen Merlin 111B, which carries a higher percentage of its weight in fuel than the other aircraft used as examples above, well illustrates the point I am making about varying approach speeds, there being a 23-knot difference between a heavy Merlin and a light one. As a general rule, the greater the variation in approach weight between maximum and minimum fuel, the greater the range of approach speeds.

Planning the approach

Selecting the correct approach speed, as described in the previous section, is only part of the story. It should be remembered that when a company takes a turboprop on the pay-roll, the world is almost its oyster. I qualify this brave statement with the word 'almost' because although the modern light turboprop can fly in and out of most of the established airfields of the world, just as some light singles cannot cope with the smallest airstrips, so there are turboprops which refuse to fit a particular runway. If the airfield offers 950 m and your company pride and joy demands 1,000 of them, landing there is rather like the experience of a man with a size 16 neck who is trying to wear a size 15 collar – uncomfortable.

To help you to avoid running out of runway, the flight manuals include several landing-distance graphs, which take into account the following variables:

1. Airfield pressure altitude.

2. Air temperature.

3. Aircraft weight.

4. Wind component.

Some also provide:

5. Obstacle height.

6. Runway incline/decline.

A separate graph is usually provided for engine-out landings, normal landings without reverse thrust, landings with reverse thrust and, sometimes, flapless landings and short-field landings. Fig. 65 shows a typical landing-distance graph assuming use of propeller reversing. I have contrived it as an approximation to a well-known Brand X turboprop, so it

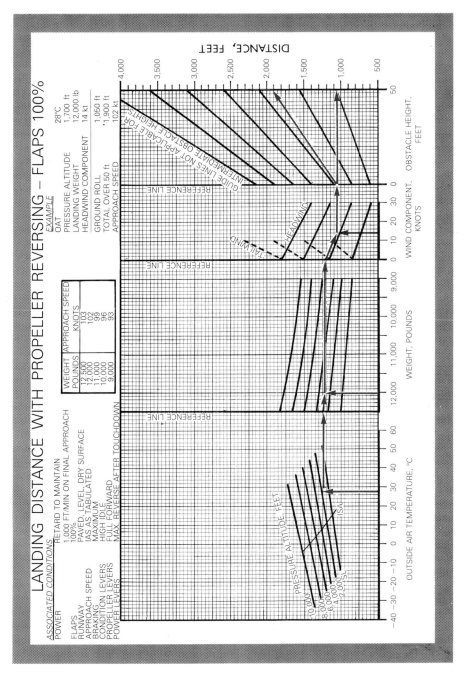

Fig. 65: Typical landing performance graph as provided in most flight manuals. This one is based on the Beech Super King Air 200.

is not to be used in practice. Note the following important features:

1. A list of associated conditions is included in the heading, and these tell you how to set up the aircraft for each type of approach and landing.

2. An example is shown in the form of arrows, blue for clarity in my drawing (but black for cheapness in the flight manual).

3. You start by feeding in the airfield conditions (pressure altitude against air temperature) on the left of the graph. Note that, for convenience, a line is shown representing ISA temperature at the various airfield levels. Where airfield level and air temperature meet, you move the point horizontally to the reference line that marks the beginning of the next section, which is:

4. Aircraft weight, starting at the maximum permitted landing weight (12,500 lb/5,700 kg for this aircraft) and reducing in steps of 100 lb (45 kg) down to 9,000 lb (4,086 kg) which represents a landing at the end of a trip when much of the fuel has been used. You feed in the calculated approach weight, as shown in the illustration, and use the sloping guide lines to extend the airfield information found in the previous section. The point where they meet is then extended to the next reference line, which marks the beginning of:

5. Wind component. In the main, this part of the graph caters for headwinds, but in case you are stuck with a tailwind, small, dotted guide lines are drawn, ascending from left to right, allowing you to take into account tailwinds of up to 10 knots, the maximum permitted for our fictitious turboprop. The reported wind component computed for down the runway, if it is a crosswind (see page 116 and Fig. 42, page 115), is transferred vertically upwards from the wind-component scale at the bottom of the graph, and your previously found reference-line point is brought along to meet it (in this case down-wards, using the printed guide lines, but upwards when there is a tailwind). By now we have taken into account airfield altitude and temperature (density altitude, in other words), aircraft landing weight and headwind/tailwind conditions. The results are moved horizontally to the final reference line and the last stage of the procedure.

6. Obstacle height, starting at zero on the left and 50 ft on the right, is

really a means of giving the answer in terms of landing roll and landing distance over the proverbial 50-ft screen, or any obstacle up to that height, although most flight manuals print the disclaimer shown, which in effect says that you can rely on the landing-roll figure and the landing distance but what you compute for, say, 10-, 20-, 30- or 40-ft obstacles may not be all that accurate. Frankly, we are splitting hairs here, because if the airfield is so tight that attempts are made to fit the aircraft on the runway by eroding the usual 50-ft screen, you would be better off landing somewhere else.

Handling turboprops on the approach

Having determined the final approach speed and satisfied yourself that the runway is long enough for your aircraft, the circuit may now be joined. Most aircraft in the turboprop league integrate better with other general aviation traffic if part-flap is lowered. It saves that faintly uncomfortable feeling that events are getting ahead as the light planes flash backwards past the flight-deck windows.

Pre-landing vital actions vary from one aircraft to the next, but even before the circuit has been reached, the usual airfield joining checks will include ensuring that the cabin altitude is not still at 10,000 ft at a time when the aircraft has descended to 1,500 ft. Some pressurization systems are capable of relatively easy mismanagement, and it only needs a minor malfunction of the depressurizing 'squat' valve to rocket-assist you out of the door (that is, if it can be opened while pressure remains in the cabin). I suggest that the pressurization check should be made while flying towards the circuit, but some flight manuals include this among the pre-landing vital actions. Other items that will be new to piston-engine pilots are:

Propeller synchrophaser	OFF
Yaw damper	OFF
Nosewheel steering	ARMED

The last item applies only to aircraft with powered steering available at the discretion of the pilot, but the landing checks in complex aircraft are bound to vary according to the systems fitted, and the complete check list will be found in the flight manual.

Assuming the final approach speed is, for example, 100 knots, the initial approach could conveniently be flown some 15 knots faster unless there is a slower aircraft on short finals. Flap settings in most (but not all) turboprops are quoted in percentages, and, once the aircraft has turned on to finals and settled into the approach, 100 per cent flap should be lowered unless there is a strong crosswind. The approach is flown as follows:

1. Trim the aircraft accurately; set the power levers to attain a steady rate of descent, and maintain the runway threshold in a fixed position relative to the windscreen; look out for drift and correct it in the normal way as described in Chapter 4.

2. If at any time the aircraft is seen to be descending below the glidepath, *immediate* steps must be taken to arrest the tendency. Add power, but avoid a situation in which the power levers must be advanced to a high setting. Remember the risk of overtorquing, and aim to settle at a steady speed, adjusting the glidepath with minor power-lever movements.

3. As the runway threshold draws near, gradually reduce to the final approach speed applicable to aircraft weight. Make full use of the trimmer.

The landing

Turboprop engines are adjusted so that, with the power levers on the idle stops, there is sufficient residual thrust to ensure a gradual sink rate after the round-out. This same residual thrust, given the opportunity, will have you devour the runway ahead unless use is made of the 'Beta' range and, of course, the brakes. For shorter landings reverse thrust should be used; this will be dealt with in the next section. In so far as the pilot is concerned, landing a turboprop is very much the same as landing a piston-engine aircraft, the only difference being confined to the landing roll. Having crossed the airfield boundary and arrived over the runway threshold at the proper speed:

1. Round out at the correct height.

2. Move the power levers to the idle stops.

3. Complete the hold-off, looking along the left of the nose, and allow the aircraft to touch down mainwheels first.

4. Lower the nosewheel to the runway, and apply brake.

5. Raise the power levers (or the power-lever latches, according to aircraft type), and move back into the 'Beta' range.

6. Bring the aircraft to a halt; clear the runway; then set the condition levers to LOW IDLE (PT6 engines), or, in the case of Garrett engines, move the propeller levers to the LOW RPM stops and complete the post-landing checks.

Use of reverse thrust

One only has to look at the propellers on a modern light turboprop, particularly those massive, four-blade windshovels that now find favour with the higher-powered aircraft, to appreciate that when the power levers are moved into the 'Beta' range, two large discs of drag are created. To illustrate the point, take a look at Fig. 66, which compares to the same scale the frontal view of three well-known aircraft in relation to propeller disc area. Considerable aerodynamic braking results from these discs during the landing roll, but when the propellers are made to provide reverse thrust, then obviously the stopping power of an aircraft will be improved to an extent that depends upon the amount of reverse thrust available.

Power available in the reverse-thrust mode is limited by the manufacturers to prevent excessive use (there may be those among us who would otherwise try their luck at taking off backwards), and here are some representative figures.

Engine type	Shaft horsepower (SHP)	Maximum reverse SHP
PT6A–11	500	200
PT6A–41	720	200

Some flight manuals recommend that reverse thrust should not be used during the landing roll at speeds below 40 knots. This is to avoid propeller-blade erosion. Conversely, the manual for the Swearingen Merlin 111B, which is powered by Garrett AiResearch engines driving large, four-blade airscrews, says, 'Do not use reverse above 40 knots', a limitation dictated by a tendency for propeller-blade vibration to occur if

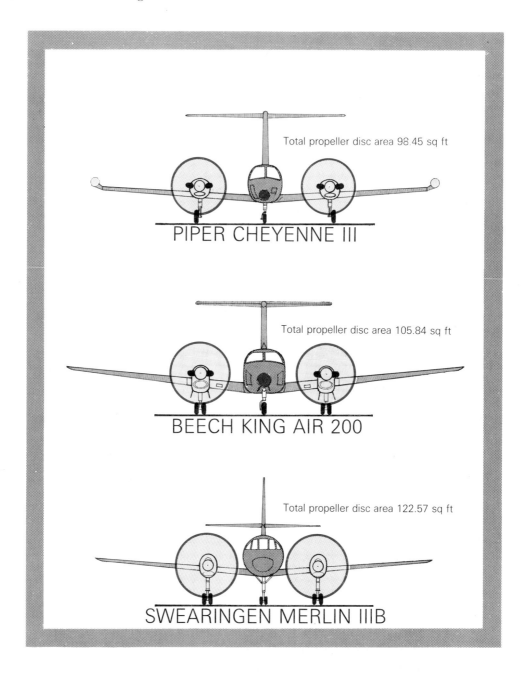

Fig. 66: Propeller disc areas of three well-known light turboprop aircraft, drawn to scale.

reverse pitch is selected at higher speeds.

When speed restrictions are mentioned in the aircraft manual, they relate to the landing roll. Obviously, reverse thrust may be used as an aid to braking while taxiing, but in so far as the landing is concerned, the following considerations must be kept in mind:

1. Reverse thrust must not be used when the aircraft is rolling at a speed that is not recommended or even prohibited by the flight manual.

2. The nosewheel must be on the runway before brake or reverse thrust is applied.

3. In an effort to make a short landing it is easy to rush, moving the power levers back beyond the idle stops. Remember: they must be lifted (or, when fitted, the power-lever latches have to be raised) before first the 'Beta' and then the reverse-pitch range can be selected. To prevent uneven application of reverse thrust, with the consequent risk of provoking a swing, movement of the power levers into the reverse-pitch range must be carried out calmly and deliberately.

4. Reverse thrust should not be used when landing on an unsealed dust or gravel runway. Serious propeller-blade erosion can result, and debris may be ingested by the engines. Furthermore, the dust likely to be thrown forward of the aircraft can obscure the vision ahead.

Anti-skid brakes are fitted to many turboprop aircraft these days, and when these are used in conjunction with reverse thrust, the landing roll can be shortened quite remarkably. Fig. 67 provides a few comparisons.

On no account should the 'Beta' range or the reverse-thrust range be selected while the aircraft is in the air. The Piper Cheyenne 111, for example, has a 'squat' switch on the landing gear to prevent such a circus act from happening either in error or by intent. However, not all turboprops have this safety device, and from time to time the unthinkable happens, as on the occasion when a test pilot, employed by the aviation authority of a certain country well-known for its airmindedness, thought fit to select reverse thrust during the hold-off in Brand X. It stopped. It dropped. And it never flew again. (Does anyone want to buy a tall, thin, Brand X?)

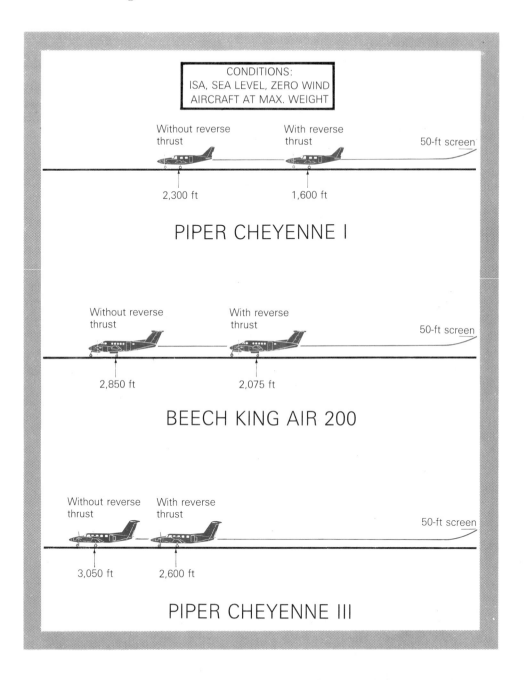

Fig. 67: Effect of reverse thrust on the landing roll of three light turboprop aircraft in widespread use.

Reverse taxiing

One of the chestnuts of aviation is that old music-hall gag, 'Joe Bloggs is an idiot. He is the only pilot ever to have crashed his plane by backing it into a mountain.' If reverse thrust will not allow even Joe Bloggs to do that, it *can* tempt pilots, wishing to impress those watching at a safe distance, with one of the turboprop's party tricks – the ability to taxi backwards. There may be occasions when it is convenient to back into a parking slot, but personally I would always prefer to enlist the help of a ground handler and his tractor. Here are the risks involved while going astern.

1. It is impossible to see behind the aircraft. Unless there is plenty of room for manoeuvre, you may easily hit another aircraft or an even more solid object, particularly since the nosewheel steering will feel strange as it resolutely swings the tail left and right at every move of the rudder pedals. If you must taxi backwards, first arrange for someone outside the aircraft to act as marshal.

2. Some aircraft tend to sit on their tails and beg if the brakes are applied too firmly while taxiing backwards. Risk is highest when the aircraft is loaded at an aft centre of gravity. Even when the brakes are applied gently, nosewheel adhesion will be reduced, and so will its directional authority. So if you must taxi backwards:

   (a) move very slowly;
   (b) avoid using the brakes unless it is essential to do so and then use them sparingly.

Although turboprop aircraft are landed in much the same way as piston-powered twins, engine handling in the air and on the ground is very different. However, like all pilot techniques the art of turboprop flying is one that can only be learned from experience. Pilots converting on to these aircraft are usually required to complete a ground course covering in detail the various systems which, unavoidably, are more complex than those of most piston-engine aircraft. In general, turboprop aircraft are quieter to fly and more reliable than those powered by the larger piston engines. Many of us believe the days of aircraft piston engines are numbered.

8. Landing jet aircraft

Looking back over the years, I have a clear recollection of my first dual instruction in a Tiger Moth. It was followed by about 70 hours on Stearmans, which seemed massive after the little de Havilland master-piece. When my fellow cadet pilots and I made the transition to the AT6A (known in the RAF as the Harvard), we really thought the big time had arrived – constant speed prop, hydraulic disappearing legs, HF radio and what was then regarded as a comprehensive instrument panel.

Really, times do not change in principle; it is the details that alter in aviation. To this day the inexperienced pilot is always impressed when he moves up the scale, from light trainer to fast tourer, from fast tourer to light piston-engine twin. Then, if he is making a career in aviation (or if he is a lucky amateur pilot), the turboprop will come his way, and after flying piston-powered equipment turboprops can feel like one's first entry through the doors of the Ritz.

This chapter sets out to provide background information on jet-engine management before explaining the landing techniques applicable to jet aircraft. They are remarkable and very satisfying to fly, for in terms of smoothness and near-silent performance, nothing can equal a jet.

Jet engines

The development of the jet engine

Early jet engines were very similar in concept to the compressor/turbine device described on page 164 and shown in Fig. 61 (page 165). During World War II the Germans were first (by a short head) to get a jetplane into the air, but they paid the price of aiming too high by opting for an axial-flow compressor at a period in history before enough knowledge and suitable materials were available. As a result, their engines failed to provide a reasonable degree of reliability. The plodding British, on the other hand, put their faith in well-understood vacuum-cleaner technol-ogy, and the early engines designed and developed by Sir Frank Whittle, which had centrifugal compressors, worked well. It was the Whittle concept that formed the basis of all early jet engines produced by Rolls-Royce, the de Havilland Engine Company and various licensed

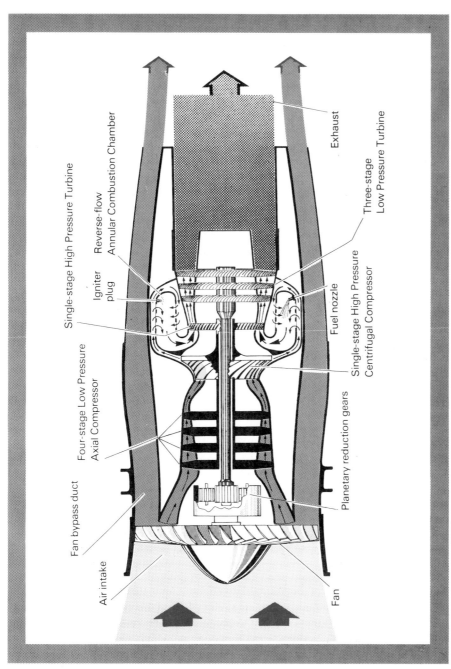

Fig. 68: Garrett AiResearch TFE 731 fanjet engine used in many small jet aircraft (guide vanes omitted for clarity). Note the tube of cold, relatively slow-moving air generated by the fan which surrounds the high-speed gas efflux from the turbines. Compare this with Fig. 62.

manufacturers in the United States. An engine such as the one illustrated
in Fig. 61 operates by taking in air, which is then compressed, heated
and expelled as a high-velocity jet. It is known as a turbojet. The concept
is, of course, delightfully simple but it has these shortcomings: (a) because
of shock waves caused by the high-energy jet, they are noisy and socially
unacceptable (many airports operate night-flying restrictions on aircraft
powered by turbojet engines); and (b) the turbojet is a thirsty engine,
particularly at low cruising levels.

It was to overcome these difficulties that the bypass and then the fan
engine were developed. In essence, a fanjet is based upon the simple
compressor/turbine unit shown in Fig. 61, but, as in the free-turbine
turboprop engine described in Chapter 7, a second assembly known as
the low-pressure turbine is rotated by the jet efflux after it has spun the
high-pressure turbine which drives the compressor stages. Much of the
energy that in a straight turbojet would provide the propulsion is
absorbed by the low-pressure turbine, which is coupled via a reduction
gear to a fan at the front of the engine in much the same way as the free
turbine drives a propeller in a two-shaft turboprop engine.

Fig. 68 is a simplified drawing of the Garrett AiResearch TFE 731
turbofan, which is widely used in business jets. Air enters the front of
the engine and is compressed by the fan. However, where the engine
differs from turbojet technology is that a large proportion of this air is
directed through a bypass duct which surrounds the unit. The remainder
of the air from the inner portions of the fan is conducted to a three-stage,
low-pressure axial compressor, then into the centre of a high-pressure
centrifugal compressor, which feeds the high-pressure air to the combustion chamber. Here a series of nozzles sprays atomized fuel at a rate
controlled by the pilot, greatly expanding the already compressed air
and endowing it with very considerable energy. These hot gases escape
at high velocity to drive the single-stage, high-pressure turbine, its sole
purpose being to drive the compressor stages (*not* the fan) via a large-
diameter tubular shaft. This part of the fanjet, the gas generator described on page 164, is sometimes known as the core of the engine.

Although a lot of power is required to drive the compressor stages,
considerable energy remains in the hot gas after it has gone through the
high-pressure turbine. From there it is led to a three-stage, low-pressure
turbine, which is coupled to the fan via a reduction gear and a drive
which runs forward within the tubular shaft of the gas generator. So a
fanjet produces two sources of propulsion: the high-energy, hot gas from

the engine tailpipe, with much of its energy absorbed by the compressor and the fan, and a tube of relatively slow-moving, cold air generated by the fan and forced through the bypass duct. The arrangement results in a fuel-efficient engine – and a quiet one at that, because the tube of slow-moving, cold air surrounds the fast-moving, hot gas efflux and provides an effective form of sound insulation.

Other than aircraft of older design, most civil jets flying today are powered by fan units similar to that described above, and those massive fan engines on the wide-bodied passenger jets provide a dramatic illustration of the way in which turbine engines have developed. The Rolls-Royce RB211 series of fan engines takes the art a stage further in having three shafts, and while the argument as to which is the better arrangement – two shafts or three – will no doubt continue as long as aircraft are powered by fanjets, the RB211 returns the most remarkable fuel economy and has proved outstandingly reliable.

Jet-engine controls

The good news for pilots is that all jet engines, turbojet or fanjet, are simple to control – very much simpler, in fact, than turboprop engines. There is no propeller to think about, no power lever that is a throttle one minute and a manual pitch control the next, and no condition lever. In many business jets, power management is limited to a single lever, the throttle, which may be lifted and brought back behind the idle stop to close the high-pressure cock, stop the flow of fuel and therefore shut down the engine. In some aircraft (the British Aerospace 125/700, for instance) a separate high-pressure cock is positioned adjacent to its associated throttle for the purpose. The following brief description of the engine controls is related to a Garrett AiResearch TFE 731 Fanjet.

Power lever

Sometimes called the throttle or the thrust lever, this alters the fuel flow and controls the amount of thrust being developed by the engine.

High-pressure fuel cock

As already mentioned, this may be a separate lever, or it can be operated by the throttle using a 20° range of movement which is provided behind the idle stop. The throttle must first be lifted out of its indent before FUEL CUT OFF can be selected.

Fuel computer

To obtain the best possible fuel economy, these engines feature a fuel computer. It compensates for temperature and barometric variations by accepting information from a number of sources (e.g., fan RPM, gas generator RPM, compressor discharge pressure, inlet temperature and pressure, interstage turbine temperature and several other parameters). Two sources of control operate in parallel, electronic and hydro-mechanical, but while it is claimed that the two systems are of equal reliability, the electronic control has a built-in safety facility which, in the event of malfunction, hands over control to the hydro-mechanical equipment. The fuel computer performs these functions:

(a) automatic turbine temperature limiting (to prevent overcooking the engine);
(b) provision of ideal fuel flow for economic operation under all conditions;
(c) overspeed protection in the event of mechanical malfunction;
(d) an improved linearity of thrust change with alterations in throttle position. In plain language, it tries to avoid the kind of lever response in which little happens during the first three-quarters of throttle movement, but everything comes to life at the end of the throttle's travel. Jet engines tend to suffer from this problem.

Starter/generator

As is the case with turboprop engines, the core of a fanjet must attain relatively high rotational speeds before sufficient air will flow through the combustion chamber for starting. The large electric motor required for this task is designed for the dual role of starting the engine and generating electric current when it is running.

Fuel-boost pump

Like any fuel system – whether piston, turboprop or jet – adequate supply must be assured, particularly when the tank is located a relatively long way from the engine. To provide sufficient fuel pressure, boost pumps are incorporated in the fuel system.

Ignition

The explanation given under this heading for turboprop engines (page 169) applies to jets.

Fanjet and turbojet engine instruments

The engine read-outs in a jet aircraft, like those in a turboprop, are arranged in a column of pairs, left and right, with the exception of those designs that feature vertical-scale presentation. While vertical presentations are claimed to offer certain advantages, some of them have an additional electronic digital read-out to compensate for the fact that it is not easy to make accurate power settings with these thermometer-like instruments. Reading from the top of the stack down, a typical layout for conventional, circular-dial engine instruments would be as follows.

Fuel flow

This is calibrated in pounds or kilograms per hour. This instrument, in conjunction with others, enables the pilot to set up a required power regime (high-speed cruise, long-range cruise, etc.).

Fan RPM

This RPM indicator reads the speed of the low-pressure or N_1 turbine which drives the fan. It is calibrated in percentages, and the power lever is used to achieve a particular fan speed according to charts included in the flight manual. These charts are produced for take-off and cruise, climb power being limited mainly by interstage turbine temperature (ITT).

ITT gauge

These gauges are red-lined for maximum starting temperature. For example the TFE-3 engines must not exceed 907° C, and the same limit applies to the take-off. The take-off rating usually has a time limit of five minutes. I remember the occasion when a cynical mate of mine, who was sales manager of an unmentionable jet aircraft (which, fortunately for us all, is no longer in production), once invited me to visit him with the words: 'You must come and have lunch during the take-off, old boy.'

N_2 RPM

This RPM indicator, which is calibrated in percentages of maximum, gives the speed of the compressor/N_2 turbine (the core assembly).

Oil pressure and oil temperature

These gauges perform the same function as those used with piston and turboprop engines. They may be separate or combined instruments.

Safety devices

Protection from ice

The fan sports a large spinner (see Fig. 68, page 189) which, like the air-intake lip formed at the front of the engine nacelle, is protected from ice by hot air supplied by the final stage of the engine compressor. In the course of compressing air there is a rise in temperature due to adiabatic heating, and this is used to prevent the formation of ice in critical regions of the air intake. Since jet aircraft may often be required to operate at flight level 400 (40,000 ft on a standard day) and above, the fuel filters are protected from icing by an engine-oil heat exchanger.

Protection from debris

At low power settings in particular, the modern jet aircraft is very quiet, and since initial approach speeds of around 160 knots are usual for the larger jets, birds can be unaware of 'big brother' until it is too late. Bird ingestion has been the cause of many engine shut-downs, and it is now common practice to switch on the landing lights while on the approach. This acts as an early warning and encourages birds to find somewhere else to play. A bird strike during take-off can, of course, be very serious. Fortunately, such incidents are rare.

Protection from debris while on the ground is mainly a design problem. Business jets have rear-mounted engines, and often their intakes are just above the trailing edge of the wing, which affords a considerable degree of protection from stones, grit, and so forth.

Handling jet engines

Before dealing with the techniques involved in landing jet aircraft, here are some brief notes on handling jet engines. In the main, they apply to the Garrett AiResearch TFE 731–3 fanjets, which are fitted in the British Aerospace 125/700 business jets and other aircraft. There is a lot more to jet-engine management than is covered below; but my intention is to provide sufficient background information for the reader to understand the techniques involved in landing jet aircraft.

Starting

The starting process with these jet engines is largely automatic. Having switched on the fuel boost pump and checked that fuel pressure is correct, the pilot then selects either ground start (external battery source) or internal start, using the aircraft's auxiliary power unit. Having checked the fuel computer, the start switch is activated. Now N_2 RPM will increase until, at 10 per cent, the fuel cut-off lever is opened. The fuel-flow indicator will show that fuel is entering the engine. Almost immediately the ITT will rise, confirming light-up. Maximum temperature is 907° C, and if it threatens to exceed that figure the fuel cut-off must be operated immediately. Oil pressure should rise within 10 seconds. At 50 per cent N_2 RPM the ignition may be turned off.

Idling

A normal characteristic of TFE 731 fanjets is their tendency to exhibit a cyclic increase and decrease in fan RPM while idling.

Use of throttle

The throttle should always be moved slowly. Although slam accelerations are permitted in an emergency, engine life will be prolonged and peak performance assured if large power changes are kept to a minimum. At all times avoid exceeding the ITT limits.

During take-off the engine will normally accelerate from idle RPM to take-off power in 5–8 seconds. If the fuel computer fails, 17–25 seconds will be required.

If at any time an increase in power setting is accompanied by expensive noises (rumbling or banging), this is probably compressor surge. Since that is unusual in a modern fanjet, the throttle must be closed, the engine shut down and the cause investigated.

Power settings

The various power settings are set as follows:

1. **Maximum Continuous Power.** This is obtained with full throttle, subject to the ITT not exceeding 885° C. If it does, the lever must be retarded slightly to bring the temperature within limits.

2. **Maximum Climb Power.** This is obtained by maintaining an ITT of 865° C up to 25,000 ft. Above that altitude the temperature may be allowed to reach 885° C.

3. **Maximum Cruise**. This is set according to N_1 (fan) RPM tables included in the flight manual. ITT must never be allowed to exceed 865° C.

Engine synchronizer

To avoid the discomfort of out-of-synchronization engine beat, the synchronizer should be on at all times except during take-off, when an engine failure would affect the live engine if this automatic device were functioning.

Stopping the engine

At the end of a flight the engines should be allowed to reach an even temperature by idling for three minutes (including taxi time). The fuel cut-off is then operated (or the throttle is brought into the cut-off range when the high-pressure cock is incorporated in the same lever). Run-down time varies from one engine to the next, but when rotation ceases in less than 60 seconds, there are grounds to suspect a mechanical problem, and this should be investigated by an engineer.

The special characteristics of jet aircraft

If turboprop and piston-engine airframes have a lot in common, the same cannot be said of their relationship to jet aircraft. Consider the special problems and talents of a jet:

1. One rarely sees a particularly high indicated airspeed in a jet. It is the ability of its engines to maintain power at heights of 30,000 or 40,000 ft or more, where lesser piston or even turboprop aircraft have long since run out of steam, that gives it an excellent TAS for a given IAS. To appreciate the advantage of maintaining a good IAS at high cruising levels, take a look at these figures. They relate to a CAS (RAS in Britain) of 228 knots and an ISA temperature.

Altitude (ft)	True airspeed (knots)
40,000	450
30,000	368
20,000	309
10,000	264
5,000	246

The added advantage of being able to cruise high is that most of the weather is left behind. On the other hand, the ability to fly at 40,000 ft and above demands very stringent engineering standards.

2. Speed means power, and power entails burning a lot of fuel. Efficient as they are, the relatively small fan engines in a BAe 125/700 have a fuel burn of around 750 lb/hr (340 kg/hr) each at 41,000 ft and considerably more at lower levels. Consequently, the proportion of total weight accounted for in terms of fuel is higher in a jet than in other types of aircraft. Here are a few examples:

Aircraft type	Max. weight	Max. fuel weight	Fuel as percentage of max. weight
McDonnell-Douglas DC10–30	572,000 lb (259,688 kg)	245,566 lb (111,486 kg)	42.93
BAe 125/700	25,500 lb (11,577 kg)	9,440 lb (4,286 kg)	37.00
Dassault Falcon 10	18,740 lb (8,508 kg)	5,910 lb (2,683 kg)	31.54
Cessna Citation 11	12,500 lb (5,700 kg)	5,009 lb (2,274 kg)	40.07
Cessna Citation 1	11,850 lb (5,380 kg)	3,807 lb (1,778 kg)	32.13

A comparison with the table of piston engine and turboprop aircraft fuel weights on page 176 will reveal that the Citation 11 carries 40 per cent of its maximum weight in fuel, whereas the King Air 200, which has the same maximum take-off weight, accounts for only 29.12 per cent of its 12,500 lb (5,700 kg) in fuel. The point has already been made about turboprops having to land at a wide variety of weights according to the amount of fuel carried. Weight variations can be even greater with jet aircraft, particularly large passenger jets, and it is essential to establish the correct approach speed with reference to the flight manual when flying jet aircraft.

3. Because of considerations 1 and 2, business jets tend to be large and heavy in relation to the number of passengers carried. This, allied to the need for clean aerodynamic design, brings with it problems of inertia, which will be mentioned in the section dealing with the approach.

Swept wings

Although the Cessna Citation 1 and 11, the Israel Aircraft Industries Westwind and the Learjets have straight wings, most other designs do not. What is the purpose of swept wings? The problem is that as we approach the speed of sound, the time comes when the aircraft is moving faster than the sound wave, which in subsonic aircraft is projected forward of the leading edge. Without this wave, the air receives no prior warning of an approaching wing; the upper and lower airstreams have no time to part ahead of the leading edge; and a shock wave occurs.

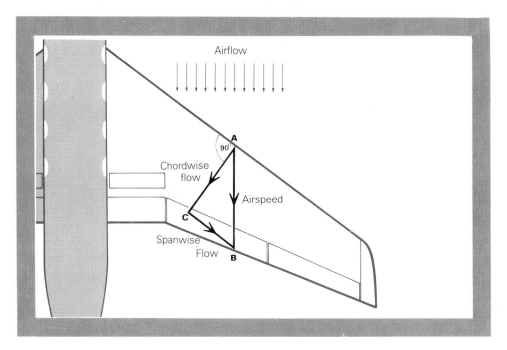

Fig. 69: Delaying shock waves by sweeping the wings. Flow at 90° to the leading edge (AC), which determines when the wing will cause shock waves, is slower than the actual airflow (AB). CB represents the usual spanwise flow.

Because the air must increase speed over the top surface of the wing, the speed of sound may be reached over some parts of the airframe although the aircraft is flying subsonic. And when they arrive, shock waves bring with them an enormous increase in drag.

One way of delaying the onset of shock waves is to have an airfoil that is thin in terms of thickness/chord ratio, but unfortunately thin wings mean thin mainspars, and while these are possible in engineering terms, the only way strength may be obtained is by using a lot of metal, a pastime that is bound to add weight at the expense of payload.

The other way of delaying the approach of shock waves and compressibility is to sweep the wing. Take a look at Fig. 69. Apparently, the pressure distribution of a wing (reduced on top, increased below) is related to its chordwise flow at 90° to the leading edge (shown as line· AC), although the actual flow is parallel to the direction of flight (line AB). The third vector, CB, represents sparwise flow, but the important thing to note is that AC is shorter than AB; consequently, the flow responsible for pressure changes over the wing, which may generate shock waves in the process, is slower than the actual airspeed represented by line AB.

Sweep-back does not only delay the formation of shockwaves; it also reduces their severity when they do occur. But sweep-back brings with it certain less desirable characteristics which materially affect the handling of a swept-wing aircraft. On the debit side there are the following disadvantages.

Poor lift at low speed

There is less up-flow towards the leading edge of a swept wing than in the case of a straight wing. This, in conjunction with the lower apparent speed across the normal chord (see Fig. 69), causes swept-wing aircraft to adopt a high nose attitude at low airspeeds (for example, while on the approach). In other words, area for area and speed for speed, swept wings produce less lift than straight wings when flying at the same angle of attack.

To compensate for the relatively poor lift performance of swept wings at low airspeeds, good flaps are essential. In some cases (e.g. Sabreliner, Falcon 10) leading-edge slats are added, and large passenger jets also make use of Kruger leading-edge flaps. Both leading-edge devices demand an even higher nose attitude on the approach. So unless the crew area is well designed, there could be a visibility problem.

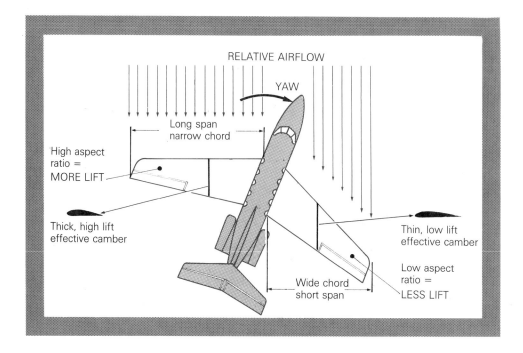

RELATIVE AIRFLOW

YAW

Long span
narrow chord

High aspect
ratio =
MORE LIFT

Thick, high lift
effective camber

Thin, low lift
effective camber

Low aspect
ratio =
LESS LIFT

Wide chord
short span

Fig. 70: Why a swept wing suffers intensified roll following yaw – one of the prices to be paid for delaying shock waves by use of sweepback.

Intensified roll following yaw

The further effect of yaw is roll, a fact known to even the most inexperienced pilot. However, with swept-wing aircraft the yaw–roll couple is more pronounced, because while the effective camber and aspect ratio of the leading wing in a yaw are increased, the trailing wing has less effective camber and a lower aspect ratio (Fig. 70). This adds up to more lift on the outer wing than on the wing on the inside of the yaw and a more pronounced roll.

Dutch Roll

In any aircraft lateral and directional stability are closely interrelated. Most modern designs tend towards predominant directional stability (with, in my opinion, insufficient lateral stability). Swept-wing aircraft, with their pronounced roll reaction following yaw, are prone to a yaw–roll motion known as 'Dutch Roll'. It may be stable (self-correcting), neutral (self-perpetuating at an even rate) or unstable, in which case it will become worse and worse unless the pilot intervenes.

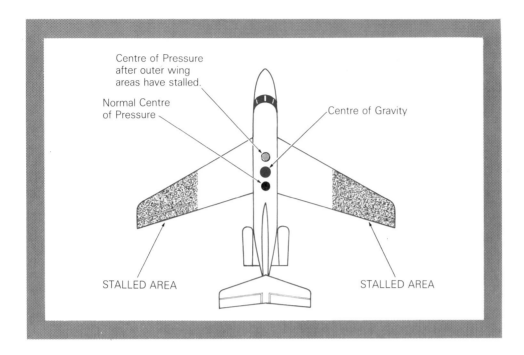

Fig. 71: Why some jets tend to pitch UP at the stall – another penalty of swept wings.

To contain Dutch Roll, most swept-wing (and some straight wing) aircraft are fitted with yaw dampers. In smaller aircraft this is the yaw-axis element of the autopilot. Generally, aircraft with insufficient fin/rudder/keel area are more prone to Dutch Roll than those with adequate vertical surface.

Poor stalling characteristics

Unless design measures are taken to counter the problem, all wings at high angles of attack create a spanwise flow that generates a large vortex at each wingtip and encourages the outer portions of the wing to stall first. Swept wings are no exception to this general rule, and reference to Fig. 71 shows that when the outer (and rearmost) portions stall, all lift is concentrated within those areas that are forward of average; the centre of pressure moves forward as a result; and, surprise, surprise, there is a nose-up pitch instead of the more familiar nose-down nod we have all come to expect at the 'g' break.

The problem of stall pitch-up with swept-wing aircraft is largely elim-inated by such devices as wash-out (smaller angle of incidence at the tip

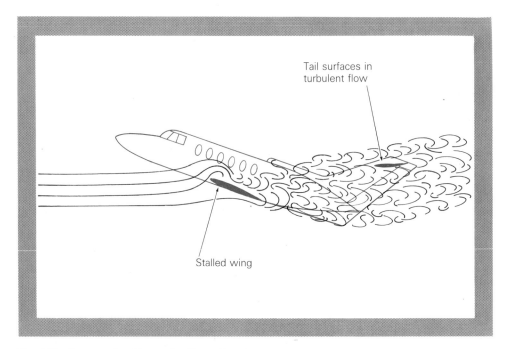

Fig. 72: Onset of a Deep Stall, a disadvantage of 'T' tails which, combined with the problem illustrated in Fig. 71 can be potentially dangerous unless a stick-pusher is fitted.

than at the wing root), leading-edge buffet inducers, and wing fences to discourage spanwise flow. However, to some extent the pitch-up tendency at the stall remains, and it is made worse (and potentially dangerous) by the introduction of 'T' tails. Fig. 72 shows that in a stall a high-set tailplane and its elevators can be materially degraded by the turbulent flow from the wing, and a so-called 'deep stall' can develop from which there is no recovery without recourse to such devices as tail parachutes. However, these are not fitted to production civil aircraft, so to guard against risk of deep stalling, aircraft capable of entering such a condition are provided with: (a) a stick shaker, which warns the pilot of the approach of a stall by vibrating the control yoke (and threatening to ruin his watch in the process); and (b) a stick pusher, which determinedly moves forward the control wheel before a situation develops from which there is no turning back.

Excessive drag build-up

The large vortex generated at each wingtip at high angle of attack has been mentioned above. This is even more pronounced in the case of swept wings – so much so that in a high-sink situation, when the airflow comes up to meet the wing, further increasing its angle of attack, so much drag may be induced that there is insufficient engine power to arrest the excessive descent rate in the height available.

Dutch Roll is controlled by yaw dampers, and deep stalls are prevented with the aid of stick pushers, but high sink rates coupled with excess drag at high angles of attack are entirely within the responsibility of the pilot. And he should never forget this unforgiving characteristic of swept wings while flying the approach. But more about this later in the chapter.

While the five characteristics described above are all peculiar to swept-wing jets, other considerations worthy of mention are a feature of all types of jet. Some are particularly important because, under certain conditions, they gang up to create situations during the approach and landing that must at all costs be avoided.

Lack of propeller slipstream

With excessive drag build-up in mind, imagine you are flying an approach in a propeller-driven aircraft (turbine or piston engine). The aiming-point starts to move up the windscreen, so immediately you remind yourself: 'Fig. 10 in that book about landing – add power.' In a twin-engine propeller aircraft a considerable area of the wing lies within the slipstream (another look at Fig. 66 on page 184 will illustrate the point I am making). So when you add power in a propeller-driven aircraft, there is an immediate increase in lift, thanks to the increased airflow over those parts of the wing that benefit from slipstream. To put some value on it, most propeller twins effect a stalling speed reduction of around 11 per cent when power is added.

The same undershoot in a jet represents a quite different ball game, because when you open the throttles there is no slipstream, just a more powerful squirt from the engines. It so happens that the effect of these jets on the surrounding air, coupled with the downward vectored thrust that occurs when an aircraft is flying in a nose-up attitude, does reduce the stalling speed by a few knots. But in practical terms, do not expect the addition of more throttle in a jet to provide more lift to arrest the rate of sink almost immediately. There is no slipstream over the wings to make that possible. The control of excessive sink in a jet is of vital importance. I would go as far as to claim that, from the handling point of view, this is the only real danger area to be faced while on the approach, particularly since the aerodynamics of the problem are compounded by the idiosyncracies of jet engines in so far as throttle response is concerned.

Jet-engine throttle response

Although spool-up times from idle to maximum RPM have improved over the years, initial engine acceleration, even with a modern fan engine, is nothing to write home about. Taking a typical example requiring eight seconds to accelerate from idle to 100 per cent RPM, six of those seconds will be needed to attain 75–80 per cent N_2 (gas-generator RPM), and not a lot of thrust will be forthcoming until the engine has spooled up to that level. From the pilotage point of view, during an approach the engines should be spooled up to around 75 per cent, ready to deliver the goods if the need arises.

What kind of need? Well, picture yourself on the approach. Through a combination of poor judgement and lack of planning, the aircraft is obviously high. So, adopting piston-engine techniques, you close the throttles and turn the exercise into a glide approach. Rate of descent increases, and too late you become aware that your overshoot has threatened to become an undershoot. For this jet bird is no light plane with a modest wing loading; it is fast, heavy and full of inertia. Throttles are opened, and for the next six seconds 'No answer' comes the loud reply, as the bits and pieces spin up without any noticeable effect on thrust.

The undershoot is beginning to look ugly, so in an effort to arrest further sink, the nose is held up. Unfortunately, drag starts to grow at a rate peculiar to swept wings, and although the engines have at last spooled up past the 80 per cent mark, there is not enough air between you and the ground to prevent — ! Fig. 73 illustrates this unhappy situation, which can be prevented by using the correct jet techniques shortly to be explained. Meanwhile, Fig. 74 shows a comparison between jet- and piston-engine throttle response. It will be seen that with jet engines, it is the final segment of lever movement that counts.

Power-unit drag

There are times in any aircraft when a little drag is like a cold beer to a man dying of thirst. You are belting along at 5,000 ft, heading in towards the destination, when, without warning, ATC tell you to descend and position over the outer marker at 1,500 ft. In a piston-engine aircraft, if you close the throttles below about 12 in manifold pressure, there is a lot of drag from the windmilling propeller. However, even when the

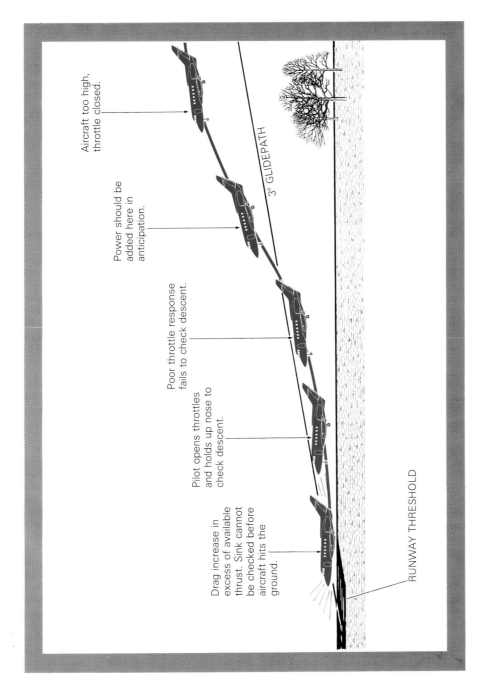

Fig. 73: High rate of sink near the ground, a situation to be avoided like the plague when flying jets.

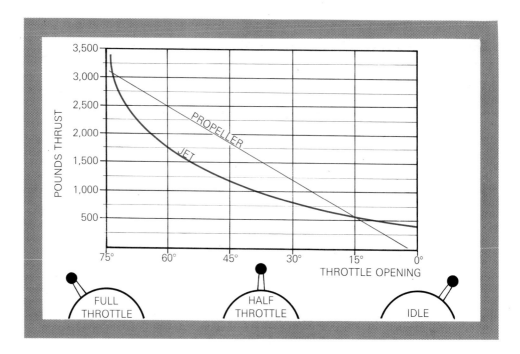

Fig. 74: Comparison of thrust response between jet and piston/propeller engines.

throttles are on the idle stops, jets continue to provide quite a lot of thrust; that, coupled with clean aerodynamic design and the inertia of a heavy aircraft, means you are hard-pressed to slow down, let alone lose height at the same time.

To cater for the problem, which affects an aircraft's ability to rid itself of unwanted speed and/or height, jets are fitted with speed brakes. These take the form of:

1. Fences which emerge from above (and sometimes below) the wing.

2. Surfaces that hinge upwards.

3. Mesh surfaces that move sideways out of the wing upper surface.

4. Surfaces that extend outwards from under the fuselage or from both sides of the tail cone.

Speed brakes, which are operated by a conveniently located control on the flight deck, are power-operated, and may be used at any speed. There is no speed limit because they may be required to prevent overspeeding when the pilot has allowed his aircraft to approach its V_{ne}/M_{ne} ('Never exceed speed/Never exceed Mach number').

Speed brakes, whatever their type, cause buffet. Since this can be a little disenchanting for passengers of a nervous disposition, the well-bred pilot will throw out the anchors only when circumstances demand a rapid reduction in speed. Having said this, speed brakes are there to be used, and they are a valuable addition to the jet pilot's stock in trade.

Speed stability

If you think about it, propeller-driven aircraft literally screw themselves through the air. To some extent, the aircraft is locked into its flight path rather like a bolt turning within a nut. The jet aircraft is locked into nothing. It is squirting itself forward rather like a toy balloon that has been allowed to deflate and fly around the room. In consequence, jets tend to enjoy less speed stability on the approach than do propeller-driven aircraft.

The situation is aggravated by another consideration – the power required to maintain the usual $1.3 \, V_s$ approach speed used in multi-engine aircraft (that is, 1.3 times stalling speed). The power-required curve for a piston/propeller aircraft flying above its minimum-power velocity shows a clearly defined 'more power for more speed – less power for less speed'. It is a steep enough curve to leave a pilot in no doubt about setting the right amount of power. A jet, on the other hand, has a rather flat power-required curve, and $1.3 \, V_s$ is actually slower than the speed for minimum power, which means that if you decrease speed, *more* power will be required to maintain height or a particular glidepath.

From the pilot's point of view, the flat power-required curve means that, unlike in piston/propeller aircraft, there is no clearly defined throttle setting in a jet because more or less the same power will provide a relatively wide range of speeds, from about $1.2 \, V_s$ to $1.55 \, V_s$. (When the stalling speed is 100 knots, this translates into a speed range of 120–155 knots.) It is not that jet aircraft are capricious; they are different.

In a nutshell, a jet on the approach must be closely controlled in speed and flightpath because there is less speed stability than in a propeller aircraft; power requirements are less clearly defined; throttle response can be sluggish if the engine has been allowed to spool down below, say, 75 per cent N_2; and if you let yourself in for a high sink/high drag situation, the ground may come up to meet you before the descent can be checked. Otherwise, jets are fine!

The approach

Planning the approach

All the considerations explained under the heading 'Planning the approach' for turboprop aircraft (page 178) apply even louder and clearer to jets because fuel accounts for an even higher proportion of a jet's total weight (see the table on page 197), and that means an even wider variation in approach speeds and minimum runway requirements. By way of illustration, look at these approach speeds, target threshold speeds (V_{at}) and runway distances required for a BAe 125/700 at various weights. Conditions assumed are a sea-level runway and zero wind.

	Aircraft weights			
	15,000 lb (6,810 kg)	17,000 lb (7,718 kg)	19,000 lb (8,626 kg)	22,000 lb (9,988 kg)
Approach (knots)	114	117	122	129
V_{at} (knots)	104	107	112	119
Landing distance (ft)	2,000	2,100	2,300	2,600

Before the landing it is therefore imperative that:

(a) you know the aircraft's weight;

(b) you have noted the approach and target threshold speeds for that weight;

(c) you have checked that the destination runway is long enough for the prevailing conditions.

Handling jets on the approach

Bearing in mind that the aim of the approach is to position the aircraft over the threshold at the right speed, right height and correct attitude, it might be as well to recap on the characeristics of a swept-wing business jet.

1. It is cleaner, faster and heavier than a piston-engine or turboprop aircraft of similar passenger capacity. A jet possesses high inertia.

2. A high-sink rate, bringing with it high angles of attack, can lead to a massive increase in drag.

3. Below 75–80 per cent N_2 RPM there is little power from jet engines, and they should not be allowed to spool down below that level because of the time required to produce thrust again.

4. It has less speed stability than a propeller-driven aircraft.

5. Jet aircraft approach at below minimum-power speed; consequently, a reduction in speed will create more drag and will demand more thrust.

6. When you open the throttles on a propeller-driven aircraft, there is an increase in thrust and lift. In a jet there is no slipstream-generated lift increase, only more thrust.

7. When you close the throttles on a propeller-driven aircraft and bring them to the idle stops, considerable drag is created by the propeller discs, and this is an asset when reducing speed at the start of a procedure. In a jet there is residual thrust, even when the throttles are on the idle stops, and to provide drag on a 'pilot-demand' basis, speed brakes are fitted.

In planning the circuit or a straight-in approach, it should be remembered that, as the aircraft is cleaner and faster, plenty of room should be allowed for manoeuvre. A crowded circuit leading to an approach that moves from one crisis to the next is not on in a jet. It is essential to become settled on both the glidepath and the runway extended centreline at the earliest possible stage. This entails planning well ahead.

Vital actions will obviously vary from one aircraft to the next, but such items as 'engine synchronizer off', 'yaw damper off', 'cabin-pressure check' and 'nosewheel steering knob clear' (in case it has become buried under a mountain of charts) will be new to most pilots converting to jets.

To align early with the runway, it is essential that the final turn should be started early to ensure a gradual transition from base leg to approach. Bear in mind that, on average, the circuit and approach speeds of a jet are somewhat higher than those of propeller-driven aircraft, and it is very easy to create the kind of situation illustrated in Fig. 7 (page 30). A small fly-through of the runway extended centreline may be corrected without difficulty; a bad one could present you with too large a correction for comfort. When this happens, or in the event of coming in above the glidepath so that drastic power reductions are required, missed-approach action should be taken without delay (see page 64).

Glide approaches cannot be tolerated in jets; it is bad practice to spool down below 75–80 per cent N_2 in all normal circumstances. Here is a blow-by-blow account of flying the approach in a jet.

1. Concentrate on maintaining the glidepath at all costs. The aircraft should be aimed at the runway threshold and flown towards it.

2. About 50 per cent flap is ideal in the early stages, while the aircraft is being established on the glidepath and the runway extended centre-line. Full flap, if it is to be used, must be lowered by a height of 500 ft on the approach, certainly not lower.

3. Check that the aircraft is trimmed at the correct approach speed for the conditions (aircraft weight, wind). Control the glidepath with the elevators and the speed with the throttles (as you would during an ILS approach in any aircraft). During a persistent undershoot, adopt-ing a higher nose attitude in isolation may lead to a serious decrease in airspeed, coupled with the risk of a high sink rate to follow. To regain the required speed, add plenty of power (quite a lot will be needed); then, at the correct IAS, reduce power immediately to a level slightly higher than that prior to speed loss. If the high power used to accelerate the aircraft is not reduced soon after the correct IAS appears, airspeed build-up will be rapid enough to cause prob-lems of a different kind. Although small glidepath deviations are handled on the elevators in a jet, a continuing tendency to undershoot demands the addition of power. The nose may then be raised slightly to check the excessive rate of descent.

4. Maintain the runway extended centreline in the usual way, avoiding any departures that would entail a major heading correction. IT IS ESSENTIAL TO BE ESTABLISHED ON THE APPROACH AS THE OUTER MARKER IS PASSED (and preferably earlier).

5. After full flap has been lowered (circumstances allowing) and just before short finals, reduce speed slightly and retrim at V_{at} (target threshold speed).

Instrument approaches

Although you might not believe it, having read my discourse on speed instability, high-sink risks and the like, a jet aircraft presents no special difficulties while flying an instrument approach, provided the glidepath and IAS are rigidly controlled. Towards the end of the approach, when the clouds may be breaking here and there to reveal green fields below and perhaps occasional glimpses of the high-intensity lights ahead, there is a natural tendency to duck under the cloudbase and to complete the landing by enlisting the 'Mk 1 eyeball' system. Understandable as it may be, this natural human ambition to establish visual contact with the runway at the earliest possible second must be resisted. Even if it were certain that there were no clouds with a lower base between you and that double gin and tonic, by ducking under you will depart from the ideal 3° glidepath, and the final part of the arrival will place the aircraft in a nose-high attitude and will result in a high-power, low-level drag, and a frantic scramble to avoid hitting such uncomfortably solid objects as trees, power lines or even houses. Stick to the twitching needles; fly down to decision height; and, if the lead-in lights cannot be seen, take instant go-round action.

The landing

Earlier in this chapter mention was made of the fact that, because of the poor low-speed lift performance of swept wings, jet aircraft, particularly those with leading-edge high-lift devices, approach in a pronounced nose-up attitude. These are usually large passenger jets, and the landing technique adopted is to fly on to the runway, closing the throttles when the wheels are near the ground. It sounds drastic, but ground effect, caused by the cushion of air that occurs between the underside of the wings and the runway, tends to reduce the rate of sink immediately before touchdown. There is no round-out in the propeller-aircraft sense, just the slightest back pressure to increase gently what is already a nose-high attitude. Intercontinental jets have grown in size to the point where it is difficult for the pilot to judge his proximity to the runway, particularly since the main wheels are a long way behind the flight deck.

In a DC10, for example, the pilot handling the landing concentrates on maintaining an accurate approach. Near the ground, use is made of the radio altimeter in determining the height of the main wheels above the runway. The other pilot (or the flight engineer) calls out, 'fifty feet . . . forty feet . . . thirty feet . . . twenty feet', at which height the three throttles are closed, the control yoke is brought back very slightly, then a combination of ground effect and a long-travel, and kind, forgiving landing gear does the rest. 'Is it difficult to land a big bird like a DC10?' I asked a training captain mate of mine; 'It's a shame to take the money,' was his reply.

All this is no more than a little light entertainment, so back to business jets. In the main, these do not have leading-edge high-lift devices, and the approach attitude, although flat, is not nose-high. Consequently, the landing proper is conducted in much the same way as for a propeller-driven aircraft.

Nosewheel steering

Other than in the smallest and lightest jets, nosewheel steering is powered. The Sabreliners have an ON/OFF switch to engage the steering with the rudder pedals during the take-off and landing and to disengage it for greater angular movement while parking.

Most business jets follow large passenger aircraft practice in having a separate steering wheel or knob, conveniently located so that it falls easily to the captain's left hand. During taxiing and the early stages of take-off, direction is maintained on the powered nosewheel-steering control until, at around 70–80 knots, the rudder has sufficient airflow to assume directional control thus allowing the captain's left hand to be released for the urgent task of holding the control yoke, ready to rotate the aircraft at the correct speed.

During the landing it will be necessary to remove the left hand from the control yoke and to take charge of the nosewheel steering *before* the rudder runs out of steam at around 80 knots or so. When there is a need to hold on into-wind aileron in crosswind conditions, the charms of two-crew operations become evident. The landing sequence is as follows:

1. As the ground approaches, make a gradual round-out and attain the level attitude.

2. Close the throttles.

3. Prevent an immediate touchdown by holding off briefly.

4. At a slight nose-up attitude, allow the aircraft to touch down, main-wheels first.

5. Immediately lower the nosewheel on to the runway; then apply the brakes and whatever ground-roll limiting devices are fitted.

6. At around 70–80 knots (according to aircraft type) remove the left hand from the control yoke, and maintain direction with the nose-wheel steering control.

The ground roll

Two methods of assisting the brakes during the landing roll are in common use:

(a) reverse thrust;
(b) lift dump.

Aircraft may be fitted with either or both features.

Reverse thrust

Two types of equipment are fitted, each of them using clamshell doors to close off the normal jet efflux. At the same time, forward-facing deflectors are opened, through which the jet emerges in a direction that is the near-reverse of the usual one. The alternative arrangement takes the form of cascades, again pointing forwards. The two types are shown in Fig. 75.

Reverse thrust is more effective when applied at high speed because:

(a) when a reverse jet acts in opposition to a high-speed airflow, as it would immediately after touchdown, more reaction is caused than when it is applied against a relatively slow airflow (remember, the retarding action is affected by the sum of two opposing flows – the reverse jet and the airflow past the aircraft);
(b) immediately after landing, when the aircraft is rolling down the runway at high speed, application of reverse thrust will reduce its kinetic energy at a high rate.

So, to obtain the best results from the thrust reversers on your wonder-plane (and not all business jets have reverse thrust), they should be applied immediately when the nosewheel touches the runway.

Reverse thrust is controlled by a separate switch in some aircraft or by small toggles positioned on the throttle levers.

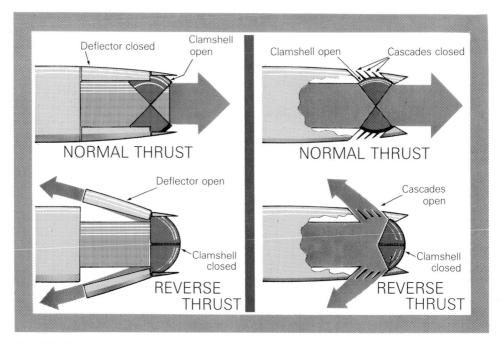

Fig. 75: Two types of thrust reversers in common use, deflector type on the left, cascade design on the right. Each makes use of clamshell doors to direct the jet efflux as required.

Lift dump

Because jets are flown on to the runway at fairly high touchdown speeds, there is little change in angle of attack between mainwheels on the ground and all wheels on the ground. Maximum braking can be assured only provided there is sufficient weight on the tyres, and the best way to ensure that is to jettison the quite considerable amount of lift being generated by the wing as the hardware charges down the runway – hence the expression 'lift dump'.

Lift dump action on large passenger jets is often automatic, being triggered when the wheels spin up. Passengers sitting near the trailing edge of the wing can see the air brakes rise to reveal vast open areas of the wing, spaces normally occupied by the Fowler flaps before they are extended backwards and depressed for the approach. A typical lift-dump system for business jets is that fitted to the BAe 125 series (illustrated in Fig. 76). It is a simple, aerodynamic method of providing additional drag, along with a substantial decrease in lift.

When the aircraft has landed and the nosewheel has been lowered on to the runway, the flap lever is lifted out of its indent and moved back

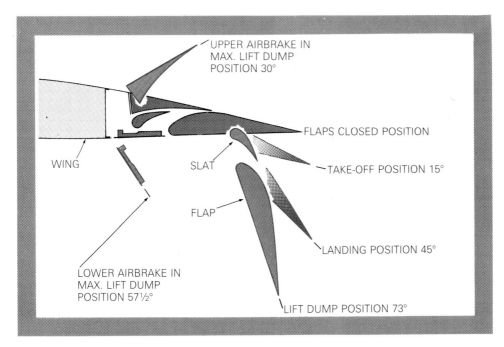

UPPER AIRBRAKE IN
MAX. LIFT DUMP
POSITION 30°

FLAPS CLOSED POSITION

WING

SLAT

TAKE-OFF POSITION 15°

FLAP

LANDING POSITION 45°

LOWER AIRBRAKE IN
MAX. LIFT DUMP
POSITION 57½°

LIFT DUMP POSITION 73°

Fig. 76: Lift dump arrangement as fitted to the BAe 125 series of business jets. Note the double slotted flaps which move through another 28° when lift dump is selected.

into the LIFT DUMP position. The flaps then depress from their normal maximum of 45° to 73°, and the airbrakes fully deploy. The brakes may then be applied to maximum effect, although stopping power will depend largely upon the state of the runway (dry, wet, covered with snow or ice – see next chapter). Thrust reversers can be fitted to the BAe 125; however, the manufacturers consider them unnecessary, since the lift-dump system will reduce the landing roll by as much as 1,000 ft.

Landing swept-wing jets in a crosswind

In so far as the approach is concerned, measures taken to compensate for a crosswind are no different from those taken in any other aircraft. One may use the crabbing or the wing-down method (see Chapter 4). It is when the aircraft is on the ground that swept wings can behave in a manner that is all their own.

Fig. 77 depicts a swept-wing jet on the runway. A strong wind is blowing from the left, in this case approaching the left wing at about 90° to its leading edge. Simultaneously, the right wing is receiving a wind component at an acute angle to its leading edge, and if you compare the

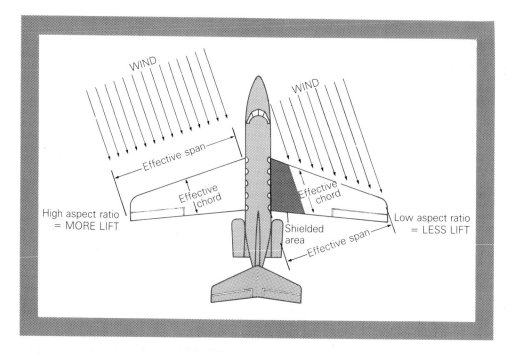

Fig. 77: Why swept wings are particularly sensitive to strong crosswinds during the landing.

aspect ratios of the two wings (span/mean chord), it is high on the left and low on the right. Furthermore, because of the wind component, part of the airflow over the right wing is shielded by the fuselage, an ungracious little complication which adds further to the imbalance of lift between the left and right wings.

Large passenger jets have been known to lift the into-wind mainplane after landing in a crosswind, simply because even experienced pilots are occasionally inclined to believe that the landing is more or less over when all wheels are on the ground. So hold on that into-wind aileron until the runway has been cleared.

Since direction must be controlled on the nosewheel-steering knob after the speed has decreased below 70–80 knots, this is a time for three-handed pilots. Although the captain may abandon the throttles and steer with his left hand while holding on aileron with his right, this is obviously a situation in which both pilots must share the workload.

Turbulence and windsheer

Because jets have a relatively high wing-loading, their gust penetration and ability to cope with thermal turbulence is generally better than that of lighter piston-engine and turboprop designs. However, windsheer must be treated with respect in any aircraft, and jets are no exception.

As a guiding rule, in turbulent conditions or when windsheer has been reported (or is expected) the approach should be flown at V_{at} plus 12 per cent.

Conclusions

If I have gone a little heavy on such aspects as throttle response, speed instability and one or two of the other swept-wing eccentricities, it is because the consequences of sloppy approach control are far more serious in a jet than in propeller-driven aircraft. I was discussing this with a Boeing 737 first officer the other day. I first made his acquaintance while testing him some years ago for his first instructor rating. 'What', I asked 'was your most profound impression while converting from light piston twins to a passenger jet?', to which he replied, 'I was shattered by the onslaught of discipline.' Nicely put, and very apt.

If business jets are handled with discipline, they are in many respects easier (if different) to handle than other aircraft, and they open up a new world to the pilot who loves his profession.

Landing a jet: note the high nose attitude prior to touchdown.

9. Landing on contaminated surfaces

The title of this chapter may well provoke thoughts of the terrible – the aftermath of a gas attack or, even worse, a runway contaminated by atomic fall-out. However, this somewhat ominous use of the word 'contaminated' is nothing more than an up-market way of describing a fouled-up runway. The mess could be snow, ice or even an over-abundance of rain. Each form of contamination brings its own special problems and the need for equally special handling techniques.

While dealing with short-field landings in Chapter 5 the subject of contamination was briefly touched upon when the damaging effect of wet grass on braking efficiency was mentioned. In the following text there will be repeated references to contaminated runways. In so far as a grass airfield can be covered by snow or ice, similar techniques apply to hard runways and grass surfaces. However, the first section, which deals with the problems of very wet surfaces, is confined to hard runways because an excess of water on those may well breed conditions that cannot be reproduced on grass.

Standing water and aquaplaning

When Everyman's family car developed the ability to cruise at high speed, we first became aware of aquaplaning or hydroplaning. Alarming stories appeared in some of the newspapers, describing how drivers entering areas of heavy rain had applied their brakes to no effect. Instead of slowing down in the normal way expected of well-mannered family chariots, theirs had carried on in a strange, unusual glide, almost as though the vehicles had taken off. In effect, they had, but at the time all one could learn of these terrifying incidents was that they were caused by a new kind of skid.

It was not until landing speed had increased to the point at which aircraft brakes really had to work for their living that aquaplaning entered the aeronautical vocabulary. Like so many of the relatively unusual experiences that afflict all manner of activities, aquaplaning (which, fortunately, is not an everyday occurrence) is regarded by most of us as something likely to bother 'the other pilot'. My first uneasy awareness of the phenomenon came when a friend of mine, a pilot of considerable skill and a solid citizen if ever there was one, landed a large, four-engine passenger plane on an adequate runway. It was one he had used on many previous occasions. This time was different. The mother and father of a cloudburst had just blown over, and the runway was swimming in water. Final approach was flown with the precision regarded by most of us as a trademark of this pilot, and the touchdown was to his consistently high standard. The brakes were applied and the aircraft went on, and on, and on, finally crossing the rail tracks outside the airport and coming to a tail-high full stop. We knew little about aquaplaning then; quite a lot is understood now.

The function of tyres during braking

Before explaining the mechanics of aquaplaning, it would be as well to consider the function of tyres while bringing an aircraft to a halt. It is not generally realized that the retarding effect of brakes is inseparable from tyre slip. The greater the braking effect, the more tyre slip will be present. However, there is a limit to the amount of slip that may be tolerated; when that limit is exceeded, braking effect will decrease. If the process is allowed to continue, a skid will develop.

Obviously, tyre adhesion is affected by the type of runway surface – the higher the friction between surface and tyre (the braking force coefficient), the better the braking effect. Other factors affecting braking are: 1. Speed at time of applying the brakes. 2. Tyre pressure, a high pressure reducing braking effect.

So far we have only considered the factors affecting a dry clean surface. Although tyre tread does not affect braking action on a dry runway, it assumes very great importance on a wet surface. Anyone who has tried to fit a new tyre to the wheel of a car will be aware that dry rubber has an intractable will of its own. The professional undermines the tenacity of rubber by applying water, lubricating the tyre and encouraging even quite large outer covers to slide on to the wheel without so much as a bruised knuckle or a tyre lever between the eyes. Likewise, a wet runway lubricates the interface between surface and tyre, causing a reduction in braking coefficient which is affected by the design of the tyre tread and its state of wear, in addition to the other factors previously mentioned which apply to a dry runway. As one would expect, braking on a wet runway is little affected at low speeds, but when the aircraft is rolling fast, stopping power may be less than one-third of what you have come to expect of a dry runway. So much for wet runways. But there comes a time, following particularly heavy rain, when a wet runway becomes *very* wet. And it only requires a sufficient depth of water to turn an aircraft into a champion water skier.

The mechanics of aquaplaning

Briefly, the mechanics of aquaplaning are as follows. An aircraft lands on a runway with areas of standing water following a heavy rain shower. It is a gentle landing, and the tyre is prevented from making direct contact with the runway surface. Instead, high-speed forward movement of the tyre turns the film of water into a wedge, and this provides a vertical component of sufficient power to support a high proportion of the aircraft's weight, leaving a very small area of rubber in contact with the runway surface. Application of brake immediately locks the wheels, even when an aircraft has anti-skid brakes, because with some systems the wheels must spin immediately after touchdown if the system is to work. The locked wheels drag along the runway, partly supported by the wedge of water, while the areas in contact with the surface heat due to friction, causing the wedge of water to boil, which emulsifies the rubber. In some cases a seal is formed, containing the water and steam, so preventing wheel-to-runway contact (Fig. 78).

Aquaplaning is a nasty business because it is often an unjust punishment for carrying out a smooth landing. Had the pilot thumped the wheels on to the runway, the film of water would probably have been pierced, allowing the wheels to spin and energize the anti-skid braking system. In the case of larger passenger jets aquaplaning is more critical since wheel spin after touchdown is essential to activate the automatic lift-dump sequence and thus bring adequate weight to bear on the tyres so that efficient braking is assured.

Factors affecting aquaplaning

Amount of water on the runway

Normally a minimum water thickness of 0.2 in (5 mm) is required to provoke the type of dynamic aquaplaning just described, although when

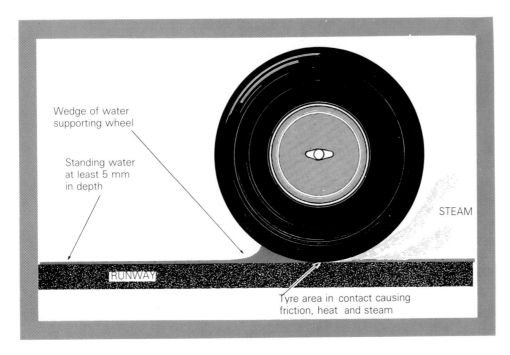

Fig. 78: The mechanics of aquaplaning. Note the wedge of water lifting most of the tyre off the runway. Sometimes a seal of reverted rubber forms around the area of contact, holding in steam and water so that no real contact exists between tyre and runway.

the runway surface is covered in rubber smears, half that thickness of water may cause aquaplaning at relatively low speeds. This is known as viscous aquaplaning. It has also been found that although a minimum water thickness of 0.2 in is required to initiate aquaplaning on an otherwise clean runway, once it has started, the aircraft may continue to skate over areas where the depth of the water is less.

Speed

The minimum speed at which aquaplaning will begin on a wet runway free of other contamination (rubber smears, grease, etc.) may be calculated by using this simple formula:

$$8.6 \times \text{square root of the tyre pressure.}$$

Here are a few examples:

Aircraft	Tyre pressure (psi)	Minimum initiating speed for aquaplaning (V_p) (knots)
BAe 125/700	127	97
Piper Cheyenne III	111	91
Cessna 421	70	72
Cessna Centurion	55	64
Robin Aiglon	33	50
Piper Tomahawk	26	44

Only when the touchdown can be made at a speed below that listed (known as V_p) will the aircraft mentioned be able to avoid the risk of aquaplaning on a wet runway. In conditions of zero wind that will rarely be possible because generally respective touchdown speeds are too high.

After aquaplaning begins it may be sustained at a lower speed.

Tyre design and condition

To some extent, the risk of aquaplaning can be reduced by suitable tyre design. It has been shown that ribs or grooves capable of providing adequate drainage can reduce water pressure at the critical time and delay the onset of aquaplaning even when the depth of water exceeds 0.2 in. It follows that tyre wear, which obviously reduces and may eventually remove the tread design, is bound to affect the speed at which aquaplaning will commence – a smooth tyre presenting the worst case.

Wheel arrangement

Light single and twin-engine aircraft have single wheels, but larger types, such as the turboprops and business jets, usually carry two wheels on each strut. The bigger passenger jets have bogies (pairs of wheels arranged in tandem), and these aircraft are at an advantage because the front pairs of wheels have a clearing action which tends to reduce the depth of water encountered by the following pairs of tyres.

Runway surface

A coarse surface texture is better able to disperse water than a smooth runway surface. It works in very much the same way as a patterned tyre tread. Runway drainage can sometimes be affected when the wind is strong enough to back the water against the slope built into the surface for the purpose of dispersing rain water. Then standing water may be deep enough to turn the runway into a mini-watershoot, and if aquaplaning starts, you will be in for an interesting ride.

Dealing with aquaplaning

Obviously, it helps if you have prior warning of the risk of aquaplaning. Fortunately, the problem is uncommon in most parts of the world, but after a particularly heavy rainstorm even the municipal airports of Hometown, USA, or the untarnished runways of rural England could be as badly affected as those of tropical Africa, where the clouds throw down water by the barrel. Here are the factors to consider when there is risk of aquaplaning:

ATC advice

Some, but not all, ATC units will on request give a statement of fact in plain language, based on braking-efficient measurements obtained with the aid of a device known as a Mu meter. Its readings, translated into the type of radio advice you may expect at suitably equipped airfields, are as follows:

Mu meter reading	ATC report
up to 0.39	'Braking action POOR'
0.40 to 0.49	'Braking action MEDIUM'
0.50 and above	'Braking action GOOD'

You may for example, be advised: 'Runway two-four has standing water on the threshold, but the surface is clear after the first intersection', or 'Water on runway two-four. Can you accept a 12-knot crosswind on runway three-zero, which is clear?' Take my advice – go for runway three-zero.

Wind effect on aquaplaning speed

It follows that you should know the minimum speed for aquaplaning applicable to your aircraft. If, for example, it is 55 knots, and your normal touchdown speed is 65 knots but there is a 20-knot wind, the odds are there is little risk of aquaplaning because on this occasion the actual touchdown will occur at around 45 knots, which is 10 knots below minimum speed for aquaplaning. However, on a calm day, watch out!

Calculating landing roll

In so far as the landing roll is concerned, it is as well to add 60 per cent to the usual length required, although this may be reduced to 25 per cent when reverse thrust is available. In the next section on slush, snow and ice, more will be said about the use of reverse thrust, but at this stage it is sufficient to say that it must be applied symmetrically and that crosswinds present special problems on contaminated runways, because if a slide across the runway begins, reverse thrust can make matters worse.

Use of brakes

Since the worst manifestations of aquaplaning include steaming the tyre into reverted rubber (the result of friction caused when a small area of tyre is dragged along the runway), it follows that the brakes must *never* be applied after touchdown until the aircraft has slowed to below the minimum speed for aquaplaning. Then use them with caution, but if a skid develops, release the brakes immediately and only apply pressure again when the slide has ceased.

The go-round decision

If, despite all the advice in this book, you have approached too fast, and your favourite plane is aquaplaning down the runway with no intention of coming to a halt within the confines of the airfield, an early decision to go round will have to be made. It will be necessary to raise the flaps and, in the case of jet aircraft, possibly to cancel the airbrakes as well. You will also have to allow time for the engines to spool up.

If a departure from the end of the runway along the ground is unavoidable, experience indicates that you are better off letting the hardware slide nose-first; in the majority of cases very little damage need result. Whereas if, following an attempt to remain on the airfield, the aircraft is slewed through 90° or so, the odds are it will continue sliding broadside in the same direction. And when firm ground is encountered, its first act of friendship will be to remove the wheels and probably the legs that go with them.

It should always be remembered that although aquaplaning has been highlighted in these pages as a landing problem, it also affects the rejected take-off situation in which something – engine noise, smoke or loss of power – encourages you to cancel the trip before lift-off.

Aquaplaning does not only affect braking; it also seriously limits the degree of directional control on the ground. So when you are faced with landing on a not overgenerous runway on which there is a risk of aquaplaning, serious consideration should be given to circling until at least some of the water has drained away. But if the situation is really bad and the airfield can offer little hope of improvement (or an alternative runway), treat yourself to a pat on the back for good old-fashioned airmanship, and divert.

Slush, snow and ice

While most of us know ice when we see it, the line of demarcation between snow and slush can vary according to the opinion of the beholder. In an attempt to clarify what is meant by snow and slush, here are a few definitions that enjoy a degree of support from within the aviation fraternity and among those in other walks of life.

Slush: Contains a high proportion of water. Stamp your foot in slush or drive a vehicle through it, and a splash can be guaranteed.

Wet snow: Does not splash when kicked or driven through. Instead it will pack down when stamped upon. Wet snow will rapidly turn into slush when it rains or if the temperature rises.

Dry snow: This is your genuine, fun-loving, Father Christmas-type white stuff. For snow to remain dry the temperature must be below 3° C. It cannot withstand bright sun because warmth turns it into wet snow. When kicked, dry snow does not splash or pack down. Instead, it scatters in a powder-like cloud.

Slush

Landing with slush on the runway

Whereas standing water may cause aquaplaning and is therefore a landing problem, slush is of more consequence during the take-off. Referring to the definitions above, it will be remembered that if you drive a vehicle through slush, it will splash. So it does when an aircraft takes off. While this book is concerned only with the landing, the following must be said because part of what happens while gathering speed through slush can affect the subsequent return to roost. During the take-off slush may cause the following difficulties:

1. Slush may be thrown on to the windscreen, obscuring the pilot's view if there are no means of clearing it.

2. Slush may be thrown into engine intakes. In the case of jets or turboprops, even when the ignition is on there could be a flame-out, causing loss of power at a critical stage of the take-off.

3. Slush may be thrown on to parts of the landing-gear retraction linkage. At the same time, the wheel wells of aircraft, having forward or backward (as opposed to sideways) retraction, can become partly filled with slush. The net result is that the landing gear may fail to retract fully. Even worse, if slush is allowed to freeze as the aircraft climbs into colder air, the gear may refuse to lower when time comes to land.

4. Slush can remain on the brake assemblies, freeze when the aircraft climbs and provide the story of the week when you land at the end of the trip.

5. Slush, which is thrown up by the wheels and whizzed around by the propeller(s) can find its way into all manner of places – like static vents, pilot head and so forth. Naturally, this can affect ASI, VSI (rate-of-climb indicator in the United States) and altimeter readings, because even when the heaters are on (as indeed they should be in these conditions), the sheer volume of part-frozen water is bound to have a detrimental affect.

6. In particularly bad cases, when slush is mixed with frozen packed snow or part-melted ice, these can be thrown up by the wheels and accelerated by the propeller(s) with sufficient velocity to damage the flaps when a take-off setting has been used. There is also a risk of damage to the tail and wing undersurfaces. To a considerable extent the risk of slush damage has been minimized by the development of chined nosewheel tyres, which deflect the slush downwards.

Safeguarding the landing after taking off in slush
Items 1, 3, 4, 5 and 6 above can all affect the aircraft when the time comes for the landing. When a windscreen wiper is fitted, this should be used to clear the slush before it has time to freeze, but it is unusual for smaller designs, even light twins, to have anything more than demist slots through which cabin heat may be concentrated. These are capable of clearing small areas of ice from the windscreen, but when it is badly obscured, the clear-vision panel will have to be opened for the landing.

After a take-off in slush it is always best to expect the worst and to assume that the wheel wells, retraction mechanism and brake systems are affected. There is little or nothing a pilot can do about the wheel wells, but defensive action may be taken on behalf of the landing gear and brakes. The drill after a normal take-off is to stop the wheels spinning with a touch of brake. This curtails any out-of-balance wheel vibration that may be present and, in the case of retractables, prevents the possibility of spinning rubber burning itself against parts of the wheel-well structure. After a take-off in slush, carry out this amended procedure:

1. Allow the wheels to spin for ten to fifteen seconds, and give them an opportunity to throw slush off the brake discs, pads and piston units.

2. Raise the landing gear, then lower it. Wait for a few seconds, and then repeat the cycle once or twice to dislodge the slush before it becomes a frozen straightjacket, capable of preventing the wheels from appearing when time comes to land.

The pilot-head/static-vent problem is one that should clear itself in all but the worse cases, provided that heat is left on. But if the airspeed indicator is obviously playing fun and games (and the pressure tube is more likely to be affected than the static source), fly attitudes on the flight panel; use familiar power settings on the approach; and get back on the ground. Fortunately, incidents such as this one are rare – but it is the rare incident that often causes unusual accidents.

The problem of flap damage during a slush-contamination take-off may be prevented by not using them unless the aircraft is of high performance and the flight manual demands that flap be used. Such demands are usually confined to the passenger jets; even quite large general-aviation equipment (business jets, turboprops and the heavier piston-engine twins) are rarely required to use flap for the take-off.

I labour the point about flaps here because aviation has been invaded by a breed of aviators that cannot live without playing at airline pilots. They line up in their two-seat tiddlers, the far end of the runway disappearing on the horizon, 20 knots of wind blowing along the dotted lines, and, for reasons I have never been able to understand, part flap is selected. If you ask them why, the stock answer is usually, 'You get a cleaner lift-off' (which is rubbish) or 'It improves the take-off run and climb', which in most cases is equal rubbish – but this is a book about landing. And when the time comes to land in the slush most reasonable-minded folk would like to believe that their aircraft is more or less intact. So if you are obsessed with using flap for take-off, even when this is not recommended, desist on a slush-covered runway, because there is a very real risk of damage if the flaps are called upon to play bat and ball with high-speed slush.

Safety measures at airports

The obvious answer to contamination is in the hands of the airports – they should clear the snow before it can turn into slush. However, to be fair, this is a massive undertaking, and even the major airports of the world can at times suffer from temporary closure. The problem can be exacerbated by rutting caused when aircraft are manoeuvring on the runway, perhaps prior to take-off. Local increases in depth can result, and a sudden temperature drop will then turn these mounds of slush into a rock-hard obstacle course fit to stop a tank. A temperature drop following heavy rain or a fall of sleet can turn a runway into an ice rink – but this will be dealt with later on in the chapter.

Several methods of assessing the degree of contamination are in use. Some airfields use a Mu meter (mentioned on page 223), which provides friction readings based upon the behaviour of a small wheel propelled along the runway. It is weaved from side to side about the centreline, so that readings are obtained across the width as well as along the length of the runway. The readings are then corrected according to the measured density of contamination, which is classified thus:

Type of contamination	Density
Standing water	1.00
Slush	0.5 to 0.8
Wet snow	0.35 to 0.5
Dry snow	0.2 to 0.35

The results of these Mu readings corrected for density are known as water-equivalent depth (WED), and they enable the airfield control service to advise pilots by radio using the terminology given on page 223.

An alternative method of assessing contamination is the good old-fashioned one of taking depth readings at approximately 300-m intervals. Snow/sleet depths are measured in millimetres on each side of centre, and an average is prepared for each third of the runway. This, together with details of contamination type, can provide the basis of ATC reports suitable for radio transmission to the pilot.

Opinions as to the value of Mu meters and other similar devices are divided, because while no doubt these gadgets are capable of accurately measuring friction or, more important, the lack of it, these days many other factors can affect an aircraft's stopping power when the runway is covered in slush or wet snow. How good are the brakes? What type of tyre is fitted? What is the tyre pressure and tyre loading? In the case of larger aircraft, to these questions must be added two others. What kind of anti-skid braking system is installed? What degree of reverse thrust is available?

Having said this, even the sceptics acknowledge that Mu meters and the like are of value in assessing the skid resistance of a runway surface, but there is a body of opinion that believes future anti-slush/wet snow developments must come from better tyres, improved runway surfaces and more powerful methods of snow clearance.

The time-honoured method of clearing snow adopted by many of the municipal authorities is to sprinkle the roads with salt, a cure regarded by those who must pay for corroded vehicles as worse than the disease. Salt can be very damaging in terms of corrosion, and obviously cannot be used for clearing runways. Instead those airports that must be kept open first clear the bulk of the snow/slush with ploughs and then spread a urea compound.

Landing on a slush-contaminated runway
When landing on slush, the following factors must be borne in mind.

1. Braking efficiency will suffer.

2. Nosewheel steering authority will be reduced.

3. Because of 1 and 2, landing-roll provision must be increased by a factor which varies from one aircraft to the next.

4. Because of 1 and 2, a swing (if one is provoked for any reason) may prove difficult to control.

5. After touchdown, slush may be thrown up by the nosewheel and given further energy by the propeller(s). A risk of airframe damage is therefore present, and the windscreen may become obscured.

Having obtained as much information as possible about runway state and about the location of the worst and best areas and, if available, recent reports from pilots who have already landed, decide whether or not there is sufficient runway length for your aircraft. Then:

1. Fly a carefully controlled approach, aiming for the best touchdown point. This may not be the runway threshold.

2. Touch down at the lowest possible speed consistent with safety.

3. Keep straight, and be prepared for the effects of one wheel running into deep contamination. A swing could result, but this must not be allowed to develop.

4. Check that the wheels are rotating (when it is possible to see them) before applying the brakes. They could have frozen after the take-off. While using the brakes, avoid locking a wheel, since this will damage the tyre, do little for your stopping power and may provoke a swing.

5. Come to a halt; carefully clear the runway; complete the post-landing checks; and then taxi with extreme caution to the parking area. Remember: airport resources are usually concentrated on the runways, so neglected taxiways and parking areas may resemble an obstacle course.

After a landing on a slush or wet-snow contaminated runway, a thorough inspection of the aircraft must be made. Remove slush/snow from the wheel wells, landing gear assemblies, control surface gaps and engine intakes, and look for damage that may have been sustained by the flaps and underskins of the wings, fuselage and tail surfaces.

Crosswind landings in slush

As already mentioned, braking effectiveness and nosewheel steering are both degraded by slush. Since these two control ingredients are essential to the pilot during a crosswind landing, only in the most pressing circumstances should one be attempted when slush is on the runway. Ice, of course, is even worse, and this topic will receive more detailed treatment later in the chapter.

All turboprops and a few of the business jets are equipped with reverse thrust. On a normal runway the ability to squirt backwards can be of great value in shortening the landing roll, but the use of reverse thrust in a crosswind when the runway is slippery can turn a bad situation into a nightmare. If you look at Fig. 79, the reason will become obvious. The

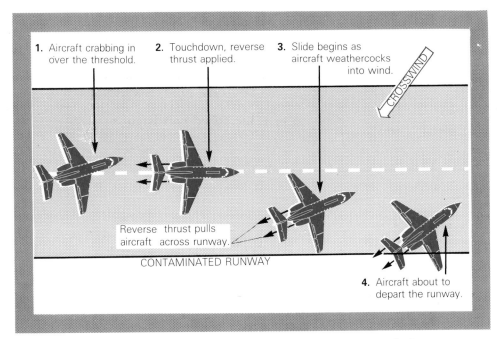

Fig. 79: Risk of using reverse thrust when landing in a crosswind on a contaminated runway.

aircraft is crabbing in on the approach (1) and is then lined up with the runway just before touchdown (2). A slide begins on the slush, together with a tendency to weathercock into wind (3). In an effort to halt his runaway horse, the pilot tries brake and nosewheel steering. Neither works because of the slippery surface, and, to make matters worse, reverse thrust helps to pull the aircraft off the side of the runway (4). In cases such as this, reverse thrust should be discontinued.

When 'braking action poor' has been reported, and in the absence of specific flight-manual advice, a maximum crosswind limit of 10 knots should be applied to all types of aircraft – whether they have reverse thrust or not – weighing up to 12,500 lb (5,700 kg). Stronger crosswind conditions should be regarded as a no-go unless the aircraft is known to enjoy considerable tolerance of slippery runways. However, if a slide begins early in the ground roll and threatens to have you across the runway, the decision to overshoot will depend upon:

1. Length of runway ahead – is it sufficient for your aircraft?

2. Type of aircraft and the actions required before a lift-off is possible (e.g., flaps up and, if it is a turboprop, out of 'Beta' or reverse pitch).

In the case of jets, lift dump may need to be retracted, and then there is the time required for engine spool-up.

So you cannot afford the luxury of wait-and-see. When a slide begins, you must decide which it is to be – the risk of departing off the side of the runway or going off the end. And the best advice I can give is this: avoid placing yourself in the position of having to make such a depressing choice.

Snow

The effect of snow on the runway

Two problems associated with snow-covered terrain are, in the main, visual. First, there is the so-called 'white-out', an odd affliction caused when an overcast sky blends with snow-covered ground. When railway lines, buildings and roads are present, the situation is tolerable, but in open, snow-covered country near-complete lack of contrast may cause disorientation. Pilots have been known to fly into rising ground simply because they were unable to see it.

On a bright day with broken cloud or large patches of blue sky, contrast is good; it is easy to tell where the ground begins – *up to a point*. And here we come to the other visual problem. If a landing is to be made on what novelists are often moved to call 'virgin snow' (snow on which no one has landed before your arrival), it can be surprisingly difficult to judge the whereabouts of the surface. In the days when we used to aviate in open cockpits, I have vivid recollections of flying over the landing area and throwing out a glove to be used as a surface marker during the hold-off to come. It worked. And so will any other marker, even the wheel ruts of a previous landing.

As with slush, snow contamination is more a take-off problem than an embarrassment while landing, although much depends on the temperature and the type of covering. Dry snow will reduce the brakes-off landing roll at a rate proportional to its depth – the deeper the snow, the more the retarding action. Used with care, the brakes may be quite effective. Wet snow represents the half-way stage between those beautiful, powder-like flakes that disperse in a mist when kicked and heavy, often dirty slush. How compacted wet snow affects an aircraft depends on the temperature, but in round figures expect the braking distance to increase by about 60 per cent when it is very cold (say, 15° C and below). Above that temperature, when it begins to soften and to become more slippery, allow double the dry runway distance. Generally, there is little risk of damage when wet snow is thrown up by the wheels.

Landing on a snow-contaminated runway

The main problem in the early stages of the approach is to identify the runway threshold. At an established airport the angle-of-approach lights will be discernible on either side of the threshold, and when contrast is poor the runway lights will probably be on. Having obtained all possible information on the state of the runway:

1. Fly the approach in the normal way. It should be flown as a continuous descent to avoid the risk of levelling off too high in the mistaken belief that the ground is a few feet below the aircraft. This is particularly important at airfields without adequate visual references near the touchdown point.

2. If difficulty is experienced in recognizing the surface, leave on a little power; raise the nose *very slightly*; and reduce the rate of descent. Allow the aircraft to fly on to the snow.

3. After touchdown, be in no hurry to apply the brakes. Instead make full use of aerodynamic braking by holding off the nosewheel with continuous back pressure on the elevator control.

4. In the case of turboprop aircraft, reverse thrust may be used on compacted snow, but there is a risk of obscuring the vision ahead when the snow is dry. Similar considerations apply to jet aircraft. When the engines are rear-mounted, the application of reverse thrust can project a curtain of dry snow forward along the cabin windows and create near-fog conditions ahead.

Having arrived in the snow with dignity and grace, it would be a pity if you were to spoil such a professional display of airmanship by skidding into a snow bank or perhaps even another aircraft. So taxi with caution, and make all turns at low speed.

Ice

Landing on an ice-contaminated runway

When a runway is reported to be covered in ice, not only will braking action be poor to the point where there is no stopping power at all but also control of direction will be limited to rudder effectiveness. The nosewheel will have little authority, and while in the early stages of the landing roll the rudder will continue to provide good control of direction, as speed decreases so will rudder effectiveness. At that stage a swing is likely to develop, and the aircraft may behave like a dog chasing its tail. In the case of single-engine aircraft, there is nothing one can do other than sit and wait for the various energies to dissipate. A burst of power against full rudder opposing the swing *might* do a little to restore the situation, but power will also discourage the deceleration process which, on ice more than at any other time, is of vital interest to the pilot. For the same reason, the use of asymmetric power when a twin-engine aircraft starts to ground-loop on ice could, if left too late, prove counter-productive. In each case, if initial attempts to check a swing prove unsuccessful, probably the most sensible things to do are:

1. Pull back the idle cut-off(s).

2. Switch off the ignition.

3. Turn off the fuel.

At least you will have minimized the risk of fire, should the aircraft hit something as it slides off the runway, sideways, backwards or any way other than sharp end first.

Most charter, air-taxi or commuter operators (which, unlike the airlines, must sometimes operate from airfields more primitive than the major airports) forbid their pilots to attempt a landing on ice, and I strongly advise you to do the same. Think about it: no braking, no steering as the aircraft slows down, and no idea of how long the hardware will slide or even which way it will be pointing when it finally comes to rest. Ice is for skaters, not pilots.

Conclusions

Aircraft flight manuals are somewhat coy about the matter of operating off contaminated runways, and to obtain expert guidance one has to take a look at some of the operators. In varying degrees, runway contamination affects all aircraft, from the tiddlers to the Jumbo Jets; but to quote an example, here are some limits for the Piper Navajo Chieftain which I have extracted from an operations manual compiled by one of the leading independent airlines:

Landing limits	
Dry snow	5 cm (2 in)
Wet snow or slush	1.5 mm (0.06 in) [=12.5 mm (0.5 in) WED]
Standing water	12.5 mm (0.5 in)
Crosswind limit	10 knots
Flooded runway	Landing prohibited
Braking action poor (below 0.2)	Landing prohibited

In round figures you should add the following safety margins to the published landing roll for your aircraft:

Wet runway	+60%
Light snow	+60%
Compacted snow, OAT above 15° C	+100%
Wet ice at or above 0° C	+166%

One way of finding how much room your favourite bomber will require to stop on a slippery runway is to touch down at or near the threshold of a dry runway (for preference, when there is no wind); leave the brakes alone, and let it roll to a halt. In turboprops select 'Beta' but no more than the minimum of reverse thrust because conditions may not allow you to make full use of your capacity to go astern. Measure the distance taken to stop, and note it for future reference.

Without doubt, landing on contaminated runways is an activity to be taken seriously – unless you want to do the skater's waltz.

Landing on skis

In some parts of the world, aircraft that land on wheels are unknown. Pilots operate in conditions of perpetual snow or ice, and although that prospect may fill the majority of us with feelings that are less than enthusiastic, to those who must take off and land on skis it is the natural thing to do. In the main, this chapter deals with landing on contaminated runways, and no doubt ski pilots will take issue with me for including their everyday activity in a section of the book devoted to abnormal operations. But snow is snow and ice is unquestionably ice, and it seemed logical to conclude this chapter with a brief rundown on the techniques of landing on skis.

Ski flying is a part of everyday life in, among other places, vast areas of Canada, the USSR and one or two mountain regions of Switzerland and France. My very limited experience of ski flying, believe it or not, was gained at Redhill, a grass airfield in Surrey, not many miles from London. Normally, this attractive little airfield is as green as they come, but for perhaps a few weeks in the year a fall of snow turns the country-side gleaming white, and the Tiger Club then fits one or two of its diminutive single-seat Turbulents with tiny skis, little bigger than those you would wear on your feet. Such flying is a fun exercise, but to those who must supply remote stations in the Antarctic or fly an accident case out of an ice runway tucked into an Alpine fold, operations on skis are a serious matter. I am therefore indebted to the very experienced ski pilot whose name appears in the acknowledgements at the beginning of this book for the following material.

Ski equipment

In the case of tailwheel aircraft, skis are attached to the airframe by fittings which allow the transition from tail-down to tail-up. Arrangements are made to ensure that in flight the skis remain parallel with the fuselage, so that drag is reduced to a minimum. When the aircraft is small, bungee chords are used, but purpose-designed spring struts are usually fitted to larger skiplanes. The need to allow for changes in pitch attitude while on the ground does not arise in the case of nosewheel aircraft, and a typical ski arrangement is that fitted to the de Havilland Aircraft Company of Canada's Twin Otter (Fig. 80). It robs the turbo-prop of about 15 knots in the cruise.

Obviously, there are no brakes on a ski plane, and power checks are normally completed while taxiing. In this respect, and indeed in others, ski flying has much in common with floatplane operations.

Visibility and contrast

Alpine weather can be gin-clear, as can that at the North and South

Poles. But in conditions of poor contrast, when the light becomes diffused, sky and ground will usually merge and, as previously mentioned, a potentially dangerous situation known as a 'white-out' can occur. In effect, there is no demarcation between sky and ground; surface reference is lost; and it becomes impossible to judge height above the landing area. Landing under these conditions, which is very similar to alighting in a seaplane on glassy water, will be discussed later.

Without suitable edge markers, landing on even a prepared snow or ice strip can be difficult because, without visual cues, a pilot must face these problems:

1. It is almost impossible to determine aircraft attitude without reference to the instruments.

2. The proximity of the ground cannot be judged.

3. Because of 1 and 2, it is very easy to become disorientated and to imagine the aircraft is flying level when it is banking and turning.

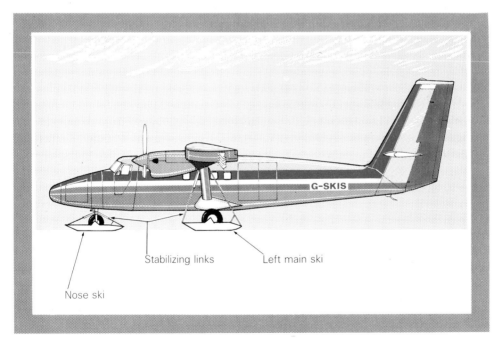

Fig. 80: Typical ski arrangement as fitted to the de Havilland Aircraft of Canada Twin Otter STOL turboprop. In this installation the skis may be raised or lowered hydraulically so that ski or wheel landings may be made according to surface.

The provision of markers (oil drums, painted posts, etc.) for reference along both edges of the landing area will perform much the same function as a simple flarepath at night. Indeed, the situation is very similar to landing on a moonless night, when runway lights are used against a dark background. In this case, dark markers are employed against a white background.

When the sky is only partly obscured – white clouds against a blue background – contrast is usually good, the surface is clearly defined and it is therefore not difficult to judge the approach. However, recognition of the surface when landing on unblemished snow can prove elusive even when contrast is good.

Flying the approach in conditions of poor contrast

Assuming the landing is to be made on a prepared strip with markers at the threshold and down the edges, it is essential to become established on the approach at an early stage. Aim for the threshold markers, using a shallow glidepath, and control the aircraft in the usual way. It is important to maintain a small rate of descent continuously until touch-down because in 'white-out' conditions there are inherent dangers in curtailing it. This is best illustrated by the case that occurred some years ago of a C130 Hercules coming to land at a South Pole airbase. Both the captain and his first officer were convinced that they had touched down. In fact, the big four-engine turboprop was still at 50 ft when it dropped out of the sky and broke in two – fortunately, without serious injury to any of its inmates. Yet here was a 2-mile long strip with edge markings. So keep flying down the glidepath. If there is uncertainty as to the nearness or otherwise of the surface, add a little power to reduce the rate of descent, and close the throttle(s) only when the skis touch the ground. Such arrivals can be surprisingly gentle, provided the final rate of descent is kept to below 250 ft/minute. For example, 200 ft/minute amounts to only 3.3 ft/second. You come down more quickly than that when jumping off a 3-ft wall.

Bringing the aircraft to a halt

Only skiplanes with reverse thrust have any form of braking other than the aerodynamic effect of flaps. When the landing is made on snow (as opposed to ice), the skis will provide a degree of retarding effect varying from quite considerable (when the snow is dry and soft) to very little (in the case of wet snow that has become compacted). Airstrips intended for skiplanes must obviously be long enough to cope with the situation. Naturally, aircraft with reverse thrust are at a distinct advantage over those without, always remembering the tendency for dry snow to turn itself into a local fog when reverse is applied.

Other than in strong crosswinds, direction may adequately be maintained via the steerable nose skid aided by *moderate* use of asymmetric thrust. Excessive power on even one engine can materially extend the landing slide. In some cases asymmetric reverse thrust can prove very effective.

Taxiing and parking

Turn radius on skis is likely to be greater than on wheels, and since it is not possible to stop decisively, it follows that taxiing speed must be kept to an absolute minimum. Allow adequate room when manoeuvring close to other objects.

Strangely enough, the skis tend to warm up appreciably while the aircraft slides to a halt after landing and during subsequent taxiing. Consequently, if the aircraft were parked and shut down immediately, the snow would melt slightly under the skids and very quickly freeze the hardware to the spot. The technique to adopt is:

1. Taxi to near the parking area, then stop for 15–30 seconds to cool the skis.

2. Move forward a little way; stop the aircraft on a fresh area of snow; then shut down.

Provided an aircraft is not parked on the same spot for more than a few days, the skis should not freeze to the surface when they have been cooled, as described, prior to engine shut-down. Much will depend upon the nature of the surface, but over a longer period of time the skis will gradually sink. Then there may be drifts or falls of snow, and these could entail digging out at least part of the aircraft.

Particularly when operating in remote areas, where battery power must be conserved, before starting the engine(s) it is good practice to dig under the skis a little to confirm that they are not frozen. If they are, the skis must be freed because there is no point in cranking up when the aircraft is firmly glued to the ground.

Open-field ski landings in remote areas

Few readers are likely to find themselves piloting skiplanes over the Arctic or the Antarctic, but although this final section of the book is based upon experience gained in those regions, the techniques that have been developed for the Poles could prove of value elsewhere.

When the aircraft is being flown into or out of a prepared strip, it is at least a known quantity, in so far as surface type and runway lengths will be notified to the pilot beforehand. But there are times, some of them dictated by emergencies, when a landing has to be made on an area never before violated by the skis of an aircraft. Nature has a habit of guarding its secrets, and some of them, if not nice to know, are nevertheless a matter of life and death for the pilot and his passengers.

When preparing to land on an unknown surface here are two serious hazards that may be hidden under a layer of dry snow: crevasses large enough to destroy the aircraft; and *sastrugi* – the Norwegian name for an undulating surface that may be difficult to see from the air and a potential hazard while landing. *Sastrugi* is caused by strong winds rather as waves are caused on the surface of the sea.

Basically open-field operations may be regarded under two headings:

1. Landings when a ground-support party is available to select an area and to mark it for the purpose. Ideally, the party should be able to radio information to the pilot about state of surface, wind direction, etc.

2. Landings without support.

Landings with ground support

The advantages of ground support need little explaining. A ground party can select a suitable landing strip, check it for crevasses and other hazards, assess the surface and determine whether or not it is level enough to accept an aircraft. It can then mark the strip with empty oil drums or the like. Provided the ground party understands what is required of it and can be relied upon to select a suitable area for an airstrip, the landing may be made without prior inspection other than an over-fly to check the layout and to assess the landing direction. A smoke generator or flare is ideal for indicating surface wind, particularly when it is light and variable. The approach and landing is flown as though the prepared strip were an established airbase.

Landing without ground support

Open-field landings in remote, unknown areas have much in common with seaplane operations on untried areas of water. The seaplane pilot faced with alighting on strange rivers or lakes is concerned with the state of the surface, the possibility of submerged rocks or floating debris, wind direction, currents and the amount of room available for the subsequent take-off. Many of these considerations are of interest to the skiplane pilot. Before attempting to land, he must satisfy himself that:

(a) there are no hidden crevasses;
(b) the surface is fit for a landing;
(c) if *sastrugi* is present, its direction is known;
(d) surface wind (speed and direction) is suitable for a landing;
(e) the area chosen is free from obstruction and large enough for both the landing and the subsequent departure;
(f) he knows of the location, nature and steepness of any inclines.

Checking the surface (Fig. 81)

One should never assume that a blemish-free carpet of gleaming snow is going to provide an ideal landing area, because those virgin flakes may conceal crevasses fit to devour a Jumbo Jet. Likewise, what may seem perfectly smooth from the air could, on closer aquaintance, prove to be covered in a series of frozen waves (*sastrugi*) of ideal length to set up destructive vibrations or other wrecking forces in the skis. Sometimes *sastrugi* is made of soft, dry snow, in which case it may present few problems, but it can also be composed of rock-hard ice and snow. A landing across the waves (as opposed to a touchdown parallel to them) could have the skis off before the pilot has time to say, 'I've heard of a ripple ice, but this is ridiculous!' Of course, if a strong wind is blowing across the *sastrugi*, then a landing parallel to the wave form will not be possible, and another alighting area will have to be investigated. How can one assess the surface and check for crevasses? The procedure demands skill, courage and a keen musical ear.

The aircraft should be slowed to around target threshold speed, using part (not maximum) flap, so that it approaches the surface in a slightly nose-high attitude. A flat descent is continued and then arrested just above the surface. Then, enough power having been set to maintain height, the aircraft is gradually lowered until the heels (rear) of the skis brush along the surface. This will perform two important services:

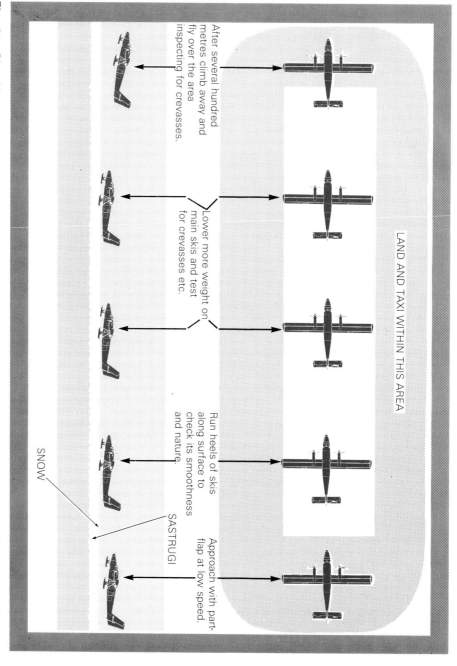

Fig. 81: Checking an unknown landing area for crevasses or unacceptable *sastrugi* which may be covered by a thin layer of smooth snow.

1. Snow will be dislodged to reveal any crevasses.

2. The nature of the surface will be recognized by the type of noise emanating from the skis: a banging and clattering noise = hard surface; a swishing, cushioning noise = soft snow.

Unless the clatter and vibration are alarming, the aircraft may be lowered a little with a view to transferring more weight to the main skis. It should be 'flown' along the surface for several hundred yards in a part-airborne condition before you add power and climb away for an inspection to see if any crevasses have appeared. Assuming no yawning gaps have been revealed by dragging the skis along the snow, a landing should be safe – provided it is confined to the immediate proximity of the ski tracks. And having safely come to a halt, avoid taxiing in the undershoot or overshoot areas (or, for that matter, anywhere other than in the immediate vicinity of your landing tracks) because a hungry crevass may be lurking in the snow waiting to gobble up an overconfident pilot and his nasty tin bird.

Checking surface wind

When dry snow is present, wind speed and direction may be determined as it drifts across the surface, but compacted snow will give no such indication. Usually, drifting dry snow denotes a wind of at least 15 knots. Moving clouds cast shadows but winds change with height, and surface direction should be modified as follows:

Northern hemisphere: 15–20° to the left of shadow track over the ground

Southern hemisphere: 15–20° to the right of shadow track over the ground

When no visual references are present, wind speed and direction can be assessed only by flying near the surface and checking drift. Without some recognizable feature to break the whiteness, this can be difficult, but a visual reference can be provided by dropping a dark object from the aircraft (a book cover or empty oil can, for example) and then flying towards it from at least three directions to determine the surface wind (Fig. 82). Apparently, after one has been flying in near-featureless regions for any time (desert, water or over snow/ice), appreciation of drift be-

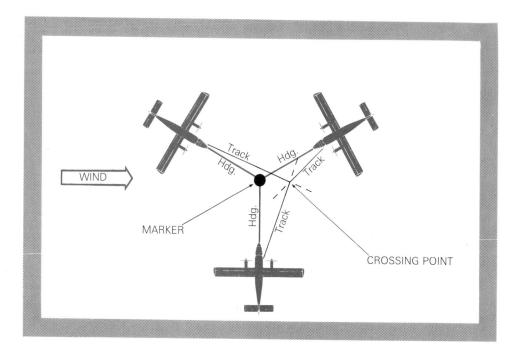

Fig. 82: Method of assessing wind conditions when no other visual references are available.

comes highly developed, and so does an awareness of wind speed and direction. It becomes second nature.

Open-field landings in poor contrast conditions

Unless a landing strip has been prepared by a competent ground party and it is adequately marked, open-field landings under 'white-out' conditions are extremely hazardous and should not be attempted. It is impossible to see cliffs, open crevasses and heavy (let alone slight) undulations. The risks are totally unacceptable.

Landing on slopes

Gentle slopes may be treated more or less as level ground, with the exception that in light or zero wind conditions the landing should be uphill and the take-off downhill.

Mountain areas or glaciers may present steep slopes, and these *demand* an uphill landing (and a downhill take-off). In extreme cases the slope may be sufficiently steep to preclude an overshoot after the final approach has commenced, so at that stage you are committed to the landing.

Faced with having to land on a steep incline, the prudent ski pilot will devote some time to casing the joint, as they say in the best criminal fiction. Look for:

1. Obstructions on the approach (high ground, etc.).

2. The possibility of turbulence caused by strong winds blowing through undulating terrain.

3. Possible constraints on landing and take-off. When the wind is moderate, landing direction may have to be downwind, relying on an uphill slide to bring the aircraft to a halt. The subsequent take-off would then provide the best of both worlds (into-wind and downhill), which is better by far than belting down the ice with the help of a tailwind, with not enough knots showing on the ASI for a lift-off but at a speed that will not allow you to stop. Remember: the landing must be planned to ensure that when the time comes you will be able to depart.

Even after the landing has been made successfully, other problems have to be faced. The danger is that the aircraft will stop, sharp end pointing up the hill; I am reliably informed that in this position it is almost impossible to make an about turn ready for take-off. To quote the words of the expert, 'You'll be left stranded like a fly on the wall.' The technique to adopt when landing uphill is as follows (see Fig. 83):

1. Having made a thorough inspection of the area and found the wind direction, fly level and approach the landing area at a height slightly below the selected touchdown point. With the aircraft in the landing configuration, adopt an approach speed that is slightly higher than usual to ensure that after touchdown it will reach the top of the landing area.

2. Gently apply back pressure on the elevator control, and fly the aircraft up the slope, keeping about 50 ft above its surface.

3. Power should be adjusted to fly the aircraft level with the slope.

4. Having arrested closure with the up-slope, make a *small* reduction in power, and let the aircraft fly on to the surface.

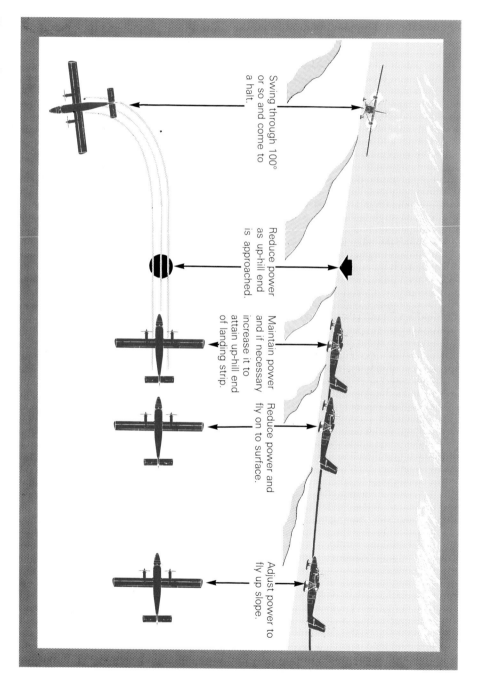

Swing through 100°
or so and come to
a halt.

Reduce power
as up-hill end
is approached.

Maintain power
and if necessary
increase it to
attain up-hill end
of landing strip.

Reduce power and
fly on to surface.

Adjust power to
fly up slope.

Fig. 83: Ski landing uphill, and safeguarding the subsequent downhill take-off.

5. After touchdown, keep the aircraft moving. *On no account be tempted to reduce power until you are certain that the uphill end of the strip will be reached.* On a steep slope it may be necessary to apply almost full power in an effort to prevent the aircraft from stopping part-way up the strip in a position that would make it possible to take off again.

6. As the uphill end of the landing strip is neared, reduce power; swing the aircraft through 100° or so; and bring it to a halt, with the nose pointing *slightly* downhill ready for take-off.

There are plenty of traps in this procedure: failure to establish the aircraft on an uphill approach that gently closes with the slope; allowing the aircraft to run out of momentum half-way up the strip, with the nose pointing towards the unattainable; and, having done it all nicely, turning through too large an angle at the end of the landing run, so that with the nose pointing downhill, the hardware begins to slide and nothing in the world will make it stop!

Experienced pilots have an in-built urge to close the throttles or power levers after landing, but this must be resisted when landing uphill on skis, otherwise the outcome could mean many hours of digging, back-breaking work with ropes and anchors (if there are enough able-bodied souls to man them) or the loss of a good aircraft, frozen to the spot as a permanent reminder of how not to do it.

Ski flying as a recreation can be great fun, but when it entails operating in remote areas without adequate ground support, opportunities for mishap are many – and the consequences can be very serious. Clearly, any pilot contemplating such occupations as Arctic flying, to quote an example, must first get himself alongside an expert, because past experiences at first hand is the only saviour when the point of no return arrives.

So we come to the end of *Make Better Landings*. Early on I mentioned that some might question whether a book of this size could be devoted entirely to the subject. But the topic of landing (and we have not discussed seaplanes because they do not land – they alight) is vast by any standards. No doubt one or two readers will claim that I should have mentioned this or that. Trouble is, where does one stop?

Appendix: Landing accident statistics

1 UK REGISTERED AIRCRAFT 1970–9

Accident type	1970	1971	1972	1973	1974	1975	1976	1977	1978	1979	TOTAL	Percentage all accidents
Loss of control (ground)	5	12	15	9	14	15	15	9	22	26	142	5.9
Wheels up	11	6	6	10	8	8	5	7	14	14	89	3.7
Gear collapsed	20	23	24	16	24	11	18	31	16	9	192	7.98
Gear retracted	4	3	8	7	10	5	9	8	10	3	67	2.78
Heavy landing	30	38	47	27	31	32	37	41	34	29	346	14.38
Nose-over	12	22	21	20	24	16	16	14	8	8	161	6.69
Overshoot (overrun)	14	11	14	12	14	17	12	10	17	11	132	5.49
Undershoot	1	7	6	8	3	4	4	5	4	3	45	1.87
TOTAL	97	122	141	109	128	108	116	125	125	103	1174	48.79
Percentage all accidents	45.9	50.5	48.6	47.9	50.2	51.8	52.5	50.4	47.1	43.2	48.79	

2 AUSTRALIA 1975–9

Accident type	Charter	Agricultural flying	Flying training	Other airwork	Private	Commuter	Business	TOTAL	Percentage all accidents
Ground-loop	5	11	37	10	52	–	1	116	10.12
Wheels up	24	–	9	10	52	3	2	100	8.73
Gear collapsed	5	5	5	9	15	2	1	42	3.66
Gear retracted	9	–	8	1	24	1	1	44	3.84
Hard landing	6	–	52	7	84	–	–	149	13.00
Nose-over/roll-over	2	1	1	4	11	–	–	19	1.66
Overshoot (overrun)	10	4	4	4	50	–	1	73	6.37
Undershoot	2	3	2	1	21	–	–	29	2.53
Collision with aircraft	5	–	3	–	7	–	–	15	1.31
Collision with ground	4	6	4	9	31	3	1	58	5.06
Collision with objects	17	50	10	31	94	1	3	206	17.98
TOTAL	89	80	135	86	441	10	10	851	74.26
Percentage all accidents	7.77	6.98	11.78	7.5	38.48	0.87	0.87	74.26	

3. SOUTH AFRICA 1970–9

Accident type	1970	1971	1972	1973	1974	1975	1976	1977	1978	1979	TOTAL	Percentage all accidents
Swung off runway	16	5	9	11	14	8	10	18	16	13	120	7.57
Wheels up	6	5	8	6	6	11	10	9	9	10	80	5.05
Gear collapsed	7	5	5	6	12	8	10	11	16	9	89	5.61
Gear retracted	–	1	–	–	–	10	–	2	6	3	22	1.39
Heavy landing	7	14	15	18	11	12	16	18	6	13	130	8.20
Overshoot (overrun)	3	3	–	2	11	5	11	5	5	3	48	3.03
Undershoot	3	2	5	1	5	4	4	3	3	1	31	1.96
Landed off runway	–	1	3	2	5	2	2	2	2	4	23	1.45
Collision with objects	15	9	2	4	12	8	8	5	10	8	81	5.11
TOTAL	57	45	47	50	76	68	71	73	73	64	624	39.37
Percentage all accidents	41	30.6	33.09	41.32	41.76	39.08	41.76	40.56	42.94	40	39.37	

4 USA 1975–9

Accident type	Phase of flight								TOTAL	Percentage all accidents
	VFR traffic pattern	VFR final approach	IFR initial approach	IFR final approach	Round-out/touchdown	Landing roll	Go-around	Missed approach		
Ground-loop/Water-loop	–	–	–	–	257	1554	24	–	1835	10.60
Wingtip/float dragged	–	2	–	1	16	3	–	–	22	0.13
Wheels up	–	1	–	–	363	17	2	–	383	2.21
Gear collapsed	–	–	–	–	47	183	1	–	231	1.33
Gear retracted	–	–	–	–	40	156	–	–	196	1.13
Hard landing	–	–	–	–	1216	4	16	–	1236	7.14
Nose-over	–	–	–	–	80	371	9	–	460	2.66
Overshoot (overrun)	–	7	–	–	927	12	–	–	946	5.47
Undershoot	5	603	–	15	5	3	–	–	631	3.65
Collision (air & ground)	26	80	–	1	52	44	3	–	206	1.19
Collision with ground/water	45	48	20	71	57	–	53	26	320	1.85
Collision with objects	25	178	9	62	174	370	173	11	1002	5.79
Stall	39	88	2	7	8	–	55	3	202	1.17
Spin	35	27	1	7	–	–	20	–	90	0.52
Spiral	6	4	1	–	–	–	3	–	14	0.08
High sink	19	49	–	5	5	1	69	1	149	0.86
Turbulence	2	18	–	2	6	1	1	–	30	0.17
Evasive action	1	–	–	–	–	4	–	1	6	0.03
Miscellaneous	1	4	1	1	11	11	2	–	31	0.18
TOTAL	204	1109	34	172	3264	2734	431	42	7990	46.16
Percentage all accidents	1.18	6.41	0.20	0.99	18.86	15.79	2.49	0.24	46.16	

5 CANADA 1976–80

Accident type	TOTAL	Percentage all accidents
Ground-loop/water-loop	268	8.72
Wingtip/float dragged	39	1.27
Wheels up	52	1.69
Gear collapsed	84	2.73
Gear retracted	41	1.33
Hard landing	166	5.40
Nose-over	87	2.83
Overshoot (overrun)	122	3.97
Undershoot	63	2.05
Collision (air & ground)	14	0.46
Collision with ground/water	35	1.14
Collision with objects	130	4.23
Stall	9	0.29
Spin	42	1.37
Spiral	3	0.10
High sink	18	0.59
Landing off runway	12	0.39
TOTAL	1185	38.56

Phase of flight	TOTAL	Percentage all accidents
VFR traffic pattern	19	0.62
VFR final approach	126	4.10
IFR intermediate approach	2	0.06
IFR final approach	15	0.49
Round-out/touchdown	349	11.36
Landing roll	567	18.46
Go-around	48	1.56
Missed approach	2	0.07
VFR long finals	1	0.03
VFR base leg	3	0.09
Final turn	20	0.65
Baulked landing after touchdown	31	1.01
Others	2	0.06
TOTAL	1185	38.56

Index

Why don't you get a *horse*,

SAM ADAMS?

by Jean Fritz

illustrated by Trina Schart Hyman

COWARD, McCANN & GEOGHEGAN, Inc.
NEW YORK

In the early days of America when men wore ruffles on their shirts and buckles on their shoes, when they rode horseback and swore allegiance to the King of England, there lived in Boston a man who cared for none of these things. His name was Samuel Adams. His clothes were shabby and plain, he refused to get on a horse, and he hated the King of England.

Samuel Adams was known as a talker and a walker. Six days of the week he would walk about Boston, talking to anyone who would listen—talking about England, always about England. What he thought about was independence, but it was a long time before he dared say "independence" out loud. Americans were still loyal to the king, even though they were often angry at the way England treated its colonies. And Samuel Adams made it his business to keep the people angry.

From one end of the town to another Samuel walked. Indeed, how else was he to travel? A man cannot say much from the top of a horse except good morning, good evening, or giddyap, and Samuel Adams had a great deal more than that to say. Still, he did not travel alone. At his side was Queue, his shaggy Newfoundland dog.

Together they went to the docks, and while Samuel Adams talked to merchants about the wrongs of the English government, Queue smelled the good smells of Boston Harbor—drying codfish, wet rope, and sometimes, if he was lucky, a giant turtle in a crate shipped up from the South. (New Englanders doted on turtle soup.)

Together Samuel and Queue called on shopkeepers. Generally Samuel went inside and talked about the wickedness of England; generally Queue stayed outside and chased a stray chicken or stopped at a hitching post to visit with a horse.

Together Samuel and Queue would drop in at a tavern. Samuel would sit down and talk about American rights; Queue, blinking through the hair that fell over his eyes, would search the floor for crumbs—a morsel of cheese, a bite of plumcake, and sometimes, if he was lucky, a discarded bone.

Samuel's younger cousin John Adams often became impatient with all his walking. "Why don't you learn to ride a horse?" he would ask.

11

But Samuel would not learn. Winter and summer he walked and he talked. Indeed, he paid so little attention to his private business that he became quite poor. His house fell into disrepair; his clothes became shabbier; his shoe leather wore thin.

14

Meanwhile, England was imposing taxes on America. First a stamp tax on printed matter. No one could obtain a marriage license now or a college diploma or even buy a newspaper without paying England a share of the money. This made the people of Boston so angry they tore down the governor's house, set fire to the tax office, and elected Samuel Adams a representative to the Massachusetts legislature.

Being a member of the government, Samuel had a chance to talk to more people, but still he walked. Even when England withdrew the stamp tax, Samuel talked and walked, warning the merchants and the shopkeepers and the people at the taverns not to trust England. It had taxed America once, he said; it would try it again. And indeed a year later it did. This time Americans had to give England money whenever they bought paint, glass, lead, or tea. This made the people so angry that the king decided to send soldiers to Boston to keep order.

They arrived in Boston on October 1, 1768—two regiments of soldiers in red coats. From the harbor they marched—one thousand strong, their drums beating, fifes playing, flags flying, and bayonets fixed. They marched straight to Boston Common, a park in the center of town where people were accustomed to take walks, play games, and graze their cows. There the soldiers set up tents and settled down for the winter.

It was a long winter. Every time he turned around, it seemed to Samuel Adams, there was a redcoat. He woke up hearing redcoats drill; he went to bed hearing their bugles. Redcoats stopped him on his walks to ask his name and business. Samuel Adams longed for America to fight the redcoats then and there, but he knew the country was not ready yet for war or independence.

But Queue could fight. Under Samuel's careful training, Queue learned to hate redcoats. He growled and snarled when they passed; he barked and snapped when they came near. And sometimes, if he was lucky, he came home with a piece of red cloth in his mouth.

Meanwhile, Samuel kept on talking and walking.

"Why can't you ride a horse like everyone else?" his cousin John asked.

But Samuel shook his head.

WITH APOLOGIES TO PAUL REVERE, ORIGINAL ARTIST

Twice in the next few years Americans came close to fighting.

Once a mob of young men swung clubs and threw rock-filled snowballs at the redcoats until the redcoats finally fired back. (Samuel Adams did his fiercest talking against the redcoats in this instance.)

Another time a band of men, dressed up like Indians, dumped a boatload of tea into Boston Harbor rather than see the tea taxed. (Samuel was the one who gave the signal to go down to the docks.)

By the fall of 1774 Americans were so alarmed about England that they called a meeting in Philadelphia to discuss what to do. Samuel Adams was chosen to go as one of the representatives from Massachusetts. He had never been out of Massachusetts before.

"You are now a traveler," his friends pointed out, "and you should learn to ride a horse."

But Samuel said that would not be necessary; the representatives were going to Philadelphia in a coach. He stood before his friends, his coat frayed, his shoes scuffed, his cotton stockings darned. His friends said nothing about his appearance, but within a few day gifts began arriving at his house:

  1 maroon-colored broadcloth suit
  6 pairs of buckled shoes
  6 pairs of white silk stockings
  2 ruffled shirts
  1 wig

When Samuel Adams left for Philadelphia, he was dressed as a representative of Massachusetts should be dressed. He was as stylish as his cousin John Adams, or his friend John Hancock, or indeed any of the other representatives. And if the others could ride a horse and he couldn't, he didn't care.

Actually, it was lucky that Samuel could at least look nice because he couldn't say much at the meeting. Many of the representatives from other colonies still weren't ready for talk about independence so Samuel had to be patient awhile longer. There was a time, he knew, for throwing snowballs and a time for dumping tea, but there was also a time for sitting still under your new wig and holding your tongue. This was such a time.

Library
St. Nicholas Ave. School

25

But of course he couldn't be still forever. By 1775 Samuel was talking openly of independence. He was fifty-three years old now and at the top of the king's "most wanted" list of American traitors. John Hancock was on the list, too. As for Queue, unfortunately he was dead. He had fought his last battle with the redcoats before the real fighting began.

On April 18 the redcoats marched out of Boston, looking for American cannon that was hidden in Concord and looking (so it was said) for Samuel Adams and John Hancock,

who were hidden in a friend's house in Lexington. Samuel wasn't afraid of trouble. The more trouble there was with the redcoats, the sooner Americans would be willing to declare their independence and the better he'd like it. But of course, he preferred not to be caught.

Fortunately for Samuel and John, the Americans had discovered what the English were up to. Ahead of the redcoats rode Paul Revere. He galloped up to the house where Samuel Adams and John Hancock were staying.

"The redcoats are coming!" he cried.

Samuel jumped out of bed, ready to fly for his life. (He was in such a hurry that he left his watch under his pillow.) John also jumped out of bed, but he was more eager to fight than to fly. He grabbed his sword and began to polish it.

Samuel told him to put his sword away. "We aren't meant to be soldiers," he said. "We are the brains behind the Revolution. It is our duty to escape."

Reluctantly John put his sword away and made ready to escape. Now, of course, as everyone knows, the way to escape from an enemy is on the back of a horse. You lean forward and with hooves thundering behind, you streak into the night. But Samuel Adams couldn't ride a horse.

In the end there was nothing for John Hancock to do but call for his carriage and his driver. The two men took their seats and rolled sedately away to a neighboring town. (Eventually they found a swamp to hide in.) It was not a heroic escape, but it was an escape. The only thing Samuel Adams regretted was that he'd left his watch behind.

Even now he would not ride a horse.

In September on the way to another meeting in Philadelphia, John Adams tried again to persuade him. This time they were traveling alone—John and Samuel and their two servants. John and his servant, Fessenden, were on horses; Samuel and his servant were in a two-wheeled chaise. Under such cir-

cumstances, it was hard for John and Samuel to talk. John suggested that Samuel could ride Fessenden's horse and Fessenden could get in the chaise. Samuel suggested that his servant could ride John's horse and John could get in the chaise, but John loved to ride. So John trotted along to Philadelphia, and Samuel rolled along, each with his own thoughts.

JOHN HANCOCK'S FLINTLOCK RIFLE (USED)

It took a week or more to go from Boston to Philadelphia, but of course there were many stops at inns, where John and Samuel could talk together. And there was much to talk about. Since the Battle of Lexington, George Washington had been put in command of an American army and there had been another battle at Bunker Hill. But there wasn't enough time to talk about all that had happened and was still to happen to the country.

At a tavern in Grafton, Connecticut, John Adams decided to make one last attempt to get Samuel on a horse.

"Riding would be good for your health," he began.

Samuel was not concerned with his health.

Riding was sociable, John suggested. Samuel said walking was sociable and riding in a chaise could be sociable, too.

Well, riding was a more convenient way to get about, John went on. As a leader of the Revolution, Samuel was a busy man and needed to get about easily.

Samuel was not interested in convenience.

Riding was the fastest way to travel, John observed. In time of war, it was sometimes important to move fast.

JOHN ADAMS'S SWORD (NEVER USED IN BATTLE)

35

36

Still, Samuel was not convinced. If he thought about his escape at Lexington, he didn't mention it.

John sighed and tried another tack. It was a pity, he said, that early man had gone to such trouble to domesticate an animal, only to have Samuel Adams come along and reject it.

Samuel didn't give two hoots for early man.

Then John Adams sat back in his chair and took a deep breath. He had one more argument. "You should ride a horse for the good of your country," he declared. America would surely be declaring its independence soon, he pointed out; if all went well, they themselves would be signing such a declaration in Philadelphia. Then they would be not just leaders of a revolution; they would be the statesmen of a new nation.

John leaned toward his cousin. "A proud new nation," he said. A great nation. A republic as Rome had been in ancient times. And whoever heard of a great nation with statesmen who could not ride horseback? John listed the heroes of Roman history. He reviewed the names of Roman senators. All were horsemen, he said. And he would not want Americans to be inferior in the least way.

For the first time Samuel looked thoughtful. After all, he told himself, he had put on silk stockings and a ruffled shirt so as not to shame the Commonwealth of Massachusetts at the meeting in Philadelphia. How could he refuse to get on a horse if the honor of his country were at stake? How could he put a stain on American history—indeed right on the opening chapter?

Samuel closed his eyes and tried to imagine the new nation

that John described. Yes, it seemed to him that he could see it—people multiplying, buildings springing up, roads unrolling. And stone statues popping up across the landscape. They were statues of the new nation's first statesmen, and they were all on horseback. There was John Adams in stone on a horse. And John Hancock. There were dozens of George Washingtons on dozens of horses. But try as he might, Samuel could not find a statue of himself. If he did not ride a horse, he asked himself, would he not even be granted a pedestal?

When they were ready to continue the journey, Samuel walked over to Fessenden's horse. He eyed it suspiciously.

"She is a very gentle creature," John assured him.

Samuel said nothing, but he allowed the two servants to boost him onto the horse. He listened to John's instructions. He did as he was told. Then the servants rolled along to Philadelphia in the chaise, and Samuel and John rode together.

Everyone agreed that Samuel did remarkably well in the saddle. There was only one trouble. At the end of the day it was discovered that at the place where Samuel Adams and the saddle met Samuel was sore. And everyone agreed that this was no way for a future statesman to feel. So at Woodstock, Connecticut, where they spent the night, John bought two yards of flannel, found a tailor, and ordered a pair of padded underpants, or "drawers," for Samuel.

The next morning John gave Samuel his final lesson in horse-manship. A statesman, he explained, should not have to be hoisted and heaved into the saddle by two servants. He should be able to mount himself.

He told Samuel to grasp the bridle with his right hand over the pummel of the saddle, to place his left foot in the stirrup, to twist his left hand into the horse's mane halfway between his ears and his shoulders, and, propelling himself upward, to throw his right leg over the saddle. Samuel did as he was told.

So mounted, in his padded drawers, Samuel rode triumphantly to Philadelphia, the very picture of a noble statesman.

And when independence was finally declared one hot July day ten months later, Samuel Adams was ready for history.

For those readers who will ask if the facts in this book are true, the answer is *yes*. I was disappointed that there was no more information to be found about Queue, but I am grateful to John Adams for telling us in such detail about how Samuel Adams finally learned to ride a horse. On September 17, 1775, John wrote all about it, including the specific instructions for mounting a horse given on page 42, in a letter to his friend James Warren.

For those readers who would like to know more about Samuel Adams, here are some additional facts.

Samuel Adams' anger at England started early in his life. His father, a wealthy and prominent businessman, was at the center of a political movement that wanted to give more power to the American people and less to England. Samuel was eighteen and a student at Harvard University when a new bank that his father and his friends had started suddenly failed. Samuel's father lost so much money that in order to pay his way through college, Samuel had to take a job waiting on table. Samuel didn't mind the job; he never cared about having money for himself, but the bank had failed because England had declared it illegal and in a way that many people thought was unfair. This was what Samuel objected to. Then and there he decided it was not right for a country across the ocean to have so much power in the life of Americans.

Yet Samuel Adams did not look like an agitator. He was a rather short, portly, blue-eyed, mild-mannered, slow-moving, polite man with a nice singing voice. He went to church regularly and was strict about his own and everyone else's morals as long as this did not interfere with his political plans. In many ways he was old-fashioned. Although he wanted America to be rid of England, he was not interested in establishing a country with new ideas. All he wanted was a free nation and one that would exhibit the virtues that he believed had existed among the first Puritan settlers.

Samuel Adams had no part in the actual writing of the Declaration of Independence, but because he had started so early to work for it, he has sometimes been called "the father of independence." He continued in politics all his life, was elected lieutenant governor and then governor of Massachusetts in the 1790's, but his real contribution was in the early years before the war. He died in 1803, at the age of eighty-one, in Boston, the city he had known and loved so well.

Samuel devoted all his energy to politics. After college, he tried business life, but he was not interested and did not do well. He was married twice (his first wife died in 1757), had two children, and although his family seemed happy and devoted, they had to manage much of the time on very little money. Samuel became known as an agitator, a people rouser, or, as the English called him, an "incendiary"—one who starts fires. And indeed, he was behind most of the disturbances and demonstrations in Boston before the war, including the famous Tea Party. He used every means he could find—fair means and often not so fair—to oppose England and to lead the people toward independence.